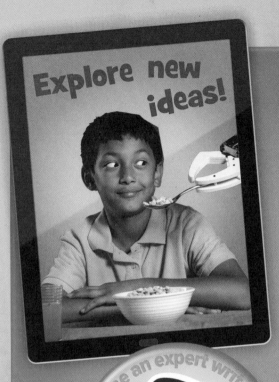

# Explore new ideas!

# Welcome to your
# California
## Reading/Writing
# Workshop

Read exciting literature, science and social studies texts!

D0604089

Become an expert writer!

Build vocabulary and knowledge to unlock the Wonders of reading!

Use your student login to explore your interactive Reading/Writing Workshop, practice close reading, and more.

*Go Digital!* www.connected.mcgraw-hill.com

# Wonders

## An English Language Arts Program

### Program Authors

| | |
|---|---|
| Diane August | Jan Hasbrouck |
| Donald R. Bear | Margaret Kilgo |
| Janice A. Dole | Jay McTighe |
| Jana Echevarria | Scott G. Paris |
| Douglas Fisher | Timothy Shanahan |
| David Francis | Josefina V. Tinajero |
| Vicki Gibson | |

Mc Graw Hill Education

**Cover and Title Pages:** Nathan Love

# www.mheonline.com/readingwonders

Send all inquiries to:
McGraw-Hill Education
Two Penn Plaza
New York, NY 10121

ISBN: 978-0-02-133171-0
MHID: 0-02-133171-5

Printed in the United States of America.

4 5 6 7 QVS 20 19 18 17        C

# Unlock the
# Wonders
## of
# Reading

## With your *Reading/Writing Workshop* you will:

- Closely read and reread literature and informational text

- Discuss what you have read with your peers

- Become a better writer and researcher

- Look for text evidence as you respond to complex text

## Get Ready to Become:

- Lifelong Learners

- Critical Thinkers

- Part of the Community of Learning

# READ and REREAD

## Exciting Literature

Waiting inside every book is an adventure! You will find fabulous fables, fun folktales, and marvelous myths. Stories, poems, and dramas will excite your imagination.

## Informational Texts

Build knowledge as you read about wonders of nature, the secrets of the planets, and events from history. Here you can explore all this and more!

Different kinds of texts can be challenging. First you need to figure out why the text is hard for you. Once you determine what the problem is, you can try to solve it. Look at the tips below. They can help you move in the right direction.

### VOCABULARY

If you come across an unfamiliar word, look for context clues. Some texts contain special words to know, such as science words. You might want to look these words up in a dictionary.

### MAKE CONNECTIONS

Sometimes you may need to make inferences about the text. For example, the reasons a character does something are not always stated. In nonfiction, you can connect information to find the essential idea.

### ILLUSTRATIONS AND TEXT FEATURES

Are there any illustrations that can give you clues about the plot or how the characters feel? In nonfiction, are there any maps or diagrams that can help you understand information in the text?

### TEXT STRUCTURE

How is the text organized? Does the author compare and contrast information? Is there a problem and a solution? Is there a sequence of events?

COLLABORATE

How could a chart or map help you understand information in a nonfiction text?

# L👀k for Text Evidence

When you answer a question about your reading, you often have to look for evidence in the text to support or even find the answer. Here are some tips to help you find what you are looking for.

Rosa and Eddie Hernandez huddled close to the radio and listened carefully to the scratchy voice of the news announcer. "The blizzard of 1947 is the biggest snowstorm in New York City history!"

**Stated**
Here I can locate information that tells me that this story is historical fiction. It is set in the past.

"Oh, mamá!" whispered Rosa. "Will papá ever get home from work?"

Mamá gave Rosa a big hug. "He must be stuck at work and unable to get home," she said.

**Unstated**
This text evidence allows me to figure out that Rosa is very worried about her father.

# Text Evidence

Let's search for some answers! Sometimes you find answers "right there" in the text. Sometimes you need to look for details or clues in different parts of the text and put the answer in your own words.

## It's Stated — Right There!

Some questions ask you to locate details. Sometimes the answers can be found stated in a sentence you can point to. For example, *When do the events of this story take place?*

To answer other questions, you may have to combine clues from more than one place. A question, such as *How is the blizzard affecting the Hernandez family?* means you have to look in the beginning, middle and end of the paragraph or selection to find the answer.

## It's Unstated — Here Is My Evidence

The answers to some questions are not stated. To answer a question, such as *Why does Rosa ask about her father?* you look for details or clues in the text. You can then use the clues to answer the question in your own words.

How do you look for text evidence? For theme, think about what the characters do and say. In a nonfiction text, look for signal words and phrases.

. . . . . . . . . . . . . . . . . . . . . . . . . . . . . . . . . . . . . . . . . . . . . . . . . . . . . . . .

What is Rosa's problem? Find evidence in the text.

# Be an Expert Writer

Remember that good writing presents clear ideas. It is well organized and contains evidence and details from reliable sources. See how Gina answered a question about a text she read.

## Gina's Model

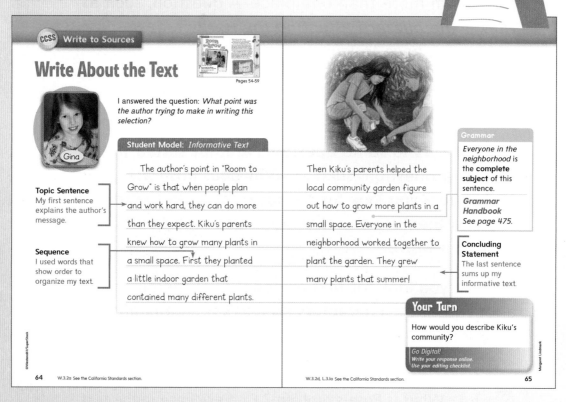

**CCSS Write to Sources**

### Write About the Text

Pages 54-59

I answered the question: *What point was the author trying to make in writing this selection?*

**Student Model:** *Informative Text*

**Topic Sentence**
My first sentence explains the author's message.

**Sequence**
I used words that show order to organize my text.

> The author's point in "Room to Grow" is that when people plan and work hard, they can do more than they expect. Kiku's parents knew how to grow many plants in a small space. First they planted a little indoor garden that contained many different plants.
>
> Then Kiku's parents helped the local community garden figure out how to grow more plants in a small space. Everyone in the neighborhood worked together to plant the garden. They grew many plants that summer!

**Grammar**
*Everyone in the neighborhood* is the **complete subject** of this sentence.
*Grammar Handbook*
See page 475.

**Concluding Statement**
The last sentence sums up my informative text.

### Your Turn

How would you describe Kiku's community?

*Go Digital!*
*Write your response online.*
*Use your editing checklist.*

64  W.3.2a See the California Standards section.

W.3.2d, L.3.1a See the California Standards section.  65

# Write About the Text

When you write about something you have read closely, you should introduce your topic clearly. Cite evidence from the text that supports your opinions. When you do research, make sure you use different reliable sources. Then give a list of the sources you have used. Use the question checklist below.

**Opinions** Did I support opinions with facts and details?

**Informative Texts** Did I clearly group information in paragraphs? Did I make a closing statement connecting all of my information?

**Narrative Texts** When you write a narrative, you use your imagination to develop real or made-up events. The checklist below will help make your stories interesting.

- **Sequence** Did I use a sequence of events that unfolds naturally? Did I make use of clue words and phrases?

- **Dialogue** Did I use dialogue and description to develop characters, experiences, and events? Did I show how characters act in different situations?

What is your favorite thing to write about? Tell a partner why.

# Unit 1

# Growing and Learning

**The Big Idea**

How can learning help us grow? . . . . . . . **16**

 *Go Digital!* Find all lessons online at www.connected.mcgraw-hill.com.

Margaret Lindmark

# Unit 2

# Figure It Out

**The Big Idea**

What does it take to solve a problem? .. **96**

(t)Elwood Smith; (c)Janet Broxon; (b)Tristan Elwell

 *Go Digital!* Find all lessons online at www.connected.mcgraw-hill.com.

(t)©Richard Hutchings/Corbis; (b)Dara Goldman

# Unit 3

## One of a Kind

**The Big Idea**

Why are individual qualities important? . . . . . . . . . . . . . . . . . . . . . . . **176**

(t)Jago Silver; (b)Peter Ferguson

SOCIAL STUDIES

(t)5155ystems/iStock/Getty Images Plus/Getty Images; (b)Nik Wheeler/Alamy

# Unit 4

# Meet the Challenge

**The Big Idea**

What are different ways to meet challenges? . . . . . . . . . . . . . . . . . . **256**

 **Go Digital!** Find all lessons online at www.connected.mcgraw-hill.com.

SCIENCE

SCIENCE

(t)Photographs By Les Piccolo/Getty Images; (c)Everett Collection/SuperStock; (b)Diverse Images/Universal Images Group/Getty Images

# Unit 5

# Take Action

**The Big Idea**

(t)Melissa McGill; (c b)Chris Vallo

  *Go Digital!* Find all lessons online at www.connected.mcgraw-hill.com.

# Unit 6 Think It Over

**The Big Idea**

How do we decide what's
important?.........................**400**

*Go Digital!* Find all lessons online at www.connected.mcgraw-hill.com.

(t)PHOTOLIFE/a.collectionRF/Getty Images; (tc)Image Source/Getty Images; (b)Stacey Schuett

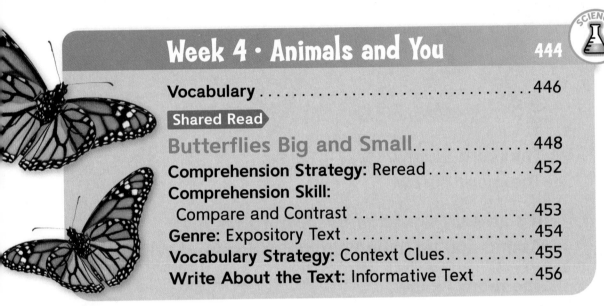
(t)NASA/JPL; (tc bc)Don Farrall/Photographer's Choice RF/Getty Images; (b)Daryll Collins

# Growing and Learning

## The More I Know

The more I know,
The more I grow.

It's an easy equation to solve if I try,
Asking and learning help me understand WHY.

The more I know,
The more I WANT to know.

It's an easy equation without a doubt,
Wondering and learning help me figure things out.

— George Samos

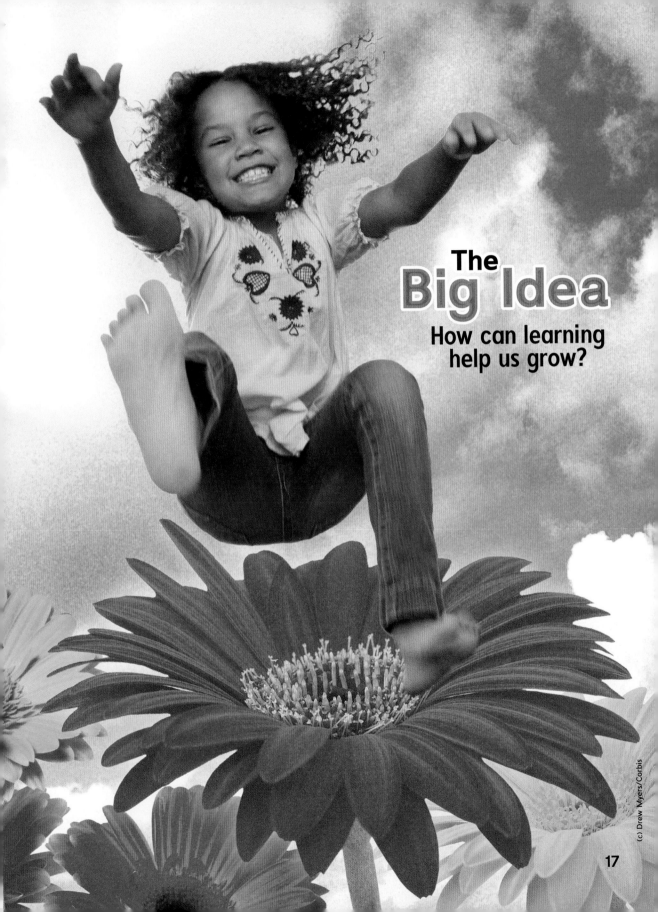

# The
# Big Idea

**How can learning
help us grow?**

(c) Drew Myers/Corbis

17

**Essential Question**

What can stories teach you?

Go Digital!

# Read and Learn

Hi. I'm Katie. Reading is so much fun. I love to read stories for many different reasons.

▶ Stories make me laugh.

▶ They teach me how to do new things.

▶ Stories inspire me to learn about other people.

## Talk About It

Write words you have learned about stories. Talk with a partner about other things you can learn from stories.

Stories

1 of 1

# Vocabulary

Use the picture and the sentence to talk with a partner about each word.

**ached**

My head **ached** and hurt when I had a bad cold.

When has your head ached?

**concentrate**

Tom can **concentrate** in the quiet library.

Name places where you can concentrate.

**discovery**

Matt and June made a fun **discovery** at the beach.

What fun discovery have you made?

**educated**

Jan went to school to be **educated**.

Why does someone become educated?

**effort**

Learning to ski takes lots of hard work and **effort**.

Name something else that takes effort.

**improved**

Sam's soccer skills **improved** with practice.

Tell how you improved at doing something.

**inspired**

My grandmother **inspired** me to learn to knit.

Who has inspired you to try something new?

**satisfied**

I am happy and **satisfied** with the good job I did.

What word means almost the same as satisfied?

## Your Turn

COLLABORATE

Pick three words. Then write three questions for your partner to answer.

*Go Digital!* *Use the online visual glossary*

# BRUNO'S NEW HOME

### Essential Question
**What can stories teach you?**

Read how one story taught a bear an important lesson.

John Hovell

Bruno shivered. A frosty wind blew through the forest. Bright red and orange leaves danced around the trees. His paws felt like blocks of ice. It was almost winter. Bruno needed a warm, safe place to hibernate, and he needed it now.

Bruno moved slowly through the woods. He grumbled and growled to himself. Finding a new place to sleep was harder than he thought.

Bruno climbed up a small hill. He hiked around a pond and walked on a path. No place was right. Finally he made an exciting **discovery**.

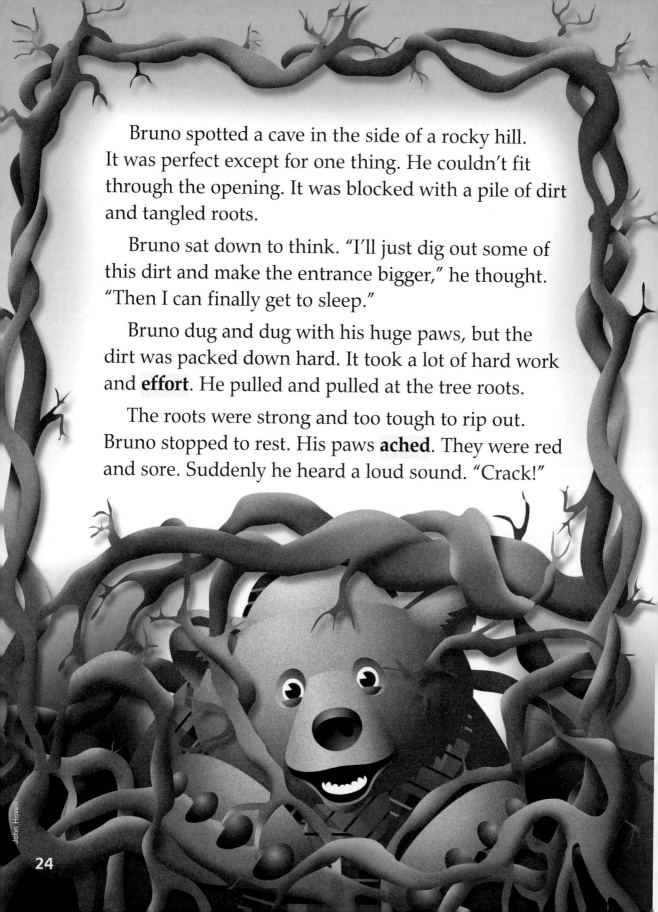

Bruno spotted a cave in the side of a rocky hill. It was perfect except for one thing. He couldn't fit through the opening. It was blocked with a pile of dirt and tangled roots.

Bruno sat down to think. "I'll just dig out some of this dirt and make the entrance bigger," he thought. "Then I can finally get to sleep."

Bruno dug and dug with his huge paws, but the dirt was packed down hard. It took a lot of hard work and **effort**. He pulled and pulled at the tree roots.

The roots were strong and too tough to rip out. Bruno stopped to rest. His paws **ached**. They were red and sore. Suddenly he heard a loud sound. "Crack!"

Bruno turned quickly and saw a small squirrel eating a nut. He stopped eating and smiled at Bruno.

"You look like you need help," said the squirrel.

Bruno sighed. "I have been trying to fit into this cave, but it's hopeless. I've been digging and digging, but I haven't **improved** the opening at all."

"I'm Jack, and I can help," said the squirrel.

"But you are too small," said Bruno.

Jack told Bruno to sit down and rest. Bruno sat and yawned as Jack scampered away. A few minutes later, he came back.

"What you need is a book," said Jack. "Reading can help you become **educated**. Books are filled with knowledge." He handed Bruno a thick red book.

Bruno moved to a bright, sunny spot. He put on his glasses and tried to **concentrate** on the story. He paid careful attention to the plot.

The story was about a lion and a mouse. The lion thought the mouse was too small to help him. One day the lion got caught in a net. The mouse chewed the net's ropes and helped the lion escape.

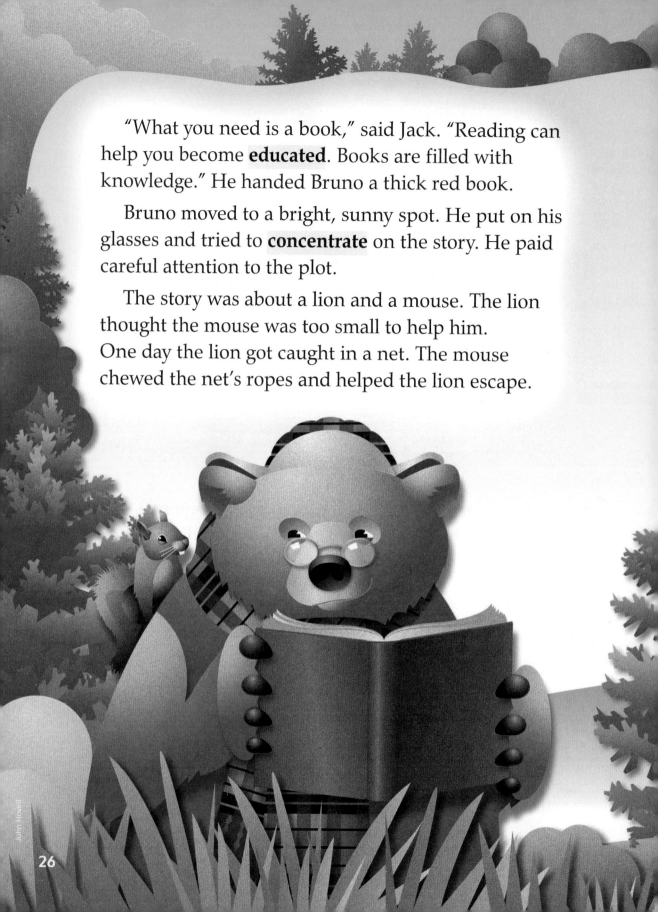

"Well, the lion in this story learned an important lesson," said Bruno. "I think I did, too."

The story **inspired** Bruno. The mouse had sharp teeth, and so did Jack. Jack could help.

The new friends made a fine team. Jack chewed through the thick roots and Bruno dug out the dirt. They worked together all afternoon. Finally, Bruno could fit through the opening.

"Are you **satisfied** and happy with your cozy new home?" asked Jack.

"I sure am!" said Bruno. "And I learned something, too. Good friends come in small packages."

## Make Connections

Talk about the story of the lion and the mouse. How did it help Bruno solve his problem? ESSENTIAL QUESTION

Discuss how you and your friends help one another. TEXT TO SELF

# Visualize

Look for colorful words as you read "Bruno's New Home." Use these words to visualize, or form pictures, in your mind.

### Find Text Evidence

Why does Bruno need to find a new home? Use the details in the first paragraph on page 23.

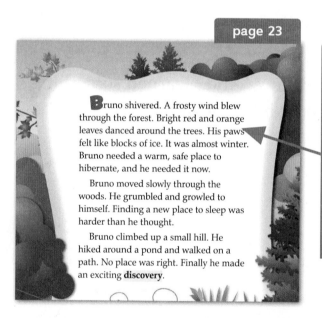

page 23

Bruno shivered. A frosty wind blew through the forest. Bright red and orange leaves danced around the trees. His paws felt like blocks of ice. It was almost winter. Bruno needed a warm, safe place to hibernate, and he needed it now.

Bruno moved slowly through the woods. He grumbled and growled to himself. Finding a new place to sleep was harder than he thought.

Bruno climbed up a small hill. He hiked around a pond and walked on a path. No place was right. Finally he made an exciting **discovery**.

_Bruno shivered. A frosty wind blew through the forest. His paws felt like blocks of ice._ From these details, I can figure out how cold Bruno feels. He needs to find a warm home so he can hibernate.

## Your Turn

COLLABORATE

How does Bruno make the cave's entrance bigger? Reread the story. Visualize what happens. Then answer the question.

John Howell

# Character

A character's actions and feelings make the events in a story happen. Traits are the special ways the character behaves.

 **Find Text Evidence**

*Bruno is the main character in the story. I will reread page 23 to find out what he wants and how he feels.*

| Character: Bruno | |
|---|---|
| **Wants or Needs** | **Feelings** |
| Bruno needs a new home for the winter. | Bruno is cold, tired, and grumpy. |
| **Actions** | **Traits** |
| | |

## Your Turn

Reread "Bruno's New Home." Think about what Bruno does next. What are his actions? What are his traits? Visualize and fill in the graphic organizer.

*Go Digital!*
*Use the interactive graphic organizer*

# Fantasy

The story "Bruno's New Home" is a fantasy. A **fantasy**:
- Has characters, settings, or events that do not exist in real life
- Has illustrations that help tell the story
- Teaches a lesson

 **Find Text Evidence**

*I can tell that "Bruno's New Home" is a fantasy. The characters are animals that talk and read. The story teaches a lesson. Illustrations show the story could not happen in real life.*

**page 25**

**Illustrations** Illustrations give more information. They show the characters doing things that are not real.

Bruno turned quickly and saw a small squirrel eating a nut. He stopped eating and smiled at Bruno.

"You look like you need help," said the squirrel.

Bruno sighed. "I have been trying to fit into this cave, but it's hopeless. I've been digging and digging, but I haven't **improved** the opening at all."

"I'm Jack, and I can help," said the squirrel.

"But you are too small," said Bruno.

Jack told Bruno to sit down and rest. Bruno sat and yawned as Jack scampered away. A few minutes later, he came back.

25

COLLABORATE

**Your Turn**

Describe two examples from "Bruno's New Home" that help you know it is a fantasy. Tell your partner.

# Synonyms

Synonyms are words that have the same meaning. In "Bruno's New Home," you may read a word you don't know. Use its synonym to figure out what it means.

 **Find Text Evidence**

*On page 23, I'm not sure what* grumbled *means. I see the word* growled *in the same sentence. I know that* growled *means "to make a deep, rumbling sound." I think* grumbled *and* growled *are synonyms. They have almost the same meanings. Now I know what* grumbled *means.*

He grumbled and growled to himself.

**Your Turn**

Find synonyms for these words from "Bruno's New Home."

**bright,** *page 26*
**satisfied,** *page 27*

Talk about what each word means with a partner.

John Howell

Pages 22-27

# Write About the Text

Alicia

I responded to the prompt: *Write a descriptive paragraph to add to the story. Have Bruno thank Jack and tell why Jack is a good friend.*

**Student Model:** *Narrative Text*

Jack's quick thinking was a big help. Bruno smiled. He raised his giant paw to give Jack a high five. He wanted to show Jack that he was grateful. Smack! Jack slapped Bruno's huge paw with his little paw. "Let's celebrate!" exclaimed Bruno happily.

### Grammar

This **complete sentence** tells a complete thought.

*Grammar Handbook*

*See page 474.*

**Describe Characters**
I described Bruno's thoughts and feelings.

quavondo/iStock/360/Getty Images

"We can decorate my new home with a colorful bed of leaves. We can make a pillow from pine cones. Will you help me?" Bruno knew he had found a friend for life when Jack agreed.

**Describe Details**
I included details to help readers visualize the story.

**Focus on an Event**
I explained how Bruno and Jack became good friends.

## Your Turn

Add a paragraph to the end of the story describing Bruno's new home. Use colorful words to help readers visualize the home.

*Go Digital!*
*Write your response online.*
*Use your editing checklist.*

John Hovell

**Essential Question**

What can traditions teach you about cultures?

*Go Digital!*

# SHARING TRADITIONS

My family and I live in Alaska. Today my grandpa is teaching us how to drum and use traditional Yupik dance fans.

▶ Traditions are passed down in my family.

▶ Traditions help me learn about my culture and customs.

▶ My family's traditions make me proud.

## Talk About It

Write words you have learned about traditions. Then talk with a partner about how your family shares traditions.

Traditions

# Vocabulary

**Use the picture and the sentence to talk with a partner about each word.**

### celebrate

Jim and his friends like to **celebrate** the Fourth of July together.

How do you like to celebrate?

### courage

Firefighters show bravery and **courage**.

What word means the same as courage?

### disappointment

Jason felt **disappointment** when it rained.

How would you show disappointment?

### precious

This **precious** necklace is special to my grandmother.

What does the word precious mean?

**pride**

I take **pride** in the vegetables I grow in my garden.

Name one time you felt pride in something you did.

**remind**

Mom will **remind** me to clean my room.

When do you need someone to remind you to do something?

**symbols**

The eagle and the flag are **symbols** of our country.

Name some symbols you know.

**tradition**

Our Sunday **tradition** is eating dinner together.

Name a tradition that people share.

COLLABORATE

## Your Turn

Pick three words. Then write three questions for your partner to answer.

*Go Digital!* *Use the online visual glossary*

# The Dream Catcher

### Essential Question

**What can traditions teach you about cultures?**

Read how Peter learns about his culture.

Richard Johnson

Peter walked home from school. Salty tears ran down his cheeks, and his stomach hurt. He didn't know what to do. Grandmother was waiting for him on the front porch.

"What's wrong, Biyen?" said Peter's grandmother. Biyen was the Ojibwe name for Peter. He called her Nokomis, which means grandmother.

Peter looked up. "I have to give a presentation where I talk about a family **tradition**. I know we have lots of beliefs and customs. Can you **remind** me of one?"

Nokomis smiled and nodded her head.

"Come with me," she said.

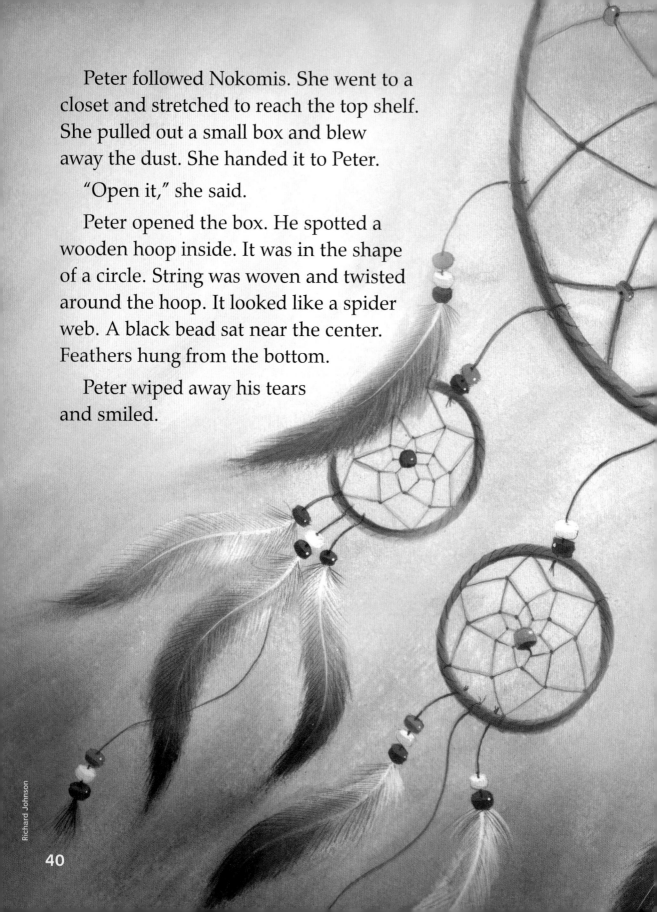

Peter followed Nokomis. She went to a closet and stretched to reach the top shelf. She pulled out a small box and blew away the dust. She handed it to Peter.

"Open it," she said.

Peter opened the box. He spotted a wooden hoop inside. It was in the shape of a circle. String was woven and twisted around the hoop. It looked like a spider web. A black bead sat near the center. Feathers hung from the bottom.

Peter wiped away his tears and smiled.

Richard Johnson

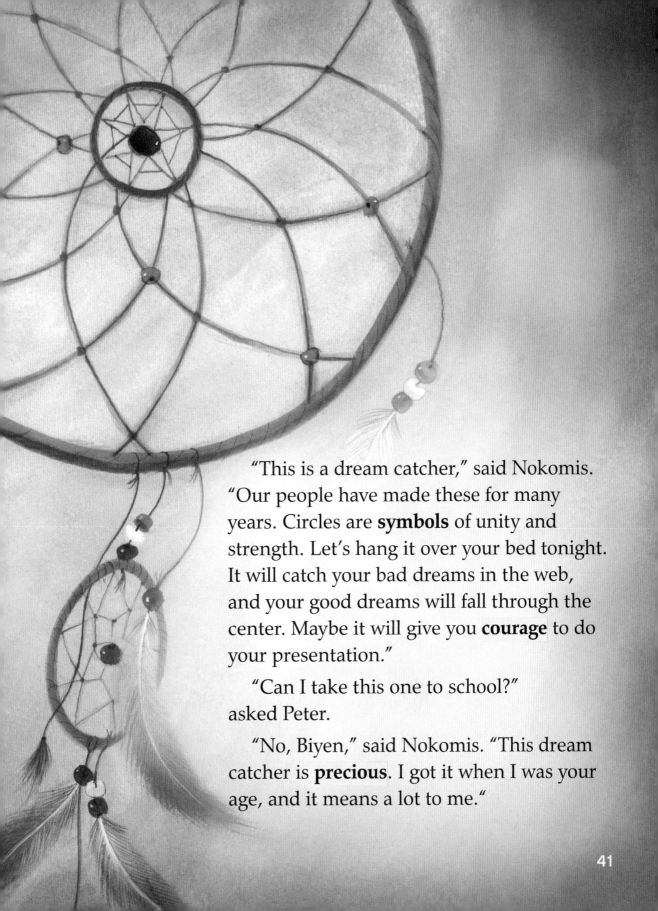

"This is a dream catcher," said Nokomis. "Our people have made these for many years. Circles are **symbols** of unity and strength. Let's hang it over your bed tonight. It will catch your bad dreams in the web, and your good dreams will fall through the center. Maybe it will give you **courage** to do your presentation."

"Can I take this one to school?" asked Peter.

"No, Biyen," said Nokomis. "This dream catcher is **precious**. I got it when I was your age, and it means a lot to me."

Peter felt **disappointment** because he wanted to share the dream catcher with his class.

"We could make you one," said Nokomis.

"I'd like that!" cried Peter.

Nokomis and Peter worked together and made a dream catcher. That night, as he gazed and looked at the dream catcher over his bed, he made a plan.

The next morning he told Nokomis his plan. "I'm going to show my class how to make a dream catcher," he said.

"That's a great idea!" said Nokomis. "Let's **celebrate** after your presentation. I will bake corn cookies and we will have a traditional Ojibwe party."

Peter shared his dream catcher with his classmates and showed them how to make their own. Peter didn't feel nervous or scared at all. He felt pride in his culture. He felt **pride** in himself, too.

## Make Connections

 What tradition did Peter learn about? How did it help him? ESSENTIAL QUESTION

What traditions do you take part in? TEXT TO SELF

# Visualize

Use details to help you visualize the characters and their actions in "The Dream Catcher." Form pictures in your mind as you read.

## Find Text Evidence

How does Peter feel at the beginning of the story? Use the details in the first paragraph on page 39.

page 39

Peter walked home from school. Salty tears ran down his cheeks, and his stomach hurt. He didn't know what to do. Grandmother was waiting for him on the front porch.

"What's wrong, Biyen?" said Peter's

*I can visualize how Peter feels at the beginning of the story. He walked home. Salty tears ran down his cheeks. His stomach hurt. These details help me figure out that Peter feels sad and upset.*

COLLABORATE

## Your Turn

How did Peter feel when he first saw the dream catcher? Reread page 40. Visualize what happened. Then answer the question.

Richard Johnson

RL.3.3 See the California Standards section.

# Sequence

A character's actions make up the plot, or events, in a story. Plot events are told in the order they happen. A plot always has a beginning, middle, and end.

 **Find Text Evidence**

*At the beginning of the story, I read to see what the characters say and do. Then I read on to see what happens in the middle of the story.*

Character
Peter and Nokomis

The events are in sequence, or time order.

Setting
Nokomis's house

Beginning
Peter is crying. Nokomis asks him what is wrong. He says he has to give a presentation at school.

Middle
Nokomis shows Peter a dream catcher. Then they make one.

End

**Your Turn**

Reread pages 42 and 43. What happens at the end of the story? List the events in order in your graphic organizer.

*Go Digital!*
*Use the interactive graphic organizer*

# Realistic Fiction

"The Dream Catcher" is realistic fiction. **Realistic fiction**:

- Is a made-up story that could really happen
- Has a beginning, middle, and end
- Has illustrations and dialogue

## Find Text Evidence

*"The Dream Catcher" is realistic fiction. I know because the events could really happen. It also has realistic illustrations and dialogue.*

page 39

**Illustrations** Illustrations give more information or details about characters and setting.

**Dialogue** Dialogue is what the characters say to each other.

Peter walked home from school. Salty tears ran down his cheeks, and his stomach hurt. He didn't know what to do. Grandmother was waiting for him on the front porch.

"What's wrong, Biyen?" said Peter's grandmother. Biyen was the Ojibwe name for Peter. He called her Nokomis, which means grandmother.

Peter looked up. "I have to give a presentation where I talk about a family **tradition**. I know we have lots of beliefs and customs. Can you **remind** me of one?"

Nokomis smiled and nodded her head.

"Come with me," she said.

39

COLLABORATE

## Your Turn

Find two things in the story that could happen in real life. Tell your partner why "The Dream Catcher" is realistic fiction.

# Context Clues

If you come across a word you don't know, use context clues. Look at other words in the same sentence. They can help you figure out the word's meaning.

 **Find Text Evidence**

*I read this sentence on page 39. I'm not sure I know what the word* presentation *means. I see the words* talk about. *This clue helps me figure out what* presentation *means. A* presentation *is a talk or speech.*

I have to give a presentation where I talk about a family tradition.

## Your Turn

Find context clues. Figure out the meanings of these words.

woven, *page 40*
gazed, *page 42*

Talk about which nearby words helped you figure out their meanings.

Richard Johnson

Pages 38–43

# Write About the Text

Walter

I responded to the prompt: *Add a paragraph to the story. Describe what happened in Peter's dreams and include the dream catcher.*

**Student Model:** *Narrative Text*

That night Peter had a dream that he was walking in the woods. A spider dropped on his shoulder. It growled, "Look up, Peter." There were spiders all around him! A huge, sticky web surrounded Peter. He tried to run, but it was harder and harder to move.

## Grammar

This text has an example of both a **command** and an **exclamation**.

*Grammar Handbook*

See page 474.

## Details

I included details about what happened in the dream.

©Jose Luis Pelaez Inc/Blend Images LLC

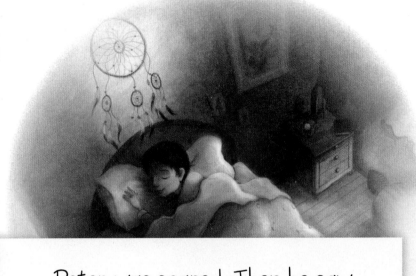

Peter was scared. Then he saw his dream catcher up ahead. He reached out his arms as far as he could. When Peter finally touched the dream catcher, the spiders and their sticky web melted away.

**Point of View**
I showed what Peter was thinking and feeling.

**Order of Events**
I told the events in the dream in order.

## Your Turn

Add a paragraph to the end of the story. Write about what happened when Peter got home from school after his presentation.

*Go Digital!*
*Write your response online.*
*Use your editing checklist.*

Richard Johnson

**Essential Question**
How do people from different cultures contribute to a community?

Go Digital!

50

Philip Scalia/Alamy

# MAKING A CONTRIBUTION

David is sharing his culture with the people in his community.

- ▶ Learning about different cultures is important.
- ▶ Different cultures make a community more interesting.
- ▶ Communities grow when people share their cultures.

## Talk About It

Write words you have learned about cultures and communities. Talk about what you can learn from other people.

Communities

# Vocabulary

**Use the picture and the sentence to talk with
a partner about each word.**

### admires

My family **admires** my good
test grades.

What do you admire about a friend?

### classmate

Don and his **classmate** Maria always
eat lunch together.

What things do you do with a
classmate?

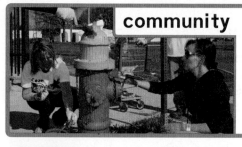

### community

Many people in my **community**
work together.

What do you like about your
community?

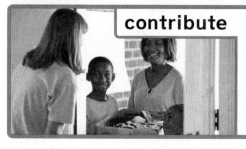

### contribute

Mom will **contribute** clothes to
people who can use them.

What could you contribute to a
bake sale?

**practicing**

Kyle has been **practicing** and now he can play lots of songs.

What skill can you improve by practicing?

**pronounce**

Cindy can **pronounce** her name in another language.

How do you pronounce your last name?

**scared**

Our dog hides during storms because he is **scared**.

What do you do when you feel scared?

**tumbled**

The ripe tomatoes **tumbled** out of the big basket onto the ground.

What does tumbled mean?

## Your Turn

COLLABORATE

Pick three words. Then write three questions for your partner to answer.

*Go Digital!* *Use the online visual glossary*

(t) Intl St. Clair/Photodisc/Getty Images; (tc) Creatas/PictureQuest; (bc) Talena Sanders/Flickr/Getty Images; (b) Food and Drink/Superstock

# Room to Grow

Our new home in Portland

## Essential Question

How do people from different cultures contribute to a community?

Read how one family helps their community grow.

# Spring in the City

My name is Kiku Sato. Last spring, my family and I moved from the country to the big city.

Our new home in Portland had no yard. There wasn't even a tiny plot of land. So Mama made an indoor garden. First she and Papa planted seeds in pots. Then they hung them from hooks. Next they crammed plants onto shelves. Green vines **tumbled** over desks. Soon our house had plants everywhere.

At first I was **scared** to start school. I was afraid no one would be my friend. But I soon met a **classmate**. Jill Hernandez and I were **practicing** reading aloud one day. She helped me say her last name, and I helped her **pronounce** mine. The next day we were best friends. Jill spent lots of time at my house.

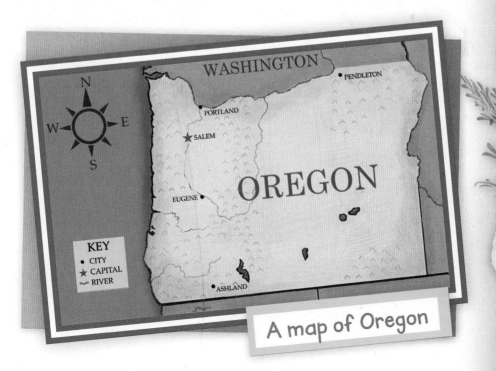

A map of Oregon

# An idea for a garden

One afternoon, Jill and her mother came to visit Mama and Papa and me. First they saw our beautiful potted plants. Jill's mother said, "Jill **admires** your indoor garden. She has told me so much about it."

We all sat down while Mama served tea. First she put green tea into the tea bowl. Then she added hot water and stirred. She handed the bowl to Jill's mother and bowed.

Mama's special tea bowls

Grandmother in Japan

"My mother taught me how to make tea," said Mama. "She also taught me how to plant a traditional Japanese garden. I learned to make the most of a small, compact space."

All of a sudden, Jill's mother smiled. "Can you help us with a project?" she asked. "Our **community** wants to plant a garden. Our plot is very small. There is so much we want to grow."

Papa looked at Mama, and they both bowed.

"Yes," they said.

# A Garden Grows

First we had a meeting with the community. Everyone agreed to **contribute**. Some people brought seeds, tools, and dirt. Then the next day we met and started our garden.

Papa built long, open boxes. Next, we filled them with dirt. The tallest box went close to the back wall. The boxes got shorter and shorter. The shortest box was in the front. "All the plants will get sunlight without making shade for the others," Mama said.

Papa building boxes

Jill and I planting seeds

Then, we used round, flat stones to make a rock path. Papa said that in Japan, stones are an important part of a garden. Finally, we planted the seeds.

Jill and I worked in the garden all summer. Our community grew many different vegetables. At the end of the summer, we picked enough to have a cookout. Mama brought a big pot of miso and vegetable stew. Everyone thanked Mama and Papa for their help. They brought a bit of Japan to Portland. I was so proud.

Look what we picked!

## Make Connections

What did Kiku's family do to help their new community? What parts of their culture did they share? ESSENTIAL QUESTION

How can you and your family contribute to your community? TEXT TO SELF

# Ask and Answer Questions

Ask yourself questions as you read. Then look for details to support your answers.

## Find Text Evidence

Look at the section "Spring in the City" on page 55. Think of a question. Then read to answer it.

page 55

### Spring in the City

My name is Kiku Sato. Last spring, my family and I moved from the country to the big city.

Our new home in Portland had no yard. There wasn't even a tiny plot of land. So Mama made an indoor garden. First she and Papa planted seeds in pots. Then they hung them from hooks. Next they crammed plants onto shelves. Green vines **tumbled** over desks. Soon our house had plants everywhere.

At first I was **scared** to start school. I was afraid no one would be my friend. But I soon met a **classmate**. Jill Hernandez and I were **practicing** reading aloud one day. She helped me say her last name, and I helped her **pronounce** mine. The next day we were best friends. Jill spent lots of time at my house.

WASHINGTON

*I have a question. Why were there so many plants in Kiku's house? I read that they did not have a yard. Mama and Papa planted lots of seeds. I can answer my question. Kiku's family liked to grow things and didn't have the space to do it outdoors.*

## Your Turn

COLLABORATE

Reread "An Idea for a Garden." Think of one question. You might ask: Why did Jill's mother ask Kiku's mother for help? Read the section again to find the answer.

# Sequence

Sequence is the order in which important events take place. Look for words, such as *first, next, then,* and *finally.* These signal words show the sequence of events.

 **Find Text Evidence**

*In this autobiography, the events are told in sequence. I see the signal word* first *in "Spring in the City" on page 55. I will read to find out what happens next. I will look for signal words to help me.*

> Event
>
> First Mama and Papa planted lots of seeds.

⬇

> Event
>
> Then they hung pots from hooks.

⬇

> Event

**Your Turn** COLLABORATE

Reread "Spring in the City." What happens next? List the events in order in your graphic organizer.

*Go Digital!*
*Use the interactive graphic organizer*

# Narrative Nonfiction

"Room to Grow" is an autobiography. An **autobiography**:

- Is a kind of narrative nonfiction
- Tells the true story of a person's life in order
- Is written by that person and uses *I* and *me*

 **Find Text Evidence**

*I know "Room to Grow" is an autobiography. It is a true story written by Kiku about her life. She uses the words* I *and* me. *Kiku's story also has headings and a map.*

**page 55**

### Spring in the city

My name is Kiku Sato. Last spring, my family and I moved from the country to the big city.

Our new home in Portland had no yard. There wasn't even a tiny plot of land. So Mama made an indoor garden. First she and Papa planted seeds in pots. Then they hung them from hooks. Next they crammed plants onto shelves. Green vines **tumbled** over desks. Soon our house had plants everywhere.

At first I was **scared** to start school. I was afraid no one would be my friend. But I soon met a **classmate**. Jill Hernandez and I were **practicing** reading aloud one day. She helped me say her last name, and I helped her **pronounce** mine. The next day we were best friends. Jill spent lots of time at my house.

A map of Oregon

55

## Text Features

**Headings** Headings tell what a section of text is mostly about.

**Map** A map is a flat drawing of a real place.

COLLABORATE

## Your Turn

Find parts of "Room to Grow" that show you it is an autobiography. Tell your partner what you learned about Kiku and her culture.

# Compound Words

A compound word has two small words in it. Put together the meanings of the two smaller words. Figure out the meaning of the compound word.

## Find Text Evidence

*I see the compound word* afternoon *on page 56. It has two smaller words,* after *and* noon. *I know what* after *means. I know* noon *means 12 o'clock. I think* afternoon *means a time after 12 o'clock.*

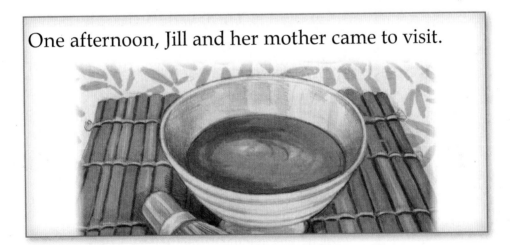

One afternoon, Jill and her mother came to visit.

## Your Turn

COLLABORATE

Figure out the meanings of these compound words.
**sunlight,** *page 58, "A Garden Grows"*
**cookout,** *page 59, "A Garden Grows"*

Margaret Lindmark

Pages 54–59

# Write About the Text

Gina

I answered the question: *What point was the author trying to make in writing this selection?*

## Student Model: *Informative Text*

**Topic Sentence**
My first sentence explains the author's message.

**Sequence**
I used words that show order to organize my text.

The author's point in "Room to Grow" is that when people plan and work hard, they can do more than they expect. Kiku's parents knew how to grow many plants in a small space. First they planted a little indoor garden that contained many different plants.

Then Kiku's parents helped the local community garden figure out how to grow more plants in a small space. Everyone in the neighborhood worked together to plant the garden. They grew many plants that summer!

## Grammar

*Everyone in the neighborhood* is the **complete subject** of this sentence.

*Grammar Handbook* *See page 475.*

**Concluding Statement**
The last sentence sums up my informative text.

## Your Turn

How would you describe Kiku's community?

*Go Digital!*
*Write your response online.*
*Use your editing checklist.*

Margaret Lindmark

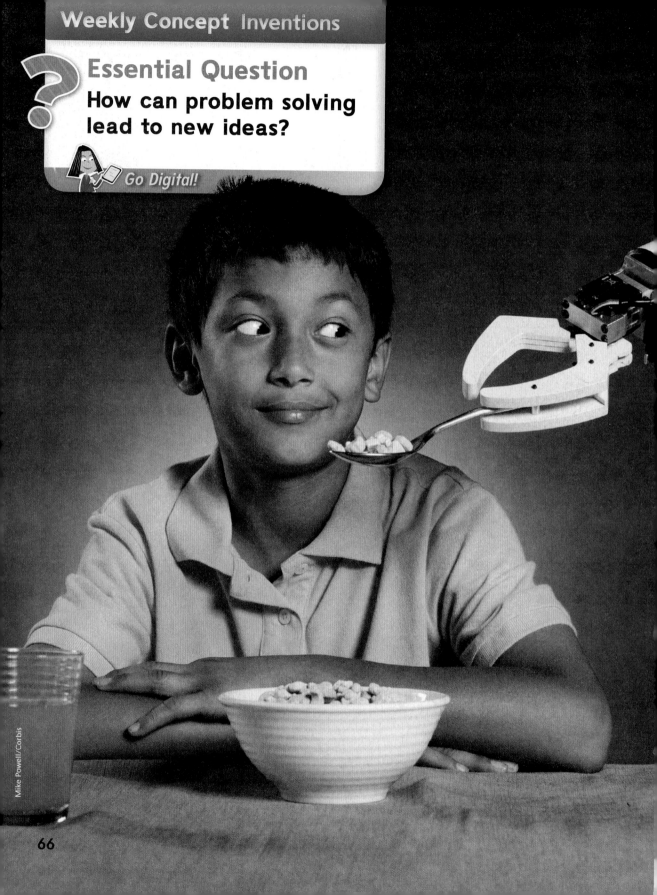

**Essential Question**
How can problem solving lead to new ideas?

Go Digital!

Mike Powell/Corbis

# Inventing Something New

Almost every new invention starts with a problem and a new idea.

▶ Inventions make our lives better.

▶ Some inventions help us learn.

▶ Other inventions entertain us.

## Talk About It

Talk with a partner about inventions. Write words that tell how inventors think up new ideas.

Inventions

# Vocabulary

Use the picture and the sentence to talk with
a partner about each word.

**design**

Jake and Andy are helping to **design** a picture for the school's new wall.

How would you design something new?

**encouraged**

My teacher **encouraged** us to eat healthy snacks.

Name something someone has encouraged you to do.

**examine**

The vet will **examine** my dog to make sure he is healthy.

What does the word examine mean?

**investigation**

Tom did a careful **investigation** of the spider web in his yard.

What can you do during an investigation?

**quality**

A good **quality** helmet helps keep me safe.

Why do people buy good quality things?

**simple**

Walking my dog is a **simple** and easy way to have fun.

What word in the sentence means the same as simple?

**solution**

Marco found a **solution** that helped him get better grades.

What does it mean to find a solution?

**substitutes**

Fruit and popcorn are healthful **substitutes** for candy.

Name two more healthful substitutes for sweets.

COLLABORATE

## Your Turn

Pick three words. Then write three questions for your partner to answer.

*Go Digital!* **Use the online visual glossary**

# Mary Anderson's
# GREAT
# INVENTION

**Essential Question**

How can problem solving lead to new ideas?

Read about how someone solved a problem and invented something new.

Malene Laugesen

You might think that a ride in a bus or car is the same today as it was long ago. That isn't true. The first cars were not as fast. They were noisy. Cars didn't even have windshield wipers!

When it rained, drivers rubbed their windshields with an onion. The oil from the onion would repel, or keep off, rain and sleet. It wasn't the best **solution**, but there were no better **substitutes**. Nothing else worked. Then a woman named Mary Anderson solved the problem.

## It Started with Snow

Mary Anderson grew up in Alabama. In the winter of 1902, she went to New York City. It was a cold and windy day. The sky was a gray curtain. Snow was a white blanket on the ground. Mary was cold and wet. Because she wanted to warm up and get dry, she rode a streetcar.

Back then, some streetcar windshields had two parts. They opened with a push. From her seat, Mary watched snow and ice build up on the windshield. The streetcar driver could not see. So, he pushed open the windshield. This helped him to see better. As a result, snow and ice blew in his face. Soon his nose and ears were ice cubes.

Other cars kept stopping, too. Sometimes the drivers hopped out. They wiped off their windshields. Then, they got back in and drove. As a result, traffic moved slowly.

Malene Laugesen

# The Next Step

Mary thought about this problem. How could drivers clean their windshields without stopping? Could they do it without opening their windshield?

Back home in Alabama, Mary sketched her idea. Then she added notes. She wanted to **examine** her solution to make sure that it worked. Next, Mary did her own **investigation**. She looked for facts about what drivers needed. She invented a windshield wiper that a driver could use from inside the car. Then she worked out a **design**, or plan. On paper, Mary's invention looked **simple**. She hoped drivers would find it easy to use.

## Mary Anderson's Windshield Wiper

Window

Wiper

The first windshield wiper was moved by a handle inside the car.

Mary had a model built. It was made of **quality** wood, rubber, and metal. Soon the model was ready to test. It was fitted on a windshield. The driver moved a handle inside the car. The handle caused a blade to move back and forth across the glass. It worked! Mary's idea was a gem! She felt **encouraged** and was sure it would sell.

## Solving the Problem

Mary's windshield wipers solved a problem. But it took many years before people used them. That's because most people did not own cars.

By 1913, more people bought and drove cars. Those cars had windshields. Finally windshield wipers began to sell. Driving became safer and easier because of Mary Anderson's idea.

# Safer to Drive

Cars from long ago were different from cars we ride in today. Here are some more inventions that helped make driving safer.

- The first seat belts were used in 1885.
- Cars stopped at the first stop sign in 1915.
- Cars first used turn signals in 1938.

## Make Connections

Talk about how Mary Anderson's solution to a problem led to a new idea. ESSENTIAL QUESTION

What inventions can you think of that have made your life better? TEXT TO SELF

# Ask and Answer Questions

Ask yourself questions as you read "Mary Anderson's Great Invention." Then look for details to support your answers.

## 🔍 Find Text Evidence

Look at the section "It Started with Snow" on page 72. Think of a question. Then read to answer it.

page 72

**It Started with Snow**

Mary Anderson grew up in Alabama. In the winter of 1902, she went to New York City. It was a cold and windy day. The sky was a gray curtain. Snow was a white blanket on the ground. Mary was cold and wet. Because she wanted to warm up and get dry, she rode a streetcar.

Back then, some streetcar windshields had two parts. They opened with a push. From her seat, Mary watched snow and ice build up on the windshield. The streetcar driver could not see. So, he pushed open the windshield. This helped him to see better. As a result, snow and ice blew in his face. Soon his nose and ears were ice cubes.

Other cars kept stopping, too. Sometimes the drivers hopped out. They wiped off their windshields. Then, they got back in and drove. As a result, traffic moved slowly.

*I have a question. Why did drivers push open their windshields? I read that windshields had two parts. The driver pushed it open. This helped him see where he was going. Now I can answer my question. Opening the windshield helped the driver see better.*

COLLABORATE

## Your Turn

Think of one question about Mary Anderson's invention. You might ask: How did it work? Reread page 74 to answer it.

Malene Laugesen

# Cause and Effect

A cause is why something happens. An effect is what happens. They happen in time order. Signal words, such as *because* and *as a result*, show cause and effect.

 **Find Text Evidence**

*On page 72 I read that Mary rode a streetcar. This is the effect. Now I can find the cause. Mary was cold and wet. She wanted to warm up and get dry. The signal word* because *helped me find the cause and effect.*

| Cause | ➡ | Effect |
|---|---|---|
| **First**<br>Mary was cold and wet and wanted to warm up. | ➡ | Mary rode a streetcar. |
| **Next**<br>Snow and ice built up on the streetcar's windshield. | ➡ | |

## Your Turn

Reread "Mary Anderson's Great Invention." Use signal words to find more causes and effects. Fill in the graphic organizer. Make sure events are in time order.

*Go Digital!*
*Use the interactive graphic organizer*

# Biography

"Mary Anderson's Great Invention" is a biography.
A **biography**:
- Tells the true story of a real person's life and is written by another person
- Is told in sequence, or time order
- May have diagrams or sidebars

## Find Text Evidence

*"Mary Anderson's Great Invention" is a biography. It is a true story about a person's life. It is written by another person. The events are told in order.*

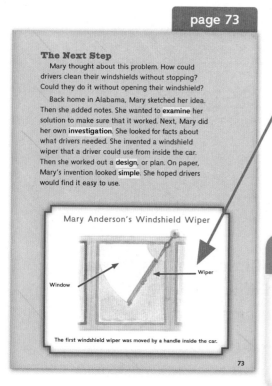

page 73

**The Next Step**

Mary thought about this problem. How could drivers clean their windshields without stopping? Could they do it without opening their windshield?

Back home in Alabama, Mary sketched her idea. Then she added notes. She wanted to **examine** her solution to make sure that it worked. Next, Mary did her own **investigation**. She looked for facts about what drivers needed. She invented a windshield wiper that a driver could use from inside the car. Then she worked out a **design**, or plan. On paper, Mary's invention looked **simple**. She hoped drivers would find it easy to use.

Mary Anderson's Windshield Wiper

Window

Wiper

The first windshield wiper was moved by a handle inside the car.

73

## Text Features

**Diagrams** Diagrams are simple drawings with labels.

**Sidebars** Sidebars give more information about a topic.

COLLABORATE

## Your Turn

Reread "Mary Anderson's Great Invention." Find text features. Tell what you learned from each of the text features.

Malene Laugesen

# Metaphors

"The sun is a yellow ball" is a metaphor. A metaphor compares two things that are very different. Look for metaphors as you read.

 **Find Text Evidence**

*On page 72, I see the sentence "The sky was a gray curtain." This is a metaphor. It compares the sky to a gray curtain. It means that the sky was dark and cloudy. This metaphor helps me picture a dark and gloomy sky.*

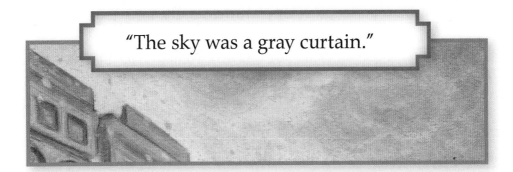

"The sky was a gray curtain."

## Your Turn

Talk about these metaphors from the story. What two things do they compare?

*Snow was a white blanket on the ground.*
page 72
*Soon his nose and ears were ice cubes.*
page 72

Malene Laugesen

Pages 70–75

# Write About the Text

David

I answered the question: *What problem was Mary Anderson trying to solve with her invention? Explain using text evidence.*

**Student Model:** *Informative Text*

Mary Anderson thought that drivers needed to see better in bad weather. Rain and snow would hit a car's windshield. That made it hard to see the road. Mary decided to solve this problem. Her idea was a windshield wiper that was controlled from inside a car.

**Topic Sentence**
My first sentence tells about the problem Mary Anderson saw.

**Grammar**

*Decided to solve this problem* is the **complete predicate** of this sentence.

*Grammar Handbook*

*See page 475.*

**Supporting Details**
I used text evidence to answer the question.

bobbieo/E+/Getty Images

First she sketched her ideas. Next she added notes to her sketches. Then she had a model made of her invention. Last, a driver tested the new windshield wiper. It worked!

**Time-Order Words**
I added words to connect ideas and put events in order.

## Your Turn

Where do ideas for inventions come from? Use evidence from the text to support your answer.

*Go Digital!*
*Write your response online.*
*Use your editing checklist.*

## Essential Question

How do landmarks help us understand our country's story?

*Go Digital!*

Ronnie James/Alamy

SL.3.lb  See the California Standards section.

# UNDERSTANDING HISTORY

Martin Luther King, Jr. played an important role in American history. This monument in Washington, D.C. honors his life.

▶ People visit monuments to learn about important people and events in history.

▶ Landmarks and monuments help us remember and understand history.

## Talk About It

Write words you have learned about landmarks. Talk with a partner about how these monuments help people learn about history.

Landmarks

# Vocabulary

**Use the picture and the sentence to talk with a partner about each word.**

**carved**

A strong river **carved** this canyon out of rock.

What other things can be carved?

**clues**

These paw prints are **clues** that a dog walked here today.

What clues tell you that it might rain?

**grand**

Diane sat and gazed at the **grand** view of the river.

What do you think would make a grand view?

**landmark**

The Statue of Liberty is an American **landmark**.

What other landmarks can you name?

**massive**

The boaters looked up at the **massive** stone cliff.

What is another word for massive?

**monument**

This **monument** honors the leaders of our country.

Describe a monument you have seen.

**national**

The Fourth of July is a **national** holiday.

Name another national holiday.

**traces**

In the morning we found **traces**, or small amounts, of snow on the plants.

What is another word for traces?

COLLABORATE

## Your Turn

Pick three words. Write three questions for your partner to answer.

*Go Digital!* *Use the online visual glossary*

## Essential Question

How do landmarks help us understand our country's story?

Read about what one national landmark teaches us.

Kristy-Anne Glubish/Design Pics

# A Natural Beauty

It is a famous **landmark** in the United States, and it's huge! It is one mile deep and ten miles wide. It was **carved** out of rock by the Colorado River. It stretches across parts of four states. What is it? It's the **Grand** Canyon!

## Exploring the Canyon

Many tourists visit the Grand Canyon. In fact, almost five million people take a trip to this **national** treasure each year. People come from around the world to hike the dusty trails. They take boat rides down the Colorado River. They gaze across miles of **massive** red and brown cliffs.

Nature lovers visit the Grand Canyon, too. They come to look for animals. They peek at the hundreds of different kinds of plants. They may spot eagles and see mountain lions. They may spy snakes and spiders, and some may even see bats. Some visitors also come to learn about the canyon's history.

# History of the Canyon

Explorers from Europe first saw the Grand Canyon in 1540. But Native Americans were the first people to explore the Grand Canyon. Groups of Native Americans settled there long before 1540.

One group was the Ancestral Puebloans. They lived in the canyon for more than one thousand years. They were farmers and hunters. Scientists have found **traces**, or parts, of their old homes still standing.

Grain was stored in buildings like these.

Scientists have also found ancient rocks in the Grand Canyon. These rocks are some of the oldest in the world. They are clues to how the canyon was formed. Some scientists look for **clues** about the people who lived there. They have found tools and pieces of pottery.

## A Great Big Park

This map shows where the Grand Canyon is located.

UTAH

NEVADA

GRAND CANYON NATIONAL PARK

Colorado River

N
W · E
S

Lake Mead

○ Las Vegas

15

Colorado River

North Rim

Grand Canyon ○ Village

ARIZONA

○ City
— Highway
Grand Canyon National Park

Kingman

40

Flagstaff

# It's a Landmark

President Theodore Roosevelt visited the Grand Canyon in 1903. He saw how beautiful it was. He said it was a special place. As a result, he made it a national monument. Then in 1919, the Grand Canyon was declared a national park. That means the land is protected. No one can build homes on it. The Grand Canyon is a place all Americans can enjoy.

## Protect the Canyon

It is important for people to take care of national landmarks. We can do our part by following the rules when we visit. Animals and wildlife are safe there and should not be touched. Rivers must be kept clean.

There is still a lot to learn about this beautiful landmark. It is important that we protect it.

Bighorn sheep live in the Grand Canyon.

## Make Connections

How does the Grand Canyon teach us about America's story? ESSENTIAL QUESTION

What do you find most interesting about the Grand Canyon's history? Why? TEXT TO SELF

# Ask and Answer Questions

Stop and ask yourself questions as you read. Then look for details to support your answers.

 **Find Text Evidence**

Reread the section "Exploring the Canyon" on page 87. Think of a question. Then read to answer it.

page 87

### Exploring the Canyon

Many tourists visit the Grand Canyon. In fact, almost five million people take a trip to this **national** treasure each year. People come from around the world to hike the dusty trails. They take boat rides down the Colorado River. They gaze across miles of **massive** red and brown cliffs.

Nature lovers visit the Grand Canyon, too. They come to look for animals. They peek at the hundreds of different kinds of plants. They may spot eagles and see mountain lions. They may spy snakes and spiders, and some may even see bats. Some visitors also come to learn about the canyon's history.

87

*I have a question. Why do people visit the Grand Canyon? I read that people like to hike trails and take boat rides. They like to look at the animals and cliffs. They go to learn about its history. Now I can answer my question. People visit the canyon for many reasons.*

## Your Turn

 COLLABORATE

Reread "History of the Canyon." Think of one question. You might ask: How do we know about people who once lived in the canyon? Read the section again to find the answer.

# Main Idea and Key Details

The main idea is the most important point the author makes about a topic. Key details tell about the main idea.

## Find Text Evidence

*What details tell about why people visit the Grand Canyon? I can reread page 87 and find important details. Then I can figure out what these key details have in common to tell the main idea.*

| Main Idea |
|---|
| |
| **Detail** |
| People hike the trails and take boat rides down the river. |
| **Detail** |
| They like to gaze across the massive red and brown cliffs. |
| **Detail** |
| |

**Your Turn**

COLLABORATE

Reread. Find more key details about why people visit the Grand Canyon. List them in your graphic organizer. Then use the details to figure out the main idea.

*Go Digital!*
**Use the interactive graphic organizer**

# Expository Text

"A Natural Beauty" is an expository text.
**Expository text:**

- Gives facts and information about a social studies topic
- Includes text features such as photographs, captions, sidebars, and maps

## Find Text Evidence

*I can tell that "A Natural Beauty" is an expository text. It gives facts and information about the Grand Canyon. It also has photographs, captions, a sidebar, and a map.*

page 88

### History of the Canyon

Explorers from Europe first saw the Grand Canyon in 1540. But Native Americans were the first people to explore the Grand Canyon. Groups of Native Americans settled there long before 1540.

One group was the Ancestral Puebloans. They lived in the canyon for more than one thousand years. They were farmers and hunters. Scientists have found **traces**, or parts, of their old homes still standing.

Grain was stored in buildings like these.

Scientists have also found ancient rocks in the Grand Canyon. These rocks are some of the oldest in the world. They are clues to how the canyon was formed. Some scientists look for **clues** about the people who lived there. They have found tools and pieces of pottery.

A Great Big Park

This map shows where the Grand Canyon is located.

## Text Features

**Captions** Captions give extra information that is not in a text.

**Map** A map is a flat drawing of a real place.

**Sidebar** A sidebar gives more information about a topic.

COLLABORATE

### Your Turn

Find more text features in "A Natural Beauty." What else did you learn?

# Multiple-Meaning Words

Multiple-meaning words have more than one meaning. Find other words in the sentence to help you figure out the meaning of a multiple-meaning word.

 **Find Text Evidence**

*On page 87 I see* bats. *This word can mean "wooden sticks used to hit a ball" or "small animals that fly." The context clues, "spy snakes and spiders" can help me figure out that* bats *are animals in this sentence. Now I know that* bats *here are "small animals that fly at night."*

They may spy snakes and spiders, and some may even see bats.

## Your Turn

COLLABORATE

Use context clues to figure out the meanings of the following words.

**spot,** *page 87*
**safe,** *page 89*

Kristy-Anne Glubish/Design Pics

**A Natural Beauty**

Pages 86-89

# Write About the Text

Patrick

I answered the question: *In your opinion, does the author convince readers that the Grand Canyon is an important landmark? Use text evidence in your answer.*

**Student Model:** *Opinion*

The author gives facts that convinced me that the Grand Canyon is an important landmark. What facts does the author include? The canyon is a mile deep. It was carved out of rock by the Colorado River. Mountain lions and eagles live in the canyon.

**State an Opinion**
My first sentence tells what I think about the text.

**Sentence Types**
I used statements, questions, and exclamations to make my text more interesting.

**Supporting Reasons**
I based my opinion on evidence from the text.

Some visitors come to enjoy nature, but other people come to learn about history. The author says that the Grand Canyon was made a national park in 1919. Now I know why!

**Grammar**

Two **simple sentences** can be combined with the conjunction *but* to make a **compound sentence.**

*Grammar Handbook*

*See page 476.*

## Your Turn

In your opinion, what are the most interesting things to see in the Grand Canyon? Use evidence from the text to support your answer.

*Go Digital!*
*Write your response online.*
*Use your editing checklist.*

Kristy-Anne Glubish/Design Pics

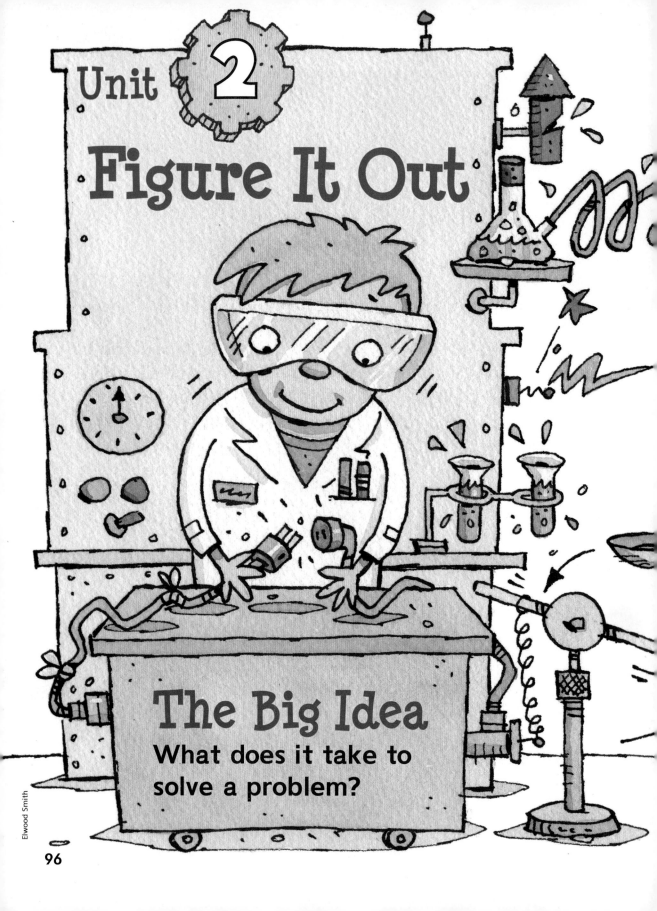

# Figure It Out

## The Big Idea

What does it take to solve a problem?

Elwood Smith

# The Problem Solver

If you have a problem,
    Super-sized or small,
I've got some suggestions,
    Just give me a call.

Do a lot of reading,
    Study every fact,
Write down some solutions,
    Think before you act.

If the problem is too hard,
    Ask a friend or two,
Teamwork's always better,
    When there's work to do.

Problems always pop up,
    Do not scream or cry,
You'll find a solution,
    If you only try.

— Constance Andrea Keremes

97

**Essential Question**
Why is working together a
good way to solve a problem?

Go Digital!

Leland Bobbé/Fuse/Getty Images

98

# WORKING TOGETHER

There was a problem, and these friends figured out what to do. Now they are working together to solve it.

▶ Working together is a good way to solve problems.

▶ Cooperation makes the job easier.

## Talk About It

Write words you have learned about working together. Talk with a partner about how cooperation helps get things done.

Cooperation

# Vocabulary

**Use the picture and the sentence to talk with a partner about each word.**

**attempt**

Maria made an **attempt** to run a mile.

When have you made an attempt to do something new?

**awkward**

The penguin looked **awkward** and clumsy.

What word in the sentence means the same as awkward?

**cooperation**

I cleaned the floor faster with Becky's **cooperation**.

Tell about a time when cooperation made a job easier.

**created**

Jim and his grandfather **created** a home for birds out of wood.

What is another word for created?

**furiously**

The rattlesnake shook its tail **furiously** as a warning.

What might make a rattlesnake shake its tail furiously?

**interfere**

The rain is going to **interfere** with our ballgame.

What kind of weather might interfere with your plans?

**involved**

Our class is **involved** in the school play.

What activity are you involved in?

**timid**

The shy, **timid** kitten hid under a blanket.

What is the opposite of timid?

## Your Turn

COLLABORATE

Pick three words. Then write three questions for your partner to answer.

*Go Digital!*  *Use the online visual glossary*

# Anansi
# Learns a Lesson

102

Anansi the Spider lived alone and made his lunch the same time each day. One afternoon, Turtle stopped by.

"I hate to get in the way and **interfere** with your meal, but those bananas look wonderful," said Turtle. "I am so hungry."

Anansi knew he should share with others. It was a big part of his culture. But he was hungry and didn't want to share. He decided to play a trick on Turtle.

"Please, help yourself," Anansi said with a sly grin.

Turtle reached for the food. "Shouldn't you wash your hands?" asked Anansi.

"Oh, yes!" Turtle said. When Turtle returned, Anansi had eaten half of the bananas.

"I didn't want the bananas to spoil," said Anansi.

Turtle got closer and made another **attempt** to eat. Anansi stopped him again.

"Turtle, please go wash your hands," he said.

Turtle knew his hands were clean, but Anansi still thought they were filthy. However, Turtle was too shy and **timid** to say no. When he returned Anansi had eaten the rest of the fruit.

"Ha, ha, I tricked you, Turtle," said Anansi. "You didn't get any bananas!"

Janet Broxon

Turtle was angry at Anansi. He decided to teach that nasty spider a lesson. "Please come to my house at the bottom of the lake for dinner tomorrow," said Turtle.

Anansi quickly said yes. He loved free food.

Turtle couldn't trick Anansi alone, so he decided to ask Fish to get **involved** and help make a plan.

Turtle found Fish at the lake. "Fish, I need your help," he said. "With your **cooperation**, we can trick Anansi." Anansi had tricked Fish many times so Fish was happy to help. Together the two friends **created** a clever plan.

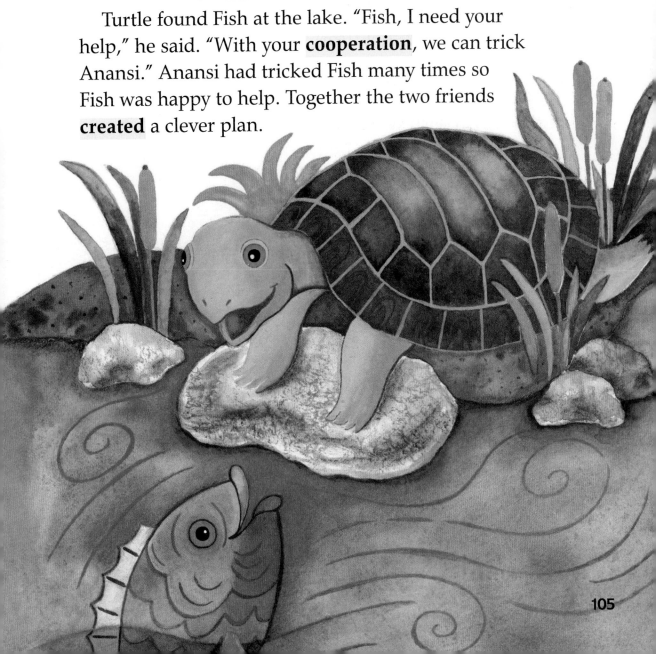

The next day, Anansi went to the lake. Fish met him at the water's edge. "Come Anansi," said Fish. "We will swim to Turtle's house together." Anansi jumped into the water. He was a clumsy and **awkward** swimmer. He was also very light.

"How will I ever get down to Turtle's house?" he cried.

Fish knew what to say. "Grab some heavy stones. Then you will sink, not float."

Anansi picked up two big stones, jumped into the lake, and sank down, down, down. Fish swam at his side. At Turtle's house, Anansi saw a wonderful feast of berries.

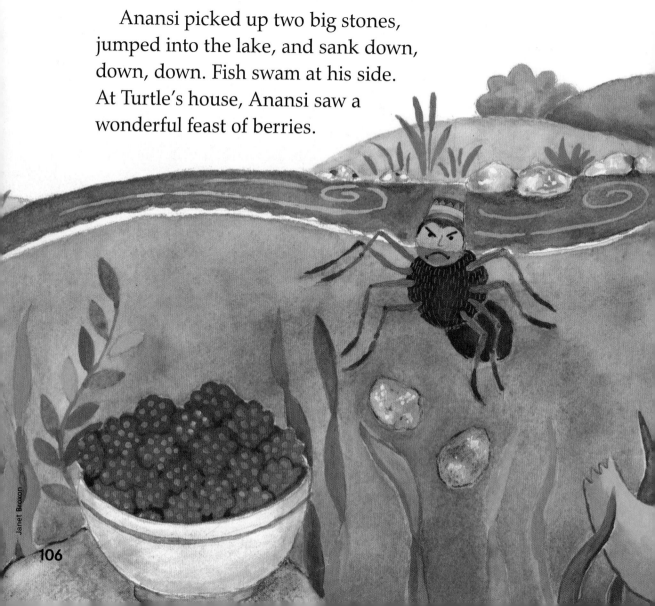

Janet Broxon

106

"Welcome, Anansi," said Turtle. "Drop those stones and help yourself."

As soon as Anansi dropped the stones, he rocketed to the surface of the lake. Anansi sputtered **furiously**. "Fish and Turtle tricked me," he cried angrily.

Back at the bottom of the lake, Turtle and Fish laughed and laughed.

"We worked together and taught Anansi a lesson," said Turtle.

"What a good way to solve a problem," said Fish. "Let's eat!"

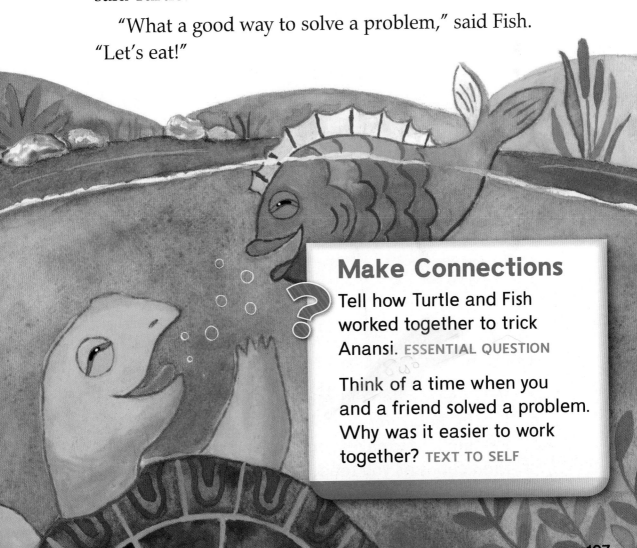

## Make Connections

Tell how Turtle and Fish worked together to trick Anansi. ESSENTIAL QUESTION

Think of a time when you and a friend solved a problem. Why was it easier to work together? TEXT TO SELF

# Make Predictions

Use clues in the story to guess, or predict, what happens next. Was your prediction right? Read on to check it. Change it if it is not right.

## Find Text Evidence

You may have made a prediction about Anansi at the beginning of "Anansi Learns a Lesson." What clues on page 103 helped you guess what might happen?

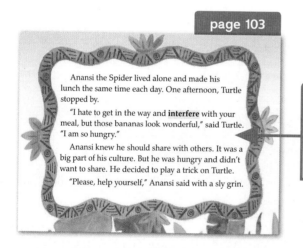

page 103

Anansi the Spider lived alone and made his lunch the same time each day. One afternoon, Turtle stopped by.

"I hate to get in the way and **interfere** with your meal, but those bananas look wonderful," said Turtle. "I am so hungry."

Anansi knew he should share with others. It was a big part of his culture. But he was hungry and didn't want to share. He decided to play a trick on Turtle.

"Please, help yourself," Anansi said with a sly grin.

*I predicted that Anansi would eat the bananas. I read that <u>Anansi was hungry and didn't want to share. He decided to play a trick on Turtle.</u> I will read on to check my prediction.*

## Your Turn

COLLABORATE

What prediction did you make after Turtle asked Fish for help? Reread to check your prediction. Remember to make, confirm, and revise predictions as you read.

Janet Broxon

# Theme

The theme of a story is the author's message. Think about what the characters do and say. Use these key details to help you figure out the theme.

## Find Text Evidence

*In "Anansi Learns a Lesson," Turtle and Fish work together to solve a problem. This is the story's theme. I can reread to find key details that help me figure out the theme.*

| Detail |
| --- |
| Anansi tricks Turtle, so Turtle decides to trick Anansi. |

↓

| Detail |
| --- |
| Turtle asks Fish to help, and they make a plan. |

↓

| Detail |
| --- |
|  |

↓

| Theme |
| --- |
| Working together is a good way to solve problems. |

COLLABORATE

## Your Turn

Reread "Anansi Learns a Lesson." List an important detail about Turtle's actions in your graphic organizer. Be sure the detail tells about the theme.

*Go Digital!*
*Use the interactive graphic organizer*

# Folktale

"Anansi Learns a Lesson" is a folktale. A **folktale**:

- Is a short story passed from person to person in a culture
- Usually has a message or lesson

## Find Text Evidence

*I can tell that "Anansi Learns a Lesson" is a folktale. I learned something about Anansi's culture. I also learned a lesson.*

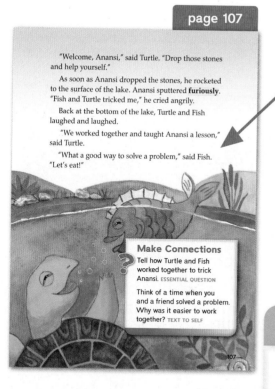

page 107

"Welcome, Anansi," said Turtle. "Drop those stones and help yourself."

As soon as Anansi dropped the stones, he rocketed to the surface of the lake. Anansi sputtered **furiously**. "Fish and Turtle tricked me," he cried angrily.

Back at the bottom of the lake, Turtle and Fish laughed and laughed.

"We worked together and taught Anansi a lesson," said Turtle.

"What a good way to solve a problem," said Fish. "Let's eat!"

**Make Connections**

Tell how Turtle and Fish worked together to trick Anansi. ESSENTIAL QUESTION

Think of a time when you and a friend solved a problem. Why was it easier to work together? TEXT TO SELF

107

The message or lesson in a folktale is sometimes found at the end of the story. It is a message the author thinks is important.

COLLABORATE

## Your Turn

Think about the lesson that Anansi learns in this story. Tell your partner the message.

# Antonyms

Antonyms are words that have opposite meanings. Look for antonyms to help you figure out the meaning of unknown words.

## Find Text Evidence

*In "Anansi Learns a Lesson," I see the word* filthy *in a sentence on page 104. I'm not sure what* filthy *means so I'll look for context clues. I see the word* clean. *I know what* clean *means. When I reread, I see that* clean *and* filthy *are antonyms. I think that* filthy *means "not clean."*

Turtle knew his hands were clean, but Anansi still thought they were filthy.

## Your Turn

Find an antonym to help you figure out the meaning of this word.
   **sink,** *page 106*
Talk about how the antonym helped you figure out what *sink* means.

Janet Broxon

# Write About the Text

Pages 102–107

Luis

I responded to the prompt: *Write an event to add to the story. Have Fish and Turtle explain to Anansi why they tricked him.*

## Student Model: *Narrative Text*

**Describe Characters**
I used dialogue to show what the characters felt and thought.

**Linking Ideas**
I included words that connect ideas.

> "Why did you play such a mean trick on me?" Anansi cried.
>
> Turtle explained, "Anansi, since you are always playing tricks on Fish and me, we decided to play one on you."
>
> Anansi asked, "When have I tricked you?"

©Wealan Pollard/age fotostock

Turtle said, "When I was hungry you made me wash my hands twice, Anansi. You did that so that I would not get any bananas."

Fish nodded and added, "Anansi, now you know how we feel!"

## Grammar

This paragraph includes examples of both **common and proper nouns.**

*Grammar Handbook*

*See page 478.*

**Strong Conclusion**
I added Fish's statement to make a good closing for the paragraph.

## Your Turn

Think about Anansi's character traits. Then write another event to add to the end of the story. Tell what Anansi would do next.

*Go Digital!*
*Write your response online.*
*Use your editing checklist.*

**Essential Question**

Why do people immigrate to new places?

*Go Digital!*

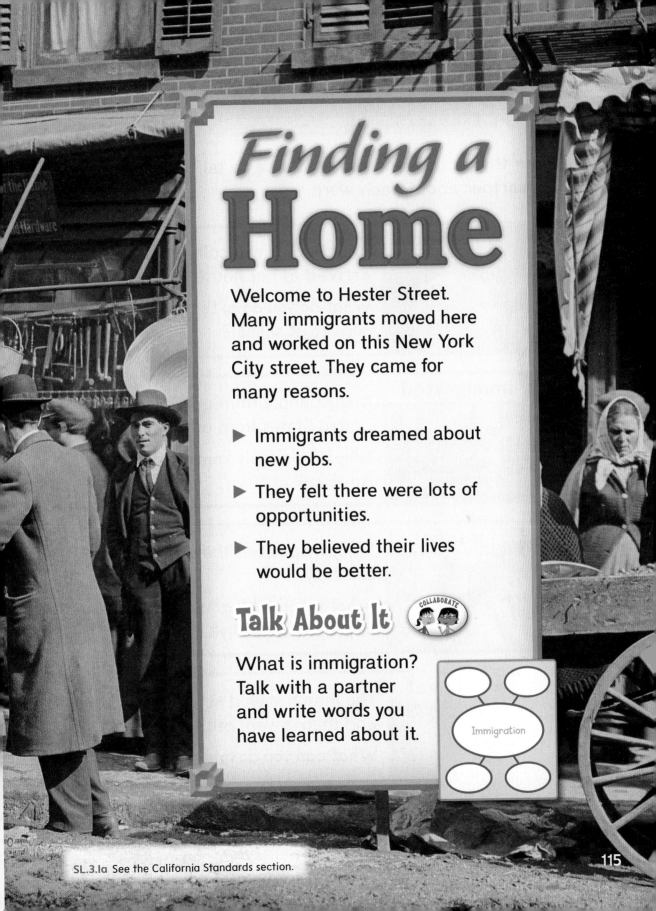

# Finding a Home

Welcome to Hester Street. Many immigrants moved here and worked on this New York City street. They came for many reasons.

▶ Immigrants dreamed about new jobs.

▶ They felt there were lots of opportunities.

▶ They believed their lives would be better.

## Talk About It

What is immigration? Talk with a partner and write words you have learned about it.

Immigration

# Vocabulary

Use the picture and the sentence to talk with
a partner about each word.

**arrived**

Aunt Sophie was so happy when we **arrived** at her house.

What do you do after you have arrived at school?

**immigrated**

Many people **immigrated** to the United States from other countries.

Why have people immigrated to America?

**inspected**

Stacy **inspected** the pine cone carefully.

What is something you have inspected carefully?

**moment**

The match stayed lit for a **moment**, and then it went out.

What can you do in a moment?

**opportunity**

Our class had an **opportunity**, or chance, to visit the museum.

What is another word for opportunity?

**photographs**

I like to look at old family **photographs**.

Why do people take photographs?

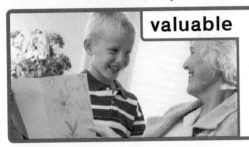

**valuable**

The card I made is very **valuable** to my grandmother.

Name something that is valuable to you.

**whispered**

Trudy **whispered** the plan to Josh so no one else could hear.

What is the opposite of whispered?

## Your Turn

COLLABORATE

Pick three words. Then write three questions for your partner to answer.

*Go Digital!* **Use the online visual glossary**

# SAILING TO AMERICA

**Essential Question**

**Why do people immigrate to new places?**

Read about why one family came to America.

Nora woke early. She hadn't slept much. It was March, 1895. Da was leaving for America today. Uncle Sean **immigrated** there last year and found work right away. He asked Da to join him. It was Mama and Da's dream to one day live in America.

Nora lit a lamp for light and sat down at the table. Her brother, Danny, joined her.

"I feel like crying," he **whispered** softly.

"I know," Nora answered. "So do I, but this is Da and Mama's dream. Da will find work and send for us. Look at the **photographs** that Uncle Sean sent. Doesn't America look grand?"

Tristan Elwell

"I don't want to ever leave Ireland," Danny said. "We won't have any friends in America. We'll be far away from Grandda, Paddy, and Colleen."

"Maybe you'll be glad it isn't Ireland," Nora said. "There will be enough food to eat. Mama and Da can relax and not worry so much. We'll all have a better life. America will be the land of our dreams."

Then Da carried a bag into the room. "Cheer up, my little loves! Why, in no time at all, you'll be joining me."

A year later, Da had saved enough money to send for his family. Mama, Danny, and Nora packed what little they had. They got on a crowded steamship and began their voyage.

The trip across the Atlantic Ocean was rough. The air inside the steamship smelled like a dirty sock. The ship tossed up and down for days. The waves were as big as mountains. Many passengers became seasick, but Nora and Danny felt fine.

Every day Nora daydreamed and reread Da's letters. She thought of the buildings and streetcars he wrote about. In her dreams, she could picture Da on a crowded street. He had a big smile on his face.

One morning, Nora awoke. A **moment** later, she realized something was different. The ocean was as smooth as glass.

A few hours later, Nora, Danny, and Mama shivered together on the ship's deck. Snowflakes drifted through the air. Another traveler noticed and gave them a blanket. It was as thin as a rag, but nothing could have been more **valuable** to them.

Suddenly, someone shouted, "There's Lady Liberty!" As the ship passed the large statue, the crowd cheered. Someone shouted, "At last, we've **arrived**! We are in America." Soon, everyone was singing and dancing.

Tristan Elwell

A ferry took the travelers to Ellis Island. In the main hall, doctors **inspected** the family. They looked for signs of illness. Mama had to answer many questions. Nora knew that people didn't get an **opportunity**, or another chance, to take these tests twice. Nora looked at Danny, then at Mama. They had to pass.

After a few hours, the family learned they could stay in America. As they filed off the ferry, Nora saw Uncle Sean's dark hair. Then she saw Da. His hands waved wildly. He had a big smile on his face. Dreams do come true, Nora thought as she waved back.

## Make Connections

Why did Nora and her family immigrate to America? How would the move make their lives better?

**ESSENTIAL QUESTION**

Has anyone in your family ever moved to a new place? How did they feel?

**TEXT TO SELF**

# Make Predictions

Use story clues to predict what happens next. Was your prediction right? Reread to confirm, or check, it. Change it if it is not right.

## Find Text Evidence

What would Da do after he left? You may have predicted that he would send for his family. Reread pages 120–121 for clues to support your prediction.

page 120

"I don't want to ever leave Ireland," Danny said. "We won't have any friends in America. We'll be far away from Grandda, Paddy, and Colleen."

"Maybe you'll be glad it isn't Ireland," Nora said. "There will be enough food to eat. Mama and Da can relax and not worry so much. We'll all have a better life. America will be the land of our dreams."

Then Da carried a bag into the room. "Cheer up, my little loves! Why, in no time at all, you'll be joining me."

*I predicted that Da would bring his family to America. Here is the clue. <u>Da says they will be joining him.</u> I read page 121 to check it. <u>A year later, Da saved enough money to send for his family.</u>*

## Your Turn

COLLABORATE

Predict what will happen when the family arrives in America. Find clues to support your prediction. Remember to make, confirm, and revise predictions as you read.

Tristan Elwell

# Theme

The theme of a story is the author's message. Think about what the characters do and say. Use these key details to help you figure out the theme.

 **Find Text Evidence**

*In "Sailing to America," Mama and Da dreamed of living in America. I think this is an important detail about the theme. I will reread to find more key details. Then I can figure out the story's theme.*

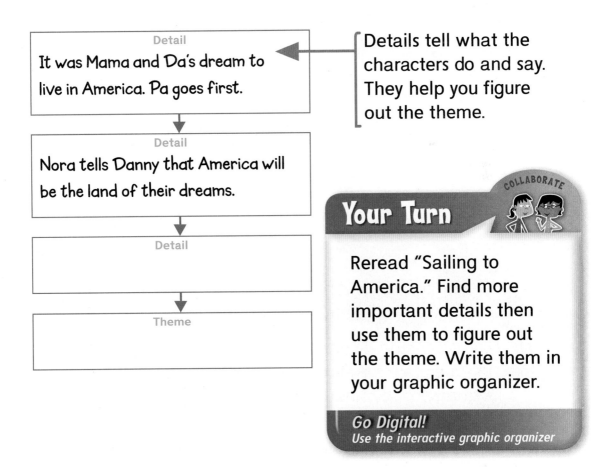

Detail
It was Mama and Da's dream to live in America. Pa goes first.

Detail
Nora tells Danny that America will be the land of their dreams.

Detail

Theme

Details tell what the characters do and say. They help you figure out the theme.

**Your Turn** COLLABORATE

Reread "Sailing to America." Find more important details then use them to figure out the theme. Write them in your graphic organizer.

*Go Digital!*
*Use the interactive graphic organizer*

# Historical Fiction

"Sailing to America" is historical fiction. **Historical fiction:**

- Is a made-up story that takes place in the past
- Has illustrations that show historical details

 **Find Text Evidence**

*I can tell that "Sailing to America" is historical fiction. The characters and events are made up. The story is based on real events that happened a long time ago.*

page 119

Nora woke early. She hadn't slept much. It was March, 1895. Da was leaving for America today. Uncle Sean **immigrated** there last year and found work right away. He asked Da to join him. It was Mama and Da's dream to one day live in America.

Nora lit a lamp for light and sat down at the table. Her brother, Danny, joined her.

"I feel like crying," he **whispered** softly.

"I know," Nora answered. "So do I, but this is Da and Mama's dream. Da will find work and send for us. Look at the **photographs** that Uncle Sean sent. Doesn't America look grand?"

119

The story and characters are made-up, but the events could happen in real life. Events in historical fiction happened a long time ago.

Illustrations show details about how people lived.

 COLLABORATE

## Your Turn

Find two things in the story that could happen in real life. Talk about why "Sailing to America" is historical fiction.

# Similes

A simile compares two very different things. It uses the word *like* or *as*. This is a simile. *Her cheeks were like red roses.* Similes are different from everyday language.

 **Find Text Evidence**

*In "Sailing to America," I see this sentence, "The waves were as big as mountains." This simile compares the way the waves looked with mountains. That means the waves looked huge and tall.*

The waves were as big as mountains.

## Your Turn

Talk about the meaning of this simile from "Sailing to America."
*The air inside the steamship smelled like a dirty sock.* page 121

Tristan Elwell

SAILING TO AMERICA

Pages 118–123

# Write About the Text

Rachel

I answered the question: *Was it a good idea for Nora and her family to immigrate to America? Tell why or why not using evidence from the text.*

**Student Model:** *Opinion*

I think it was a good idea for Nora and her family to immigrate to America. Nora told her brother Danny that in America they would have enough food to eat. They might feel hungry all the time if they stayed in Ireland.

**State an Opinion**
I gave my opinion at the beginning of my text.

**Supporting Reasons**
I used text evidence to support my opinion.

Nora called America the land of their dreams. They would have more chances there. The trip on the steamship was rough, but Nora's family made the right choice to immigrate to America.

**Grammar**

*Nora* is a **singular noun** and the word *dreams* is a **plural noun.**

*Grammar Handbook*

*See page 479.*

**Precise Nouns**
I chose interesting nouns to make my meaning clear.

## Your Turn

In your opinion, did the author do a good job of explaining why the family moved to America? Tell why or why not.

*Go Digital!*
*Write your response online.*
*Use your editing checklist.*

Tristan Elwell

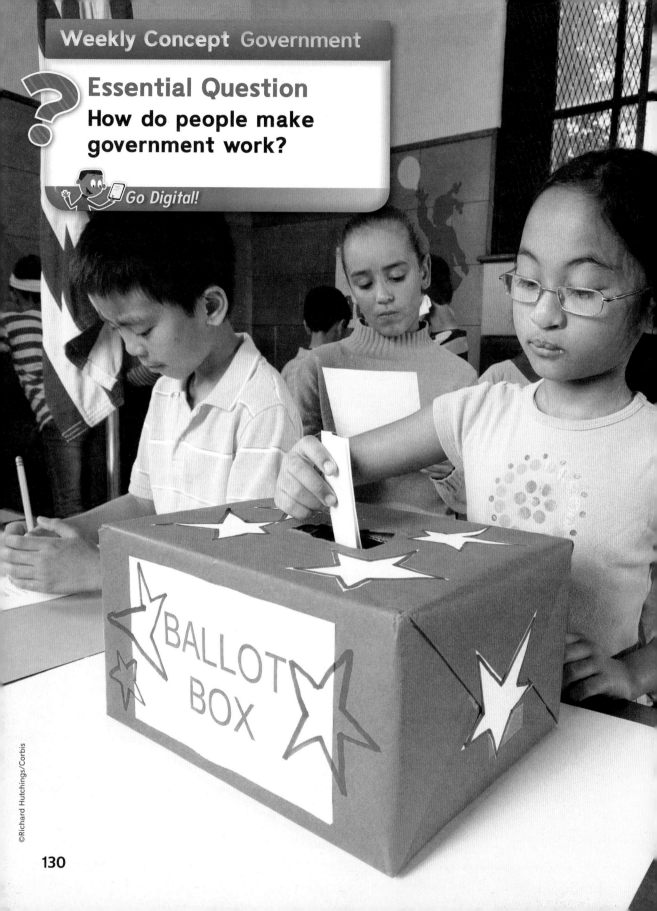

**Essential Question**
How do people make government work?

*Go Digital!*

BALLOT
BOX

# Our Voices Count

Today we are voting for class president. I will vote for Jan. I think she will do the best job. My vote will count!

▶ Voting lets people know what you think.

▶ It gives you the power to choose.

## Talk About It

Write words about voting. Talk with a partner about why voting is so important.

Vote

# Vocabulary

**Use the picture and the sentence to talk with a partner about each word.**

**announced**

Ms. Parks **announced** the winner of the contest.

When has someone announced your name?

**candidates**

Andrew is one of four **candidates** for class president.

What are some things candidates do before an election?

**convince**

Julia's mother tried to **convince** her to play soccer.

What is something someone tried to convince you to do?

**decisions**

Nick made two **decisions** about what to eat for breakfast.

Name two decisions you make every day.

**elect**

The students voted to **elect** a new class president.

What is another word for elect?

**estimate**

Sam tried to **estimate**, or guess, the number of coins he had.

What does it mean to estimate something?

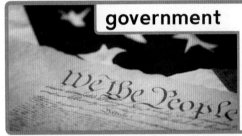

**government**

Our **government** makes laws.

Think of one law our government has made.

**independent**

It's good to be **independent** and do things on your own.

How can you be more independent at home?

COLLABORATE

## Your Turn

Pick three words. Write three questions for your partner to answer.

*Go Digital!* *Use the online visual glossary*

# Every VOTE Counts!

## Essential Question

**How do people make government work?**

Read about one group that teaches kids the power of voting.

Vote for the Class Pet

Have you ever voted? Maybe you voted to choose a class pet. Maybe your family voted on which movie to see. If you have ever voted, then you know how good it feels. Voting is important. It tells people what you think.

Many years ago, the leaders of our country wanted to know what people thought, too. They wrote a plan for our **government**. It is called the Constitution. It gives men and women in the United States the right to vote.

Each year, people who are eighteen years and older pick new leaders. They also **vote** on new laws. Voting gives Americans the **power** to choose.

135

# Teaching Kids to Vote

Did you know that only about six out of every ten Americans vote? That's sad. Some people think that voting is too hard. They are unsure where to go to vote. They think it takes too much time. Now, a group called Kids Voting USA is trying to **convince** everyone to vote.

Kids Voting USA teaches kids that voting is important. The group gives teachers lessons to use in their classrooms. First, kids read stories and do fun activities about government. They also learn how to choose and **elect** a good leader.

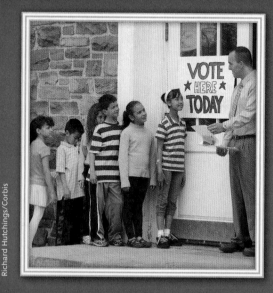

Richard Hutchings/Corbis

**Election Day is here!**

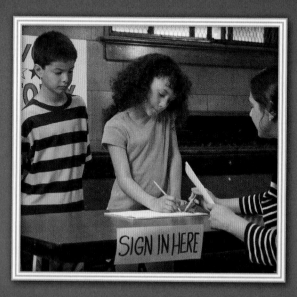

**First we sign in.**

Next, kids talk with their families. They reread stories about **candidates**. These are the people who want to be chosen as leaders. Families discuss their ideas and make **decisions**. That way, when it's time to vote, kids know who they want to vote for.

On **election** day, kids get to vote just like adults. They use ballots like the ones in real elections. A ballot is a special form with the names of candidates on it. Kids mark their choices on the ballot. Then they put the ballot into a special box. Finally, all the votes are counted and recounted. The winners are **announced**, and everyone knows who won.

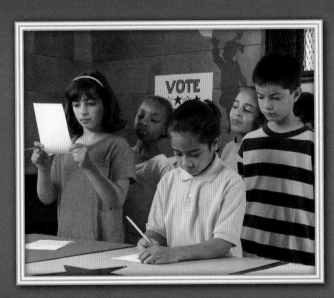

**Then we mark a ballot.**

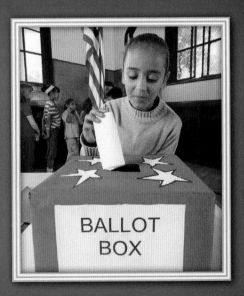

**Finally we vote!**

Richard Hutchings/Corbis

137

# Vote Now

Voting helps kids learn how to be **independent** and think for themselves. It also gives them the power to share how they feel. Kids Voting USA wants kids to vote now. There's a good reason. They **estimate** that when these kids grow up, more of them will vote.

In about ten years, kids your age will be old enough to vote. You will have the power to help elect great leaders and make new laws. Isn't that exciting?

**Elections are held in many schools to teach kids how to vote.**

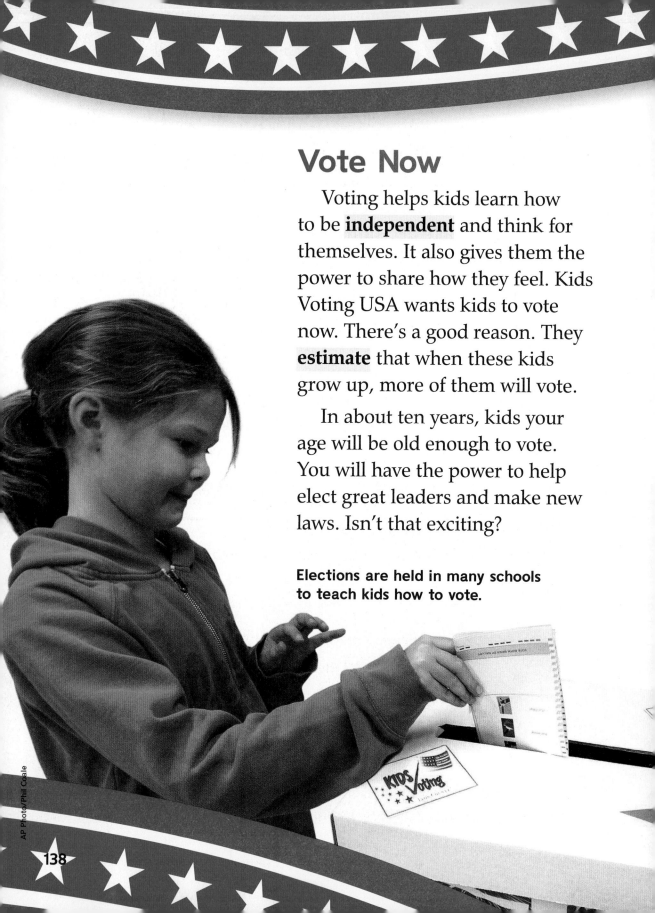

This bar graph shows the results of a class election. Which pet was the favorite?

Vote for a Class Pet

Hamster

Hermit Crab

Guinea Pig

Mouse

0  1  2  3  4  5  6  7  8

## Make Connections

Talk about voting. How does voting give people the power to choose?
**ESSENTIAL QUESTION**

Tell about a time when you voted. How did it make you feel? **TEXT TO SELF**

# Reread

Stop and think about the text as you read. Do you understand what you are reading? Does it make sense? Reread to make sure you understand.

## 🔍 Find Text Evidence

Do you understand why the author thinks voting is important? Reread the first part of page 135.

**page 135**

Have you ever voted? Maybe you voted to choose a class pet. Maybe your family voted on which movie to see. If you have ever voted, then you know how good it feels. Voting is important. It tells people what you think.

Many years ago, the leaders of our country wanted to know what people thought, too. They wrote a plan for our **government**. It is called the Constitution. It gives men and women in the United States the right to vote.

Each year, people who are eighteen years and older

*I read that <u>voting is a way to tell people what you think. It is a way for people to choose new laws and leaders.</u> Now I understand why the author thinks voting is important.*

COLLABORATE

## Your Turn

How does Kids Voting USA teach kids to vote? Reread pages 136 and 137.

TongRo Image Stock/Corbis

# Author's Point of View

An author often has a point of view about a topic. Look for details that show what the author thinks. Then decide if you agree with the author's point of view.

 **Find Text Evidence**

*What does the author think about voting? I can reread and look for details that tell me what the author thinks. This will help me figure out the author's point of view.*

| Details |
|---|
| The title of the story is "Every Vote Counts!" |
| The author thinks it's sad that only six out of every ten Americans vote. |
| Voting gives Americans the right to choose. |

Details help you figure out the author's point of view.

| Point of View |
|---|
| Voting is important. Everyone should vote. |

**Your Turn**

Reread "Every Vote Counts!" Find details that tell how the author feels about Kids Voting USA. Write them in a graphic organizer. What is the author's point of view? Do you agree with it?

*Go Digital!*
*Use the interactive graphic organizer*

# Expository Text

"Every Vote Counts!" is an expository text.

**Expository text:**
- Gives facts and information about a topic
- Has headings that tell what a section is about
- Includes text features, such as bar graphs

## Find Text Evidence

*I can tell "Every Vote Counts!" is expository text. It gives facts about voting. It also has headings and a bar graph.*

page 139

This bar graph shows the results of a class election. Which pet was the favorite?

Vote for a Class Pet

Hamster
Hermit Crab
Guinea Pig
Mouse

0 1 2 3 4 5 6 7 8

**Make Connections**

Talk about voting. How does voting give people the power to choose? ESSENTIAL QUESTION

Tell about a time when you voted. How did it make you feel? TEXT TO SELF

139

## Text Features

**Headings** Headings tell what a section of text is mostly about.

**Bar Graph** A bar graph is a special kind of picture. It helps you understand numbers and information in a quick and easy way.

COLLABORATE

## Your Turn

Look at the bar graph on page 139. Tell your partner something you learned from it.

# Prefixes

A prefix is a word part added to the beginning of a word. It changes the meaning of the word. The prefix *un-* means "not." The prefix *re-* means "again."

## Find Text Evidence

*In "Every Vote Counts!" I see this sentence.* "They reread stories about candidates." *The word* reread *has the prefix* re-. *I know that the prefix* re- *means "again." The word* reread *must mean "read again."*

**They <u>reread</u> stories about candidates.**

## Your Turn

Find prefixes. Figure out the meanings of the following words in "Every Vote Counts!"

**unsure,** *page 136*
**recounted,** *page 137*

# Write About the Text

Pages 134–139

Marlon

I answered the question: *In your opinion, does the author do a good job of convincing readers they should vote? Think about the reasons the author gave.*

## Student Model: *Opinion*

**State an Opinion**
I began by telling my opinion.

**Details**
I gave reasons from the text to support my opinion.

> I think the author did a good
> job of convincing readers they
> should vote. The author gave
> different reasons why it is
> important to vote. For example,
> voting lets people know what you
> think. Also, it gives people the
> power to choose leaders.

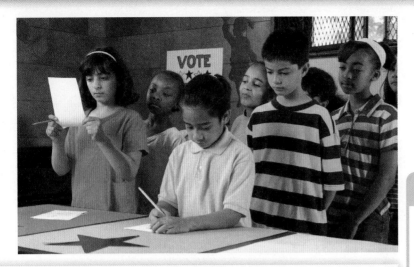

Kids who vote in school learn how to be independent and think for themselves. When they are men and women, they will elect leaders and help make new laws. These are all good reasons to vote!

**Grammar**

In this sentence, *men* and *women* are examples of **irregular plural nouns.**

*Grammar Handbook*

*See page 479.*

**Concluding Statement**
I ended with a sentence that sums up my opinion.

## Your Turn

Do you agree or disagree with the author's point of view about voting? Explain your answer.

*Go Digital!*
*Write your response online.*
*Use your editing checklist.*

**Essential Question**

How can people help animals survive?

*Go Digital!*

# SAViNG ANiMALS

These manatees look healthy and happy, but sometimes they need help. We can help threatened animals, like manatees, survive.

► We can protect their habitats.

► We can keep their habitats clean.

► We can join special groups that help animals.

## Talk About It

Write words you have learned about what animals need to survive. Talk with a partner about things you can do to save animals.

|  |  |  |
|---|---|---|

Survive

# Vocabulary

Use the picture and the sentence to talk with
a partner about each word.

**caretakers**

The **caretakers** at the zoo feed the penguins every day.

What would caretakers for a horse do?

**population**

There is a large **population** of flamingos living in the pond.

Name another animal population that might live in a pond.

**recognized**

Nola **recognized** herself in the mirror.

What is another word for recognized?

**relatives**

We invited friends and **relatives** to our picnic.

How do you spend time with your relatives?

**resources**

Plants need **resources**, such as sunlight and fresh air, to grow.

What resources do people need?

**success**

Jill's performance was a **success**.

Tell about a success you have had.

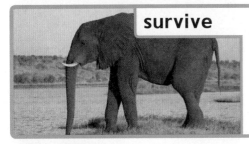
**survive**

Animals need water to **survive**.

What are some other things animals need to survive?

**threatened**

The wildfire **threatened** the trees.

Describe a time when a storm threatened your plans.

COLLABORATE

## Your Turn

Pick three words. Write three questions for your partner to answer.

*Go Digital!* *Use the online visual glossary*

# KIDS to the Rescue!

Olivia and Carter Ries,
founders of One More Generation

## Essential Question

**How can people help
animals survive?**

Read how two children helped
sea turtles survive an oil spill.

150

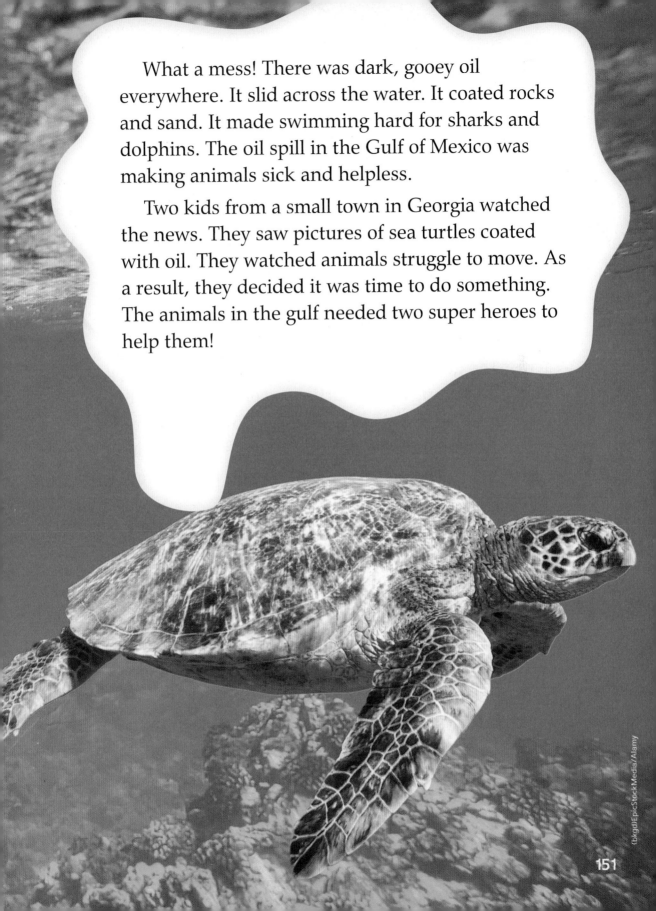

What a mess! There was dark, gooey oil everywhere. It slid across the water. It coated rocks and sand. It made swimming hard for sharks and dolphins. The oil spill in the Gulf of Mexico was making animals sick and helpless.

Two kids from a small town in Georgia watched the news. They saw pictures of sea turtles coated with oil. They watched animals struggle to move. As a result, they decided it was time to do something. The animals in the gulf needed two super heroes to help them!

# Olivia and Carter to the Rescue!

Meet Olivia and Carter Ries. They started a group that works to save animals. Olivia was seven years old, and Carter, her brother, was eight-and-a-half. They named their group One More Generation. They want animals to be around for kids in the future.

Olivia and Carter believe everyone can make a difference. They are sending an important message. Their message is that everyone can help animals.

Olivia and Carter watched oil spread for miles across the gulf. More and more animals were getting sick. The Kemp's ridley turtle was one of them. There are only a few thousand left in the world. They are endangered, and their **population** is getting smaller and smaller. The oil **threatened** to ruin their homes and their habitat.

Olivia and Carter Ries learned how oil harms Kemp's ridley turtles.

This female turtle is clean and healthy. It is being returned to the gulf.

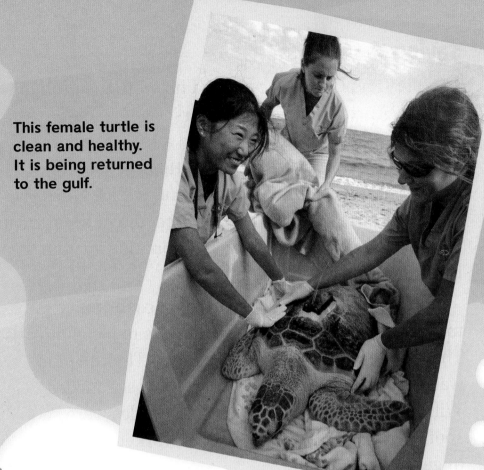

## Oil Spoils Everything

Olivia and Carter learned that the female turtles were swimming across the gulf to Mexico. They were going to lay eggs on the beaches there. But the thick oil destroyed the **resources** the turtles need to live. The harmful oil covered the sand. It made it hard for them to swim.

Sea turtles **survive** by eating seaweed, jellyfish, and small sea animals. The oil spill spoiled their food, too. Without food, the turtles die.

Steven Senne/AP Images

## Saving the Sea Turtles

Olivia and Carter **recognized** how big the problem was. The turtles needed help. First they made a thoughtful plan. Then they called a rescue group in New Orleans. They found out that the workers needed useful cleaning supplies and wipes. Next, the kids asked friends, **relatives**, and people in their town to help. They told them how the donations would help remove oil from the turtles.

Olivia and Carter collected supplies for four months. They rode with their parents to New Orleans. They carried the supplies with them. Then the kids watched **caretakers** clean hundreds of sea turtles. With the help of many people, the turtles were soon spotless. Olivia and Carter's plan worked. It was a huge **success**!

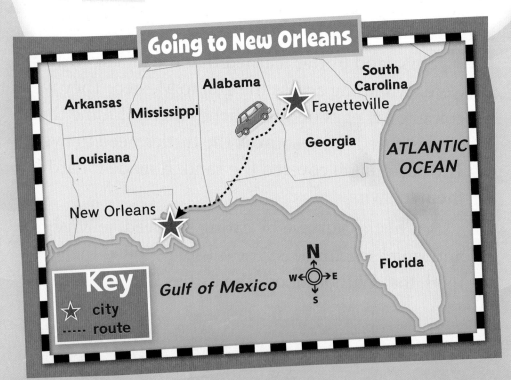

### Going to New Orleans

Arkansas
Mississippi
Alabama
South Carolina
Fayetteville
Georgia
ATLANTIC OCEAN
Louisiana
New Orleans
Florida
Gulf of Mexico

N
W E
S

**Key**
☆ city
..... route

## Keeping Busy

Olivia and Carter work with many other groups to help animals all over the world. They give talks at museums and schools. They ask community leaders to support laws that help animals. They help rescue animals in danger.

Olivia and Carter are truly super heroes to endangered animals. With their help, many animals will survive for one more generation.

Carter and his mom unpack supplies in New Orleans.

### Ways You Can Help Animals!
- Protect animal nests.
- Pick up trash at parks and wild places.
- Keep water clean.
- Stop using plastic bags.

## Make Connections

Describe the steps that Olivia and Carter took to help the Kemp's ridley sea turtles. ESSENTIAL QUESTION

What can you and your friends do to help animals? TEXT TO SELF

# Reread

Stop and think about the text as you read. Are there new facts and ideas? Do they make sense? Reread to make sure you understand.

### Find Text Evidence

Do you understand why an oil spill is harmful to animals? Go back and reread page 151.

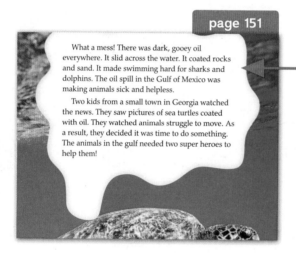

page 151

What a mess! There was dark, gooey oil everywhere. It slid across the water. It coated rocks and sand. It made swimming hard for sharks and dolphins. The oil spill in the Gulf of Mexico was making animals sick and helpless.

Two kids from a small town in Georgia watched the news. They saw pictures of sea turtles coated with oil. They watched animals struggle to move. As a result, they decided it was time to do something. The animals in the gulf needed two super heroes to help them!

*I read that <u>oil made it hard for sharks and dolphins to swim. Sea turtles were coated with oil. They struggled to move.</u> These details help me understand why oil is harmful to animals.*

## Your Turn

COLLABORATE

Reread the section "Olivia and Carter to the Rescue!" Look for details about how oil spills harm animals.

# Author's Point of View

An author often has a point of view about a topic. Look for details that show what the author thinks. Then decide if you agree with the author's point of view.

 **Find Text Evidence**

*What does the author think about Olivia and Carter's work with animals? I can reread and look for details that tell me what the author thinks.*

| Details |
| --- |
| Olivia and Carter recognize that turtles need help. |
| Olivia and Carter collected supplies to help the turtles. |
| Their plan was a huge success. |

↓

| Point of View |
| --- |
|  |

*Details from the text help you figure out the point of view.*

**Your Turn** COLLABORATE

Reread "Kids to the Rescue." Use the details in your graphic organizer. Write the author's point of view about Olivia and Carter. Do you agree with the author's point of view?

*Go Digital!*
*Use the interactive graphic organizer*

# Expository Text

"Kids to the Rescue!" is an expository text.

**Expository text:**
- Gives facts and information about a topic
- Has headings and sidebars
- Includes text features, such as maps

## Find Text Evidence

*I can tell that "Kids to the Rescue!" is nonfiction. It gives facts and information about a group that helps animals. It also has a sidebar and a map.*

page 154

**Saving the Sea Turtles**

Olivia and Carter **recognized** how big the problem was. The turtles needed help. First they made a thoughtful plan. Then they called a rescue group in New Orleans. They found out that the workers needed useful cleaning supplies and wipes. Next, the kids asked friends, **relatives**, and people in their town to help. They told them how the donations would help remove oil from the turtles.

Olivia and Carter collected supplies for four months. They rode with their parents to New Orleans. They carried the supplies with them. Then the kids watched **caretakers** clean hundreds of sea turtles. With the help of many people, the turtles were soon spotless. Olivia and Carter's plan worked. It was a huge **success**!

Going to New Orleans

Arkansas  Mississippi  Alabama  South Carolina  Fayetteville
Louisiana  Georgia  ATLANTIC OCEAN
New Orleans
Key
★ city
····· route
Gulf of Mexico  Florida
N W E S
154

## Text Features

**Sidebar** A sidebar gives more information about a topic.

**Map** A map is a picture of an area. It shows cities, roads, and rivers.

COLLABORATE

## Your Turn

Look at the text features in "Kids to the Rescue!" Tell your partner something you learned.

# Suffixes

A suffix is a word part added to the end of a word. It changes the word's meaning. The suffix *-ful* means "full of." The suffix *-less* means "having no" or "without."

 **Find Text Evidence**

*In "Kids to the Rescue!" I see this sentence, "The harmful oil covered the sand." The word* harmful *has the suffix* -ful. *I know that the suffix* -ful *means "full of." The word* harmful *must mean "full of harm."*

The <u>*harmful*</u> oil covered the sand.

COLLABORATE

## Your Turn

Find suffixes. Figure out the meanings of the following words in "Kids to the Rescue!"
    **helpless,** *page 151*
    **thoughtful,** *page 154*
    **spotless,** *page 154*

# Write About the Text

Pages 150–155

Rhett

I answered the question: *What were the effects of the oil spill on the turtles?*

## Student Model: *Informative Text*

An oil spill in the Gulf of Mexico had harmful effects on turtles living there. First it ruined important resources. The oil spill spoiled seaweed and small animals. Turtles need these for food. Then some turtles died because they could not eat.

**Sequence**
I used the words *first* and *then* to put events in order.

**Grammar**
You can **combine the nouns in two sentences** to make one sentence.

*Grammar Handbook*
See page 480.

**Linking Words**
I added linking words to connect ideas.

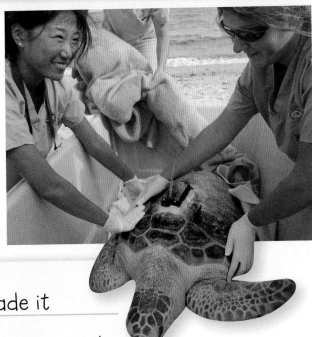

The oil spill also made it difficult for turtles to swim and move across the sand. Female turtles did not have a place to lay their eggs. These are some examples of how the oil spill hurt turtles.

**Facts and Details**
I included details from the text about the oil spill's effects on turtles.

## Your Turn

How would you describe Olivia and Carter? Use details from the text.

*Go Digital!*
*Write your response online.*
*Use your editing checklist.*

**Essential Question**

How do people figure things out?

*Go Digital!*

162

# What Do I Do Next?

When my family and I go biking, it's my job to figure out the best way to go. I use a map. It helps me imagine the best places to ride. Then we all talk about it.

▶ I also ask questions that help me decide what to do.

▶ There are many ways to figure things out.

## Talk About It

Think about how you decide what to do. Talk with a partner. Write down how you figure things out.

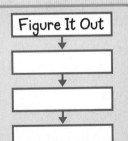

Figure It Out

↓

↓

↓

# Vocabulary

**Use the picture and the sentence to talk with a partner about each word.**

### bounce

Keith likes to **bounce** a soccer ball off his head.

How many times can you bounce a ball without stopping?

### imagine

Mandy likes to **imagine** what her dream house might look like.

What do you imagine when you daydream?

### inventor

Thomas Edison was the **inventor** of the first light bulb.

What does an inventor do?

### observer

Jason is a good **observer** and enjoys watching birds.

Tell about a time when you were an observer at an event.

# Poetry Words

### alliteration

"Poets paint precise pictures" is an example of **alliteration**.

Give another example of alliteration.

### free verse

Jeremy likes to write **free verse** poems because they don't need to rhyme.

What would you write a free verse poem about?

### limerick

Dan's **limerick** had five lines and made the class laugh.

How is a limerick different from other poems?

### rhyme

The words *cat* and *bat* **rhyme** because they end in the same sound.

Name two other words that rhyme.

COLLABORATE

## Your Turn

Pick three words. Then write three questions for your partner to answer.

*Go Digital!* **Use the online visual glossary**

# Empanada Day

One bite of Abuelita's empanadas
And my mouth purrs like a cat.
  "Teach me," I beg and bounce on my feet,
  "Teach me to make this magical treat."
Abuelita smiles,
  "Be an observer, watch and learn,
  Then you too can take a turn."

## ? Essential Question

**How do people figure things out?**

Read poems about different ways
to figure things out.

Dara Goldman

She sets before me a ball of dough,
Round and golden as the sun.
My eyes wide as saucers, I watch and follow,
Press circles flat as pancakes,
Spoon on apple slices and nose-tickling spices,
Seal it all in, a half-moon envelope of bliss.
Together we write down every step
As the empanadas bake and crisp in the oven,
My stomach rumbling like a hungry bear.
Ah, empanada day!

– George Santiago

167

# Cold Feet

An inventor with feet like ice,

And toes like ten shivering mice,

Looked at clothes, studied feet.

Read about cold and heat,

And knit the first socks, warm and nice.

# OUR WASHING MACHINE

Our washing machine is a bear

That munches up socks by the pair.

He will suds them and grumble

As they spin, turn, and tumble,

Then spit them out, ready to wear.

Dara Goldman

168

# Bugged

A creature has crawled on my knee,

It's a bug green and round as a pea.

His five wings are fish fins,

He's got teeth sharp as pins.

Just imagine him chomping on me!

I read every bug book I see,

To learn what this creature might be.

I ask scientists too,

But they don't have a clue.

So I'm bugged by this great mystery.

## Make Connections

What are different ways to figure things out? Talk about what happens in each poem.
ESSENTIAL QUESTION

Which poem has the best way to solve a problem? TEXT TO SELF

# Limerick and Free Verse

**Limerick**: • Is a short funny poem that rhymes. • Each stanza has five lines. • The first, second, and fifth lines rhyme. The third and fourth lines rhyme.

**Free verse**: • Does not always rhyme. • Can have any number of lines and stanzas.

 **Find Text Evidence**

*I can tell that "Cold Feet" is a limerick. It is funny. The stanza has five lines. The first, second, and fifth lines rhyme. The third and fourth lines also rhyme.*

page 168

**Cold Feet**

An inventor with feet like ice,
And toes like ten shivering mice,
Looked at clothes, studied feet.
Read about cold and heat,
And knit the first socks, warm and nice.

**OUR WASHING MACHINE**

Our washing machine is a bear
That munches up socks by the pair.
He will suds them and grumble
As they spin, turn, and tumble,
Then spit them out, ready to wear.

168

In this funny limerick, the first, second, and fifth lines rhyme. This limerick has one stanza. A stanza is a group of lines in a poem.

 COLLABORATE

**Your Turn**

Reread the poems "Our Washing Machine" and "Empanada Day." Explain whether each poem is free verse or a limerick.

# Point of View

A poem often shows a narrator's thoughts about events or characters. This is the point of view. Look for details that show point of view.

 **Find Text Evidence**

*I'll reread "Empanada Day" and look for details that show what the narrator thinks about making empanadas with Abuelita, his grandmother. This is his point of view.*

| Details |
|---|
| One bite of Abuelita's empanadas and my mouth purrs. |
| Teach me to make this magical treat. |
| My eyes wide as saucers, I watch and follow. |

↓

| Point of View |
|---|
|  |

**Your Turn**

Reread "Empanada Day." Think about the details. Then write the narrator's point of view in the graphic organizer. Do you agree with the narrator? Why or why not?

# Alliteration and Rhyme

Poets use alliteration and rhyme to make descriptions fun to read and poems sound musical.

### Find Text Evidence

Reread "Bugged" on page 169 aloud. Listen for beginning sounds that repeat. Listen for words that rhyme.

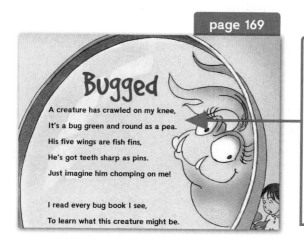

page 169

### Bugged

A creature has crawled on my knee,
It's a bug green and round as a pea.
His five wings are fish fins,
He's got teeth sharp as pins.
Just imagine him chomping on me!

I read every bug book I see,
To learn what this creature might be.

*In the first line, the words* crawled *and* creature *start with the same sound.*

*The words* knee *and* pea *rhyme. I like the way these words sound.*

## Your Turn

COLLABORATE

Find more examples of alliteration and rhyming words in "Bugged."

# Simile

A simile compares two things that are very different. Similes always have the word *like* or *as*. Two examples of similes are, "The bug is as green as grass" or "The moon is like a giant pearl."

 **Find Text Evidence**

*To find a simile, I need to look for two things that are being compared. In "Cold Feet," I see the line, "An inventor with feet like ice." The simile compares the inventor's feet with ice. That means his feet were very cold.*

page 168

An inventor with feet like ice,
And toes like ten shivering mice,
Looked at clothes, studied feet.
Read about cold and heat,
And knit the first socks, warm and nice.

 COLLABORATE

## Your Turn

Reread "Bugged." Look for a simile. Talk about the two things being compared.

Dara Goldman

Pages 166–169

# Write About the Text

Sophia

I responded to the prompt: *Pick an invention. Write a limerick or rhyming poem about it. Include a simile.*

**Student Model:** *Narrative Text*

**Simile**
I compared the scooter to a magic carpet ride.

**Details**
I added details to describe how fast the scooter goes.

### My Scooter

My scooter is like a magic

   carpet ride.

It flies me past trees as I zoom

   and glide.

My friends' bikes are a

   far-away blur

As my scooter's wheels hum

   and whir.

My scooter goes faster than

trucks and cars.

My scooter's wheels might take

me to Mars!

**Grammar**

This poem includes **possessive nouns.**

*Grammar Handbook*

*See page 480.*

**Rhyme**
I chose words that rhyme at the ends of lines.

**Your Turn**

Write your own poem or limerick that tells about an invention. Include a simile.

*Go Digital!*
*Write your response online.*
*Use your editing checklist.*

# 3

# One
## of a Kind

## The Big Idea

Why are individual qualities important?

# If Everything

If everything was just the same,
    How very dull the world would be.
No different colors, unique sounds,
    No mountain, desert, forest, sea.

Imagine everyone alike,
    How tiresome they all would seem.
No different sizes, shapes, or thoughts,
    And no one left to think and dream.

— **by Winifred Califano**

**? Essential Question**

**What makes different animals unique?**

# SPECIAL QUALITIES

Bottlenose dolphins are unique mammals. They have the right shape for gliding through the water. And they talk to each other by whistling.

▶ All animals have qualities that are unique.

▶ Animals use their special features to get what they need, protect themselves, and communicate.

## Talk About It

Talk with a partner about other animals and their unique qualities. Write words you know here.

# Vocabulary

**Use the picture and the sentence to talk with a partner about each word.**

**disbelief**

Winnie stared in **disbelief** at the huge shark.

What is another word for disbelief?

**dismay**

Marco looked at the rain with sadness and **dismay**.

What is the opposite of dismay?

**fabulous**

The fireworks were amazing and **fabulous**.

What do you think is fabulous?

**features**

Lions have special **features** that help them survive.

Name a feature that helps lions survive.

**offered**

Brian **offered** to help Donna get up.

How has someone offered to help you?

**splendid**

Katie's day at the zoo ended with a wonderful, **splendid** surprise.

List words that mean the same as splendid.

**unique**

The anteater's long nose makes it a **unique** animal.

What word is the opposite of unique?

**watchful**

The ducklings learned to swim under the **watchful** eyes of their mother.

What does it mean to be watchful?

## Your Turn

COLLABORATE

Pick three words. Write three questions for your partner to answer.

*Go Digital!* *Use the online visual glossary*

# INCHWORM'S TALE

## ? Essential Question

**What makes different animals unique?**

Read about how one animal uses its special features to solve a problem.

Long ago, Anant and his sister, Anika, went swimming. They swam all afternoon and became very tired. They were exhausted and climbed onto a large, flat rock to rest. Soon they fell asleep.

A strange and mysterious thing happened as they slept. The rock beneath them grew and expanded until it reached the clouds.

Anant awoke and looked around. "Sister, wake up!" he cried in **disbelief**. "Am I dreaming, or are we among the clouds?"

Anika rubbed her eyes. "You're not dreaming, brother. This rock has grown while we slept!" The children looked around and saw **fabulous** blue sky and wonderful white clouds.

The children were so high, Anika felt dizzy. Anant searched for a way to climb down, but he could not find a path. Anant and Anika started to cry. They felt fear and **dismay**.

Below, the villagers became worried. Where were the children? They searched the forests, meadows, river, and lakes. Then Isha, the village chief, looked around and noticed Hawk sitting on a tree branch.

"Hawk, will you help us find Anant and Anika?" he asked. "You have sharp, **watchful** eyes and strong wings. They are your best **features**. Please use them to help us find the children."

Hawk agreed to help and flew up into the sky. He tilted his head and squinted his eyes at the bright sunlight. When he was near the clouds, he spied the children on the rock.

"Don't be afraid," said Hawk. "We will rescue you!"

Hawk was unable to carry the children down the rock, so he gathered lots of food for them to eat. Then he brought large leaves to keep them warm. Hawk wanted to make sure they were safe and unharmed.

Hawk flew down to the village and spoke to Isha. Isha called all the animals together and told them they needed help to get the children down. He asked each animal to use its most special feature to climb the tall rock. Several tried and failed.

Mouse's teeth were strong and **unique**, but they couldn't help her climb up the rock.

Bear's huge claws were good for climbing up trees. However, they could not help him scale rocks.

Mountain Lion's claws were sharp and powerful, but the rock was too slippery and he slid back down.

Finally, a tiny voice filled with enthusiasm spoke up and **offered** to help. "May I try, please? It's me, Too-Tock, the Inchworm!"

Inchworm showed them all how skillful she was at climbing. Hawk volunteered to carry Inchworm to the top of the rock. Then she could lead Anant and Anika down the giant mountain. Isha agreed to the plan.

So Hawk carefully picked up Inchworm in his beak. Together they flew to the top of the rock where the children were waiting. Along the way, Inchworm planned for the trip down.

It took almost a week for the three to climb down to the village. Inch by inch, Inchworm led the children carefully down the rocky slope. Every day, Hawk brought food to the children. Every day he reappeared in the village with news for the villagers.

Finally, Inchworm, Anant, and Anika reached the bottom of the rock. Everyone cheered and called Inchworm a hero. It was a glorious, **splendid** day.

"From this day on," said Isha, "I rename the big rock, Too-Tock-Awn-oo-Lah, after the brave inchworm."

## Make Connections

What unique feature does Inchworm have? How does it help? ESSENTIAL QUESTION

What do your special features help you do? TEXT TO SELF

# Visualize

Use colorful words and details to help you visualize, or form pictures, in your mind. This will help you understand the characters' actions and feelings.

 **Find Text Evidence**

You may not be sure how Anant and Anika feel when they wake up. Reread page 183. The details will help you visualize how they feel.

> **page 183**
>
> Long ago, Anant and his sister, Anika, went swimming. They swam all afternoon and became very tired. They were exhausted and climbed onto a large, flat rock to rest. Soon they fell asleep.
>
> A strange and mysterious thing happened as they slept. The rock beneath them grew and expanded until it reached the clouds.
>
> Anant awoke and looked around. "Sister, wake up!" he cried in **disbelief**. "Am I dreaming, or are we among the clouds?"
>
> Anika rubbed her eyes. "You're not dreaming, brother. This rock has grown while we slept!" The children looked around and saw **fabulous** blue sky and wonderful white clouds.
>
> The children were so high, Anika felt dizzy. Anant searched for a way to climb down, but he could not find a path. Anant and Anika started to cry. They felt fear and **dismay**.

*I read that Anika felt dizzy and Anant searched for a way down. He could not find a way down and they both began to cry.* *These details help me figure out how scared Anant and Anika felt.*

## Your Turn

COLLABORATE

How do the children get back down to the village? Reread and visualize what happens. Then tell what happens.

# Problem and Solution

A plot often has a problem and solution. A problem is something that needs to change or be solved. The solution is how the characters fix the problem.

## Find Text Evidence

*On page 183, I read that the rock grew and Anant and Anika were stuck on top. This is the problem. I read that the villagers search for the children. Then Isha asks Hawk for help. These are steps to solving the problem. They are in sequence, or time order.*

**Problem**

The children are on top of a tall rock and cannot get down.

The villagers look for the children.

The villagers ask Hawk for help.

**Solution**

## Your Turn

COLLABORATE

Reread "Inchworm's Tale." Find more steps to solving the problem. List them in your graphic organizer in sequence. Then write the solution.

*Go Digital!*
*Use the interactive graphic organizer*

# Folktale

"Inchworm's Tale" is a folktale.

A **folktale**:

- Is a short story passed from parents to children in a culture
- Usually has a message or teaches a lesson

## Find Text Evidence

*I can tell that "Inchworm's Tale" is a folktale. I learned about how a great rock got its name. I also learned a lesson. Even small animals can solve big problems.*

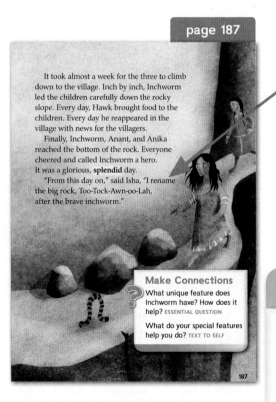

page 187

It took almost a week for the three to climb down to the village. Inch by inch, Inchworm led the children carefully down the rocky slope. Every day, Hawk brought food to the children. Every day he reappeared in the village with news for the villagers.

Finally, Inchworm, Anant, and Anika reached the bottom of the rock. Everyone cheered and called Inchworm a hero. It was a glorious, **splendid** day.

"From this day on," said Isha, "I rename the big rock, Too-Tock-Awn-oo-Lah, after the brave inchworm."

**Make Connections**
What unique feature does Inchworm have? How does it help? ESSENTIAL QUESTION

What do your special features help you do? TEXT TO SELF

187

The lesson in a folktale is sometimes found at the end of the story. It is a message the author thinks is important.

COLLABORATE

## Your Turn

What details in the story show you "Inchworm's Tale" is a folktale? Tell your partner the details.

# Synonyms

Synonyms are words that have the same meaning. Sometimes synonyms are context clues for words you don't know.

## Find Text Evidence

*On page 183, I'm not sure what* expanded *means. I see the context clue* grew *in the same sentence. I know that* grew *means "to get bigger." I think* grew *and* expanded *are synonyms. They have almost the same meanings. Now I know that* expanded *means "grew bigger."*

The rock beneath them grew and expanded until it reached the clouds.

## Your Turn

Find synonyms for these words from "Inchworm's Tale."
**unharmed,** *page 184*
**scale,** *page 185*

Jago Silver

Pages 182–187

# Write About the Text

I responded to the prompt: *Add an event to the story. Describe what the children said to Inchworm when they got to the bottom of the rock.*

**Student Model:** *Narrative Text*

Anant and Anika were so happy to be home. They knelt down and gave Inchworm a big hug. "Oh Inchworm, thank you so much!" cried Anant.

"We never would have made it without you," added Anika. "How can we repay you?"

Inchworm thought for a while. She said, "It was a very long trip.

**Dialogue**
I used dialogue to show the characters' feelings.

**Sentence Types**
I used different kinds of sentences to make my story more interesting.

**Grammar**

The word *sprang* is an example of an **action verb**.

*Grammar Handbook* See page 481.

I am hungry now. Could I have some leaves?"

The children sprang to their feet. They gathered tasty leaves from the forest. Then they sprinkled them around Inchworm. She poked her head up with a big smile.

**Order of Events**
I used a signal word to tell the sequence of events.

## Your Turn

Add another event to the story. Tell what Inchworm and the children do when a big rock blocks the path. How do they solve their problem?

*Go Digital!*
*Write your response online.*
*Use your editing checklist.*

Jackie Robinson was the first African-American major league baseball player.

Bettmann/Corbis

194

# MAKE A DIFFERENCE

Jackie Robinson changed the world one home run at a time. He was an inspiring athlete and worked hard to help change the way people treated each other. He was brave and always did his best.

▶ Brave people lead the way for others.

▶ They stand up for what they believe in.

▶ Strong leaders make a difference.

## Talk About It

Write words you have learned about leadership. Talk with a partner about what it takes to make a difference.

John F. Kennedy, U.S. President

Jane Goodall, Scientist

# Vocabulary

Use the picture and the sentence to talk with a partner about each word.

**amazement**

Kris and Lauren watched the movie with **amazement**.

What word means the same as amazement?

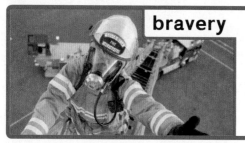

**bravery**

It takes **bravery** and courage to be a firefighter.

What other jobs take bravery?

**disappear**

I saw the turtle's head **disappear** into its shell.

What is the opposite of disappear?

**donated**

Ms. Walker **donated** her time by reading to children at the library.

What have you donated to help others?

**leader**

Abraham Lincoln was a great **leader**.

Who is another great leader?

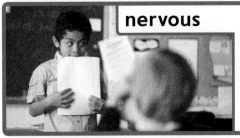

**nervous**

James is **nervous** about speaking in front of his class.

Show how you look when you are nervous.

**refused**

Tom and Kyle **refused** to eat their breakfast.

What is something you refused to do?

**temporary**

Raking leaves is a **temporary** job for Steven.

What does it mean when something is temporary?

COLLABORATE

## Your Turn

Pick three words. Then write three questions for your partner to answer.

*Go Digital!* *Use the online visual glossary*

# Jane's Discovery

## Essential Question

How can one person change the way you think?

Read how a future president changed Jane's life.

198

Jane slammed the door of the log cabin and raced toward the Indiana woods. Mother and Father insisted that Jane go to school and learn to read. It was September of 1825, and Jane wanted to help on the farm like her brothers. Therefore, she told her parents "No!" and **refused** to learn to read.

Jane scooped up her long skirts and splashed through a small stream. Running helped her collect her thoughts, so she ran for what seemed like hours. She dashed around a tree and wasn't paying attention. As a result, she tripped over a pair of long legs stretched out in the grass.

The legs belonged to her neighbor, Abe Lincoln. Abe was leaning against a tree reading a book. He smiled, stood up, and extended his arm to help Jane up.

Peter Ferguson

Jane recognized Abe and knew what a hard-worker he was. But she also heard he was not like the other sixteen-year-old boys in Perry County. Abe was different because he spent all of his spare time reading books.

"Why are you running so fast?" Abe asked. "Are you hurt?"

Jane frowned. "No, I'm all right," she said. "I'm running because I'm upset. My parents want me to learn to read, and I told them no!"

Abe looked down at his book and then at Jane.

"Reading can change your life," he said quietly. "Meet me here tomorrow, and I'll prove to you how important reading is."

Jane met Abe the next afternoon. He showed her a book about George Washington. One of his favorite teachers had **donated** it to him, and he had read it many times.

Abe began to read aloud while Jane listened carefully. He read about Washington and what a great **leader** he was. He read about Washington's courage and **bravery**.

"Someday I want to be as courageous as George Washington," said Abe proudly. "Someday I will be president of the United States, too."

"I believe you will make a great president," said Jane. "Look at what a good leader you are now. You've completely changed my mind about reading!"

Abe smiled. "Tell your parents you will learn to read," he said. "Then meet me here every day after school. We will read together and I will help you."

Peter Ferguson

At first, Jane was **nervous** and uncertain about learning to read, but she met Abe every day like clockwork. Fortunately, Jane's intense dislike for reading was only a **temporary** feeling. She was getting the hang of it. As a result, her nervousness began to **disappear**. One afternoon, Abe surprised her. To her **amazement**, he gave her his favorite book.

Peter Ferguson

"Thank you," she said. "Now that I can read, I don't ever want to stop."

Years later, Jane opened her newspaper and read the good news. Her friend, Abe Lincoln, had been elected President of the United States. She smiled and thought about the day she tripped over his long legs. That was the day that changed her life.

## PERRY COUNTY TRIBUNE

# Lincoln Elected!

## Abe Lincoln Elected 16th President

### November 6, 1860

Illinois Senator Abraham Lincoln was elected 16th president of the United States of America. He defeated three other candidates in the November 1860 election.

**?**

## Make Connections

How did Abe change Jane's life?
ESSENTIAL QUESTION

Who has helped change the way you think? TEXT TO SELF

# Visualize

Use colorful words and details to help you visualize how characters feel. Picture in your mind what they do as you read.

## Find Text Evidence

How does Jane feel at the beginning of the story? Use the details on page 199 to help you visualize.

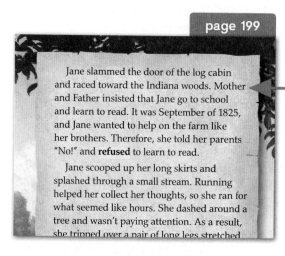

page 199

Jane slammed the door of the log cabin and raced toward the Indiana woods. Mother and Father insisted that Jane go to school and learn to read. It was September of 1825, and Jane wanted to help on the farm like her brothers. Therefore, she told her parents "No!" and **refused** to learn to read.

Jane scooped up her long skirts and splashed through a small stream. Running helped her collect her thoughts, so she ran for what seemed like hours. She dashed around a tree and wasn't paying attention. As a result, she tripped over a pair of long legs stretched

*I read that Jane slammed the door and raced into the woods. She ran for a long time.* From these details, I can figure out how Jane is feeling. She is upset and angry.

## Your Turn

COLLABORATE

What is Abe's first reaction to Jane? Reread and visualize what happens when they meet. Then answer the question.

Peter Ferguson

# Cause and Effect

Events in a story's plot are made up of causes and effects. A cause is why something happens. An effect is what happens. Words and phrases, such as *because, so,* and *as a result,* often show a cause and its effect.

 **Find Text Evidence**

*On page 199, I read that Jane is upset and angry. That's the effect. Now I need to find the cause. Mother and Father want her to learn to read, and she refuses. That is the cause. A cause and its effect happen in sequence, or time order.*

| Characters |
|---|
| Jane, Abe |

| Setting |
|---|
| the woods near Jane's house |

| Cause | Effect |
|---|---|
| Jane is upset because Mother and Father want her to learn to read. | Jane refuses and runs through the woods to calm down. |
| Cause | Effect |
|  |  |

## Your Turn  COLLABORATE

What happens next? Reread "Jane's Discovery." Look for more causes and effects. List them in sequence in your graphic organizer.

*Go Digital!*
*Use the interactive graphic organizer*

# Historical Fiction

"Jane's Discovery" is historical fiction.

**Historical fiction:**

- Is a story with made-up characters who take part in real events from history
- Has illustrations that show that the story takes place in the past

 **Find Text Evidence**

*I can tell that "Jane's Discovery" is historical fiction. Jane is made up, but she meets and talks with Abraham Lincoln. The story is based on real events that could have happened a long time ago.*

**page 200**

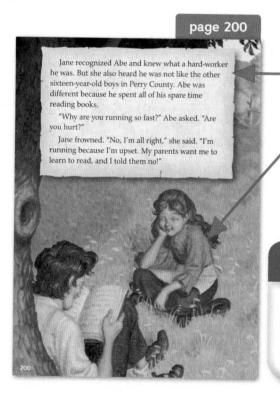

Jane recognized Abe and knew what a hard-worker he was. But she also heard he was not like the other sixteen-year-old boys in Perry County. Abe was different because he spent all of his spare time reading books.

"Why are you running so fast?" Abe asked. "Are you hurt?"

Jane frowned. "No, I'm all right," she said. "I'm running because I'm upset. My parents want me to learn to read, and I told them no!"

200

In historical fiction, made-up characters might meet with real people from the past.

The illustrations show details about how people dressed.

COLLABORATE

**Your Turn**

Find two details in "Jane's Discovery" that show this story is historical fiction.

# Idioms

An idiom is a group of words that means something different from the meaning of each word in it. The phrase *a piece of cake* is an idiom. It does not mean "a bit of cake." It means "something that's easy to do."

## Find Text Evidence

*On page 199, the phrase* collect her thoughts *is an idiom. I can use clues in the story to help me figure out that it means "to think about something."*

Running helped her <u>collect her thoughts,</u> so she ran for what seemed like hours.

## Your Turn

Talk about these idioms from "Jane's Discovery."
  **like clockwork,** *page 202*
  **getting the hang of it,** *page 202*

Peter Ferguson

# Write About the Text

Isabella

I responded to the prompt: *Think about Jane. Write a letter to Abe from Jane after she reads about Abe being elected president. Use details from the story.*

**Student Model:** *Narrative Text*

**Narrator**
My letter is written in first person from Jane's point of view.

**Descriptive Details**
I used sensory words to show action.

Dear Abe,

   I am so happy that you have been elected President of the United States. I read about it in the newspaper. I remember the day I tripped over your legs, and you changed my mind about reading.

Caterina Bernardi/Photdisc/Getty Images

**Linking Words**
I included signal words to connect ideas.

I still have the book you gave me about George Washington. I read it to my children. As a result, they enjoy books, too. Thank you for teaching me how to read. It changed my life.

Your friend,

Jane

**Grammar**

This is an example of a **present-tense verb**.

*Grammar Handbook See page 482.*

**Your Turn**

Think about Abe. Have him write a letter to a friend telling why he is teaching Jane to read. Use details from the story.

*Go Digital!*
*Write your response online.*
*Use your editing checklist.*

Peter Ferguson

**Essential Question**

What do we know about Earth and its neighbors?

Go Digital!

# Discover
## the Universe

Look up at the sky. What do you see? Astronomers first learned about Earth and its neighbors by looking up.

▶ Today scientists use telescopes, satellites, and manned spaceships to study the universe.

▶ They make new discoveries every day about Earth and our solar system.

## Talk About It

Write words you have learned about our solar system. Talk with a partner about these discoveries.

Solar System

# Vocabulary

**Use the picture and the sentence to talk with a partner about each word.**

**amount**

James drank a small **amount** of water.

What could you use to carry a large amount of juice?

**astronomy**

Kia looked at the stars when she studied **astronomy**.

What would you like to learn about astronomy?

**globe**

Our Earth is a big, round **globe**.

What is another word for globe?

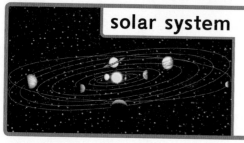

**solar system**

There are eight planets in our **solar system**.

Name one planet in our solar system.

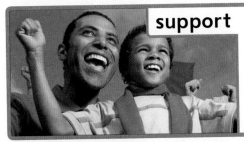

**support**

My dad and I **support** our favorite baseball team by cheering.

What can you do to show your support?

**surface**

An astronaut walks on the dry, dusty **surface** of the moon.

Describe the surface of your desk.

**temperature**

We can have fun even when the **temperature** outside is cold.

What is the temperature where you are today?

**warmth**

Will and Paul cooked marshmallows over the **warmth** of a fire.

What is another word for warmth?

COLLABORATE

## Your Turn

Pick three words. Then write three questions for your partner to answer.

*Go Digital!* *Use the online visual glossary*

# Earth and Its Neighbors

**? Essential Question**

**What do we know about Earth and its neighbors?**

Read about how we have learned about space.

Galileo studied the sky with a telescope he built.

If the Sun could talk, it might say, "Look at me! Look at my sunspots! I am so hot!" Without the Sun, Earth would be a cold, dark planet. How do we know this?

Thanks to the astronomer, Galileo, we know a lot about the Sun and the rest of our **solar system**.

## Telescopes: Looking Up

Galileo did not invent the **telescope**. However, 400 years ago he did build one that was strong enough to study the sky. When Galileo looked into space, he saw the rocky surface of the Moon. When he looked at the Sun, he discovered spots on its fiery surface.

The Moon is Earth's closest neighbor.

Astronomy, or the study of space, began with the simple telescope. But astronomers wanted to look at the sky more closely. They made bigger telescopes that could see further than the one Galileo used. Astronomers still had many questions.

## Satellites: A Step Closer

In 1958, scientists launched Explorer 1, the first American satellite, into space. It was an exciting day for America.

Explorer 1 takes off.

Soon many satellites circled the globe and took photographs of Earth, the Moon, stars, and other planets. They collected a large amount of information. Satellites even tracked the temperature on the planet Saturn.

Scientists have learned many things about the solar system from satellites. That's why they kept sending more into space. Soon there were hundreds of satellites in space making amazing discoveries, but astronomers wanted to know even more. That's why they found a way to put a man on the moon.

(bkgd) NASA, ESA, R. O'Connell (University of Virginia), and the Hubble Heritage Team (STScI/AURA); (c) NASA Marshall Space Flight Center (NASA-MSFC)

# One Giant Leap

In 1961, Alan Shepard became America's first **astronaut**. He blasted off into space in a rocket and then turned around and came back to Earth. His short trip was a big success. Shepard's flight proved that people could go into space.

After Shepard, more astronauts went into space. Some orbited the Earth. Some walked on the dusty, bumpy **surface** of the Moon. They took pictures and collected Moon rocks. Astronauts wanted to answer some important questions. Did the Sun's **warmth** heat the moon? Could the Moon **support** life someday?

Astronaut Edwin "Buzz" Aldrin walks toward the Lunar Module. Aldrin left his footprints on the Moon.

Aldrin brought home this Moon rock.

Scientists studied the photographs and Moon rocks that the astronauts brought back. They made exciting discoveries using telescopes and satellites. But it wasn't enough. Scientists wanted to get closer to the other planets. Soon they found a way!

## Hubble and Beyond

Scientists created another telescope, but this time it was gigantic. They sent it up into space. The Hubble Space Telescope was launched in 1990. It's still up there and orbits the Earth above the clouds. It takes clear, close-up photographs of stars and planets. It sends fascinating information back to Earth. The Hubble helps scientists study Earth and its neighbors. It also helps astronomers see planets outside our solar system.

It takes the Hubble Telescope 96 minutes to orbit the Earth.

## More Discoveries Every Day

Scientists are still asking questions about Earth and its neighbors in space. With the help of satellites, telescopes, and astronauts, they will continue to **explore** and find answers.

## What Can We See?

| With Our Eyes | With a Simple Telescope | With the Hubble Telescope |
|---|---|---|
| The Moon | Craters on the Moon | Planets outside our solar system |
| The Sun | Sunspots | Stars bigger than the Sun and far, far away |
| Mars | Clouds around Jupiter | Jupiter's surface |

This is a Hubble Telescope photo of an exploding star.

## Make Connections

How have we learned about Earth and its neighbors in space? ESSENTIAL QUESTION

What do you see when you look at the sky? TEXT TO SELF

(b) NASA/ESA/JPL/Arizona State Univ.

# Summarize

When you summarize, you tell the most important ideas and details in a text. Use these ideas and details to help you summarize "Earth and Its Neighbors."

 **Find Text Evidence**

How did telescopes help us learn about space? Identify important ideas and details and summarize them in your own words.

page 215

If the Sun could talk, it might say, "Look at me! Look at my sunspots! I am so hot!" Without the Sun, Earth would be a cold, dark planet. How do we know this?

Thanks to the astronomer, Galileo, we know a lot about the Sun and the rest of our **solar system**.

Telescopes: Looking Up

Galileo did not invent the **telescope**. However, 400 years ago he did build one that was strong enough to study the sky. When Galileo looked into space, he saw the rocky surface of the Moon. When he

*I read that Galileo built a telescope. He discovered sunspots and saw the Moon's surface. Details help me summarize. Telescopes helped scientists learn more about space.*

## Your Turn

COLLABORATE

Reread "Satellites: A Step Closer" on page 216. Summarize the important ideas and details about satellites.

Ian McKinnell/Photographer's Choice/Getty Images

# Main Idea and Key Details

The main idea is the most important point an author makes about a topic. Key details tell about the main idea.

 **Find Text Evidence**

*I can reread and look for important details about satellites. Then I can figure out what these details have in common to figure out the main idea.*

| Main Idea |
|---|
| **Detail**<br>Satellites take photographs of Earth, the Moon, stars, and planets. |
| **Detail** |
| **Detail** |

**Your Turn**

Reread. Find more key details about satellites. List them in your graphic organizer. Use details to figure out the main idea.

*Go Digital!*
*Use the interactive graphic organizer*

# Expository Text

"Earth and Its Neighbors" is an expository text.

**Expository text:**
- Gives facts and information about a topic
- Has text features such as headings, key words, and charts

 **Find Text Evidence**

*I can tell that "Earth and Its Neighbors" is expository text. It gives facts and information about telescopes, satellites, and space. It has headings, key words, and a chart.*

page 219

**More Discoveries Every Day**

Scientists are still asking questions about Earth and its neighbors in space. With the help of satellites, telescopes, and astronauts, they will continue to **explore** and find answers.

**What Can We See?**

| With Our Eyes | With a Simple Telescope | With the Hubble Telescope |
|---|---|---|
| The Moon | Craters on the Moon | Planets outside our solar system |
| The Sun | Sunspots | Stars bigger than the Sun and far, far away |
| Mars | Clouds around Jupiter | Jupiter's surface |

**Make Connections**

How have we learned about Earth and its neighbors in space? ESSENTIAL QUESTION

What do you see when you look at the sky? TEXT TO SELF

This is a Hubble Telescope photo of an exploding star.

219

## Text Features

**Key Words** Key words are important words in the text.

**Chart** A chart is a list of facts arranged in rows and columns across a page.

 COLLABORATE

## Your Turn

Look at the chart on page 219. Tell one way the Hubble telescope is different from a simple telescope.

# Suffixes

A suffix is a word part added to the end of a word. It changes the word's meaning. The suffix -y means "full of." The suffix -ly means "in a certain way."

 **Find Text Evidence**

*On page 215 in "Earth and Its Neighbors" I see the word* rocky. Rocky *has the suffix -y. I know that the suffix -y means "full of." The word* rocky *must mean "full of rocks."*

When Galileo looked into space, he saw the rocky surface of the Moon.

COLLABORATE

## Your Turn

Find the suffix. Use it to figure out each word's meaning.

**closely,** *page 216*
**dusty,** *page 217*
**bumpy,** *page 217*

The Granger Collection, NYC

# Write About the Text

Pages 214-219

Noah

I answered the question: *How does the author use sequence of events to explain how scientists have learned about the solar system?*

**Student Model:** *Informative Text*

**Main Idea**
My topic sentence expresses the most important point of my paragraph.

**Strong Paragraphs**
I used facts and details to support the main idea in my topic sentence.

The author describes a sequence of events in history to show how scientists have learned about the solar system. First I read that Galileo built a strong telescope 400 years ago to study the Moon and Sun. Then I read that scientists built bigger telescopes and learned more. Later they sent up satellites.

monkeybusinessimages/iStock360/Getty Images

**224**    W.3.2a, W.3.2b  See the California Standards section.

Next I read how astronauts helped to answer questions about the solar system. Today the Hubble Space Telescope sends pictures from space. Reading these events in order helped me understand how scientists learned about space.

**Grammar**

The word *helped* is an example of a regular **past-tense verb.**

*Grammar Handbook* See page 482.

**Strong Conclusion**
I ended by summing up what I learned from the text.

## Your Turn

What do the photographs and the captions add to the text? Use details from the text.

*Go Digital!*
*Write your response online.*
*Use your editing checklist.*

NASA–JSC

**Essential Question**

What ideas can we get from nature?

Go Digital!

# IDEAS FROM NATURE

This spider may be small, but it inspires big ideas. Its webs are super strong, and scientists want to know why.

▶ Scientists look to nature for new ideas.

▶ These ideas help people in many different ways.

## Talk About It

Talk with a partner about how nature inspires new ideas. Write words you have learned.

Nature

# Vocabulary

**Use the picture and the sentence to talk with a partner about each word.**

**effective**

The broom is an **effective** tool for sweeping up leaves and dirt.

What is an effective tool for cutting paper?

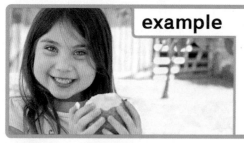

**example**

The apple is a good **example** of a healthy fruit.

Name an example of a healthy vegetable.

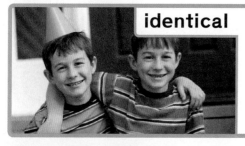

**identical**

Mark and Matt are **identical** twins because they look alike.

What makes two things identical?

**imitate**

This robot can **imitate** the way Cody moves.

What does it mean to imitate something?

**material**

The baby's blanket is made of a soft, warm **material**.

Describe the material your shirt is made of.

**model**

Kevin and I play with my **model** airplane in the park.

Why does it help to have a model?

**observed**

Meg and Joann **observed** the fish, and wrote down what they saw.

What is another word for *observed*?

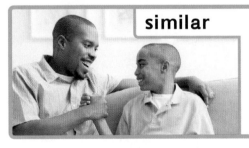

**similar**

My dad and I like to look alike, so we wear **similar** shirts.

What is a word that means the opposite of *similar*?

## Your Turn

COLLABORATE

Pick three words. Then write three questions for your partner to answer.

*Go Digital!* *Use the online visual glossary*

# BATS DID IT FIRST

(bkgd)©Radius Images/Alamy; (inset)Ewen Charlton/Moment/Getty Images

## Essential Question

What ideas can we get from nature?

Read about how bats inspired a new cane for blind people.

Nature is full of great ideas. Many inventors and scientists just step outside and look around for inspiration and ideas. They often **imitate**, or copy, what they see outdoors. They use nature to inspire their inventions.

One amazing invention was inspired by bats. It's a special cane that helps blind people navigate and get around.

This boy is blind and uses a special cane to help him get around.

## Canes Lead the Way

Many blind people use canes. They tap the canes on the ground in front of them to locate objects that may be in the way. This helps them move around safely as they do their shopping or walk outdoors.

The bat-inspired cane is different from these canes. It sends out sound waves, or signals. These signals are almost **identical** to the ones bats use to find their way in the dark.

## How Bats Get Around

The scientist that came up with the idea for the new cane was inspired by watching bats. He **observed** the way bats fly at night. The bats make high-pitched sounds that people cannot hear. These sounds create an amazing navigation system for the bats. Here's how it works.

Bats send sound waves out through their mouth or nose. These sound waves hit objects and then bounce back as an echo. The echo tells the bats how far away an object is and how big it is. This information helps bats find bugs to eat. It is also an **effective** way to keep bats from bumping into trees and other bats.

## How Bats Use Sound Waves

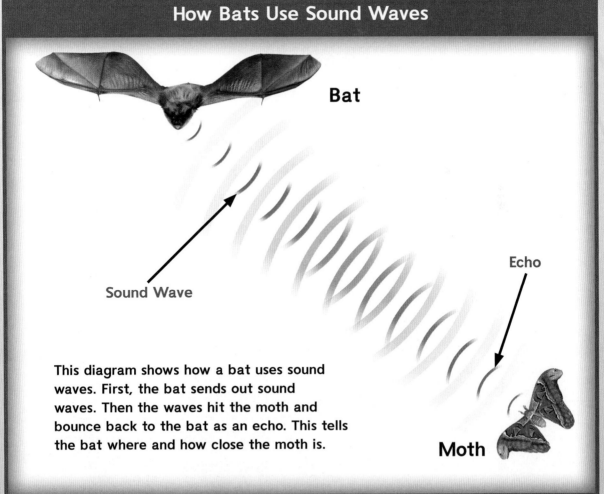

Bat

Sound Wave

Echo

Moth

This diagram shows how a bat uses sound waves. First, the bat sends out sound waves. Then the waves hit the moth and bounce back to the bat as an echo. This tells the bat where and how close the moth is.

## A Batty Idea

The scientist who invented the new cane took what he learned from observing bats. He used a **similar** idea. He started with an ordinary white cane. He wanted the cane to imitate the way bats use sound waves. So, he sketched plans and made a **model** of his invention. When he built the cane, the scientist used a special **material** that was lightweight and strong. Then he added sound waves. Finally, a team of scientists tested the cane. It worked!

## How the Cane Works

The handle of the cane sends out signals. The signals bounce off objects in front of the cane. Then an echo bounces back to the cane's handle. The person holding it feels buttons on the handle vibrate, or shake. These buttons tell the person how far away and how big the object is.

### The Bat-Inspired Cane

Sound Wave

Cane →

Echo

Mailbox

This bat-inspired cane uses sound waves. The cane alerts the man there is something in his way.

Scientists and inventors study plants and animals all the time. Their observations have led them to invent many useful things. And like many new inventions, the bat-inspired cane is a good **example** of how great ideas can come from nature.

This scientist is studying how bats fly.

## Make Connections

How did bats inspire a cane that helps blind people? ESSENTIAL QUESTION

What is something in nature that inspires you? What would you invent? TEXT TO SELF

# Summarize

When you summarize, you tell the most important ideas and details in a text. Use important details to help you summarize "Bats Did It First."

### 🔍 Find Text Evidence

How did one scientist come up with the idea for the new cane? Identify important ideas and details, and summarize them in your own words.

page 232

**How Bats Get Around**

The scientist that came up with the idea for the new cane was inspired by watching bats. He **observed** the way bats fly at night. The bats make high-pitched sounds that people cannot hear. These sounds create an amazing navigation system for the bats. Here's how it works.

*I read that <u>one scientist came up with an idea for a new cane. He watched bats use sound waves to navigate at night.</u> Those details help me summarize. The way bats use sound waves led to the invention of a new cane.*

## Your Turn

COLLABORATE

Reread "How The Cane Works" on page 234. Summarize the important ideas and details about how the new bat-inspired cane works.

# Main Idea and Key Details

The main idea is the most important point the author makes about a topic. Key details tell about the main idea. Put the details together to figure out the main idea.

 **Find Text Evidence**

*What details tell about how bats fly at night? I can reread page 233 and find key details. Then I can figure out what they have in common to tell the main idea.*

| Main Idea |
|---|
| How bats use sound waves |

| Detail |
|---|
| Bats make high-pitched sounds through their mouth and nose. |

| Detail |
|---|
| These sound waves hit objects and bounce back as an echo. |

| Detail |
|---|
| keeping bats from bumping into other objects |

## Your Turn

Reread. Find more key details about how bats fly at night. List them in your graphic organizer. Then use the details to figure out the main idea.

*Go Digital!*
*Use the interactive graphic organizer*

# Expository Text

"Bats Did it First" is an expository text.

**Expository text:**
- Gives facts and information about a topic
- Includes text features such as photographs, captions, and a diagram

### Find Text Evidence

*I can tell that "Bats Did It First" is an expository text. It has photographs with captions. It also has a diagram that shows how bats fly at night.*

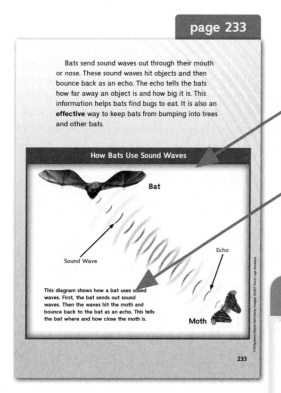

page 233

Bats send sound waves out through their mouth or nose. These sound waves hit objects and then bounce back as an echo. The echo tells the bats how far away an object is and how big it is. This information helps bats find bugs to eat. It is also an **effective** way to keep bats from bumping into trees and other bats.

**How Bats Use Sound Waves**

Bat

Sound Wave

Echo

This diagram shows how a bat uses sound waves. First, the bat sends out sound waves. Then the waves hit the moth and bounce back to the bat as an echo. This tells the bat where and how close the moth is.

Moth

233

## Text Features

**Diagram** A diagram is a picture that gives more information about the text. Labels name the parts of the diagram.

**Caption** A caption tells about a photograph or diagram.

COLLABORATE

## Your Turn

Look at the diagram on page 233. Explain how the bat finds food at night.

# Root Words

A root word is the simplest form of a word. It helps you figure out the meaning of a related word.

### Find Text Evidence

*In "Bats Did It First" I see the word* invention. *I think the root word of* invention *is* invent. *I know* invent *means "to make something new." An invention is "something new that is made."*

> One amazing invention was inspired by bats.

## Your Turn

COLLABORATE

Find the root word. Then use it to figure out the meaning of each word.

**inspiration,** *page 231*
**navigation,** *page 232*

5ISystems/iStock/360/Getty Images

# Write About the Text

Pages 230–235

Aisha

I answered the question: *Why is the new cane the scientist designed better than earlier models? Use details from the text.*

---

**Student Model:** *Informative Text*

The new cane is better than earlier models because it can tell blind people how far away objects are by using signals. Older models cannot do this. These signals are like the ones a bat sends to help it hunt in the dark.

**Topic Sentence**
I introduced the main idea in the first sentence.

**Supporting Details**
I included text evidence to develop the topic of my paragraph.

When the cane's signal bounces off an object in front of it, buttons on the cane vibrate. This tells the blind person that something is there. The new cane's design will make it safer for blind people to walk without bumping into objects.

**Strong Conclusion**
My final sentence retells the main idea in different words.

**Grammar**

This is an example of a **future-tense verb.**

*Grammar Handbook*
*See page 483.*

**Your Turn**

How does the author help us understand what sound waves are? Use details from the text.

*Go Digital!*
*Write your response online.*
*Use your editing checklist.*

## Essential Question
## How is each event in history unique?

*Go Digital!*

©Corbis

SL.3.Ia See the California Standards section.

# History Lives

Christopher Columbus sailed to America in 1492. Today, people reenact his historic voyage. Reliving past events helps us remember them and understand what happened.

▶ History is made up of many unique events.

▶ Reliving history helps us appreciate what people went through to get to new places.

## Talk About It

Think about a time in history when people moved from one place to another. Talk with a friend about what makes the event unique.

Unique

# Vocabulary

**Use the picture and the sentence to talk with a partner about each word.**

### agreeable

Lori loves cold weather and thinks it is pleasant and **agreeable**.

*What kind of weather do you find agreeable?*

### appreciate

Jan and Kayla **appreciate** everything their grandmother does for them.

*How do you show people that you appreciate them?*

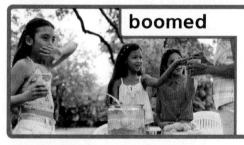

### boomed

Anita's lemonade business **boomed** when the weather got hotter.

*What does boomed mean in this sentence?*

### descendants

Ann and her family are **descendants** of the people in the photographs.

*What are descendants?*

## emigration

People who left their homes knew that **emigration** would be hard.

*What are some reasons for emigration?*

## pioneers

In 1843, **pioneers** traveled across the country by covered wagon.

*Why did pioneers travel across the country?*

## transportation

Trains are a favorite form of **transportation** for many people.

*Tell about another form of transportation.*

## vehicles

These **vehicles** are parked in a large parking lot.

*What type of vehicle do you travel to school in?*

## Your Turn

COLLABORATE

Pick three words. Write three questions for your partner to answer.

*Go Digital!* **Use the online visual glossary**

? **Essential Question**

How is each event in history unique?

Read to see how the pioneers found their way to Oregon.

Pioneers crossed America in covered wagons like these.

246

# The Long Road to Oregon

In the spring of 1843, more than 800 **pioneers** began a journey from Independence, Missouri to Oregon City, Oregon. They had 120 wagons and 5,000 cattle. This was one of the first wagon trains to travel west on the Oregon Trail.

## Land of Promise

Life was very hard in Missouri in the 1800s. Bad weather caused crops to die. Businesses closed. As a result, many people could not find jobs.

Americans wanted a more enjoyable life. They wanted to live in a place where the soil was richer and the weather was more **agreeable** and pleasant.

The United States government was giving away free land to pioneers. So, thousands of people traveled west to Oregon, a territory in the northwest part of the country.

*This map shows the Oregon Trail in 1843.*

## The Oregon Trail

Oregon City

OREGON COUNTRY

UNORGANIZED TERRITORY

IOWA

KEY
~ Trail
• Cities

MEXICAN TERRITORY

Independence

MISSOURI

REPUBLIC OF TEXAS

247

## Getting Ready to Go

Pioneers knew that **emigration** to Oregon would be difficult. The trip was more than 2,000 miles of dusty, bumpy trails and would take at least five months. The pioneers needed to be prepared.

First they gathered their cows and chickens. Then they packed many pounds of food, cooking pots, tools, and seeds.

Covered wagons were the main form of **transportation** on the Oregon Trail. The wagons were stuffed with everything a family would need. There was little room for anything else. As a result, children left books, toys, and most of their clothes behind.

## A Long, Hard Journey

Planning and packing took weeks. The first thing pioneer families did was hook a team of oxen up to their wagons. Oxen were dependable and strong and could pull the heavy **vehicles**. Next the families joined other pioneer families.

All the wagons traveling together formed a wagon train. The children and healthy adults walked. The sick or tired pioneers rode in the uncomfortable wagons.

Dirty water, sickness, and fierce dust storms made the journey challenging. Bad weather often made the trail impassable. But the pioneers were determined. As a result, they finally reached their new home in Oregon.

**This reenactment shows a wagon train on the Oregon Trail.**

Greg Ryan/Alamy

## A New Life in Oregon

When the pioneers got to Oregon, they cleared land and built houses. Then they planted crops. As more emigrants arrived, towns grew. People opened stores and restaurants. Businesses **boomed**. The pioneers worked hard to make their new towns successful. They had found a better life!

Many of the people who live in Oregon today are **descendants** of the brave pioneers who made the journey west from the 1840s to the 1880s. They **appreciate** their family members' hard work and courage. And they are grateful for the Oregon Trail.

## Learn Your History!

History is the study of people and events from the past. It's important to know our country's past. Learning about history helps us appreciate our country and the people who helped build it.

One fun way to learn about history is by reading the stories of the brave people who lived it. You can read diaries of pioneers on the Oregon Trail, or biographies of explorers. These can be more exciting and inspiring than a movie or a television show!

You can still see parts of the original Oregon Trail today.

## Make Connections

How was the Oregon Trail emigration a unique time in history? ESSENTIAL QUESTION

What is your favorite event in history? Describe why. TEXT TO SELF

# Summarize

When you summarize, you tell the most important ideas and details in a text. Use details to help you summarize "The Long Road to Oregon."

 **Find Text Evidence**

Why did pioneers leave Missouri to travel west to Oregon? Reread "Land of Promise" on page 247. Sort the details. Decide which are most important. Then summarize the text in your own words.

---

**page 247**

In the spring of 1843, more than 800 **pioneers** began a journey from Independence, Missouri to Oregon City, Oregon. They had 120 wagons and 5,000 cattle. This was one of the first wagon trains to travel west on the Oregon Trail.

**Land of Promise**

Life was very hard in Missouri in the 1800s. Bad weather caused crops to die. Businesses closed.

As a result, many people could not find jobs.

Americans wanted a more enjoyable life. They wanted to live in a place where the soil was richer and the weather was more **agreeable** and pleasant.

The United States government was giving away free land to pioneers. So, thousands of people traveled west to Oregon, a territory in the northwest part of the country.

---

*I read that <u>crops died, businesses closed, and people couldn't find jobs. They got free land. The weather and soil were better in Oregon.</u> These key details help me summarize. Pioneers left Missouri because life was hard and they wanted a better life.*

## Your Turn

 COLLABORATE

Reread "A New Life in Oregon." Find the key details. Use them to summarize the main ideas and details in your own words.

# Sequence

The sequence is the order in which events take place. Look for words and phrases that show time order, such as *first, next, then, later,* and *finally.*

 **Find Text Evidence**

The events in "The Long Road to Oregon" happen in time order. Life was hard in Missouri in the 1800s, and the United States government was giving away free land. That is the first event. I can use signal words to find more events.

| Event |
|---|
| The government was giving away free land in Oregon and the pioneers decided to go west. |

↓

| First the pioneers gathered their cows and chickens. |
|---|

↓

| Then they packed food, cooking pots, tools, and seeds. |
|---|

↓

| they were getting ready to go |
|---|

↓

| They arrived and planted crops. |
|---|

## Your Turn

COLLABORATE

Reread "A New Life in Oregon" on page 249. What happened when the pioneers got to Oregon? List details of the events in order in your graphic organizer. Use signal words to help you.

*Go Digital!*
*Use the interactive graphic organizer*

# Expository Text

"The Long Road to Oregon" is an expository text.
**Expository text:**
- May explain a social studies or history topic
- Has headings and sidebars
- May include photos, captions, and maps

## 🔍 Find Text Evidence

*I can tell that "The Long Road to Oregon" is an expository text. It gives information about the Oregon Trail. It also has headings, photographs, captions, and a map.*

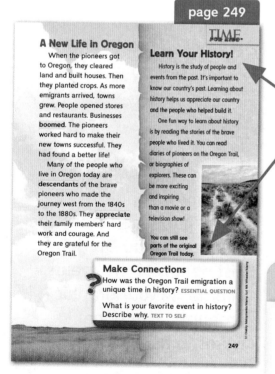

page 249

**A New Life in Oregon**

When the pioneers got to Oregon, they cleared land and built houses. Then they planted crops. As more emigrants arrived, towns grew. People opened stores and restaurants. Businesses boomed. The pioneers worked hard to make their new towns successful. They had found a better life!

Many of the people who live in Oregon today are descendants of the brave pioneers who made the journey west from the 1840s to the 1880s. They appreciate their family members' hard work and courage. And they are grateful for the Oregon Trail.

**TIME** FOR KIDS.

**Learn Your History!**

History is the study of people and events from the past. It's important to know our country's past. Learning about history helps us appreciate our country and the people who helped build it.

One fun way to learn about history is by reading the stories of the brave people who lived it. You can read diaries of pioneers on the Oregon Trail, or biographies of explorers. These can be more exciting and inspiring than a movie or a television show!

You can still see parts of the original Oregon Trail today.

**Make Connections**

❓ How was the Oregon Trail emigration a unique time in history? ESSENTIAL QUESTION

What is your favorite event in history? Describe why. TEXT TO SELF

249

## Text Features

**Sidebar** A sidebar may present the author's opinion.

**Photographs and captions** Photographs and captions give additional facts and details.

COLLABORATE

# Your Turn

Reread the sidebar on page 249. Tell your partner what the author's opinion is.

# Suffixes

A suffix is a word part added to the end of a word. It changes the word's meaning. The suffix *-able* means "is or can be."

### Find Text Evidence

*I see the word enjoyable on page 247. Enjoyable has the root word enjoy. I know that enjoy means "to be happy with." The suffix -able means "is able or can be." I think the word enjoyable means "can be happy with."*

Americans wanted a more enjoyable life.

## Your Turn

Use the suffix to figure out the meaning of each word.
  **agreeable,** *page 247*
  **dependable,** *page 248*

Oleksiy Maksymenko Photos/Alamy

# Write About the Text

Pages 246–249

Micco

I answered the question: *In your opinion, does the author do a good job of describing the pioneers' journey on the Oregon Trail?*

## Student Model: *Opinion*

I think the author does a good job of describing the pioneers' journey on the Oregon Trail. The author gives details to show how difficult the journey was. The trip was more than 2,000 miles and took five months. Oxen pulled wagons along the dusty trails.

**State an Opinion**
I introduced the topic by making my opinion clear.

### Grammar

**Combining sentences with verbs** can be done when the subject is the same.

*Grammar Handbook See page 485.*

Kali Nine LLC/iStock/360/Getty Images

The author explains that the pioneers had to walk because the wagons were full. The author describes challenges, such as dust storms and dirty water. These details helped me picture the long, difficult journey.

**Formal Voice**
I used a formal style of writing with complete sentences and correct grammar.

**Supporting Reasons**
I included facts to support my opinion.

## Your Turn

In your opinion, was it worth it to move to Oregon in the 1800s? Use details from the text.

*Go Digital!*
*Write your response online.*
*Use your editing checklist.*

Greg Ryan/Alamy

# Meet the Challenge

## The Big Idea

What are different ways to meet challenges?

# Meatballs on Wheels

Our meatballs roll from door to door,
    We go each week at half past four.
We deliver dinner on wheels,
    Bringing seniors hot, tasty meals.

Meatballs rolling from door to door,
Meatballs and a whole lot more.

— by Trevor Reynolds

Michael Moran

257

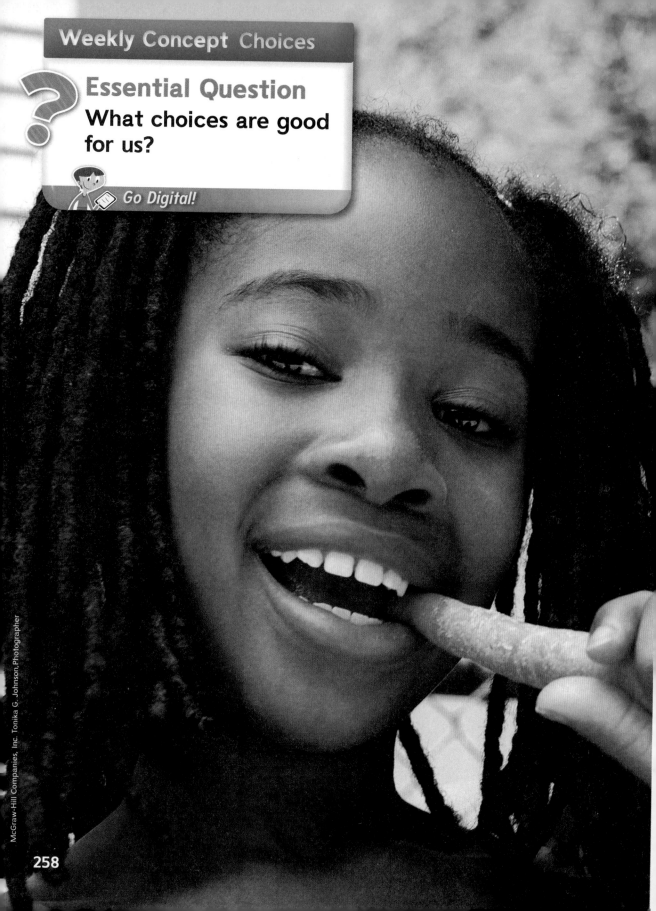

**Essential Question**

What choices are good for us?

Go Digital!

# Smart Choices

Some decisions are easy. This crispy carrot is my favorite snack, and it is delicious and healthy. Making good choices makes me feel good.

▶ We make many decisions every day.

▶ Smart choices help us live healthy lives.

## Talk About It

Write words you have learned about choices. Talk with a partner about making smart decisions.

| Smart Choices |
| --- |
| ↓ |
| |
| ↓ |
| |
| ↓ |
| |

# Vocabulary

Use the picture and the sentence to talk with a partner about each word.

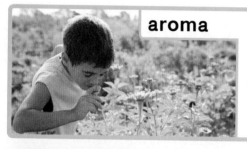

**aroma**

Carl smells the sweet **aroma** of the flowers near his house.

What is your favorite aroma?

**expect**

I see clouds, so I **expect** it will rain today.

What do you expect to do while it is raining?

**flavorful**

Jo and Tori eat lunches that are delicious and **flavorful.**

What are some of your favorite flavorful foods?

**graceful**

Katie is a **graceful** dancer.

What word means the opposite of graceful?

**healthful**

Sue chooses **healthful** foods at the market.

What is a good example of a healthful lunch?

**interrupted**

A small dog **interrupted** the soccer game.

How might you feel if someone interrupted you?

**luscious**

These strawberries are sweet and **luscious**.

What is another word for luscious?

**variety**

The bookstore has a large **variety** of books by my favorite author.

Where else could you find a variety of books?

## Your Turn

COLLABORATE

Pick three words. Then write three questions for your partner to answer.

*Go Digital!* *Use the online visual glossary*

# Nail Soup

## Essential Question

**What choices are good for us?**

Read about how choices helped a man and his wife learn a lesson.

Once long ago, Papa and I were walking for miles on a long and winding country road. Finally we approached a large farmhouse surrounded by fields of healthy vegetables.

"Papa, I'm so hungry," I said.

Papa patted my head and winked. I smiled and nodded back. I admired my Papa. I knew he would find a way to get us a warm meal. We knocked on the door, and a well-dressed man and his wife answered.

"Hello," said Papa. "My son, Erik, is hungry. Could you please spare a morsel of food?"

The man shook his head. "We have lots of food, but we cannot afford to give any of it away," he said.

"Well, I could cook my **flavorful** nail soup if you would donate a small cup of hot water," said Papa.

The woman looked at her husband. "Soup from a nail?" she said. "That's impossible." But the man's curiosity overwhelmed him, so he brought a small cup of boiling water.

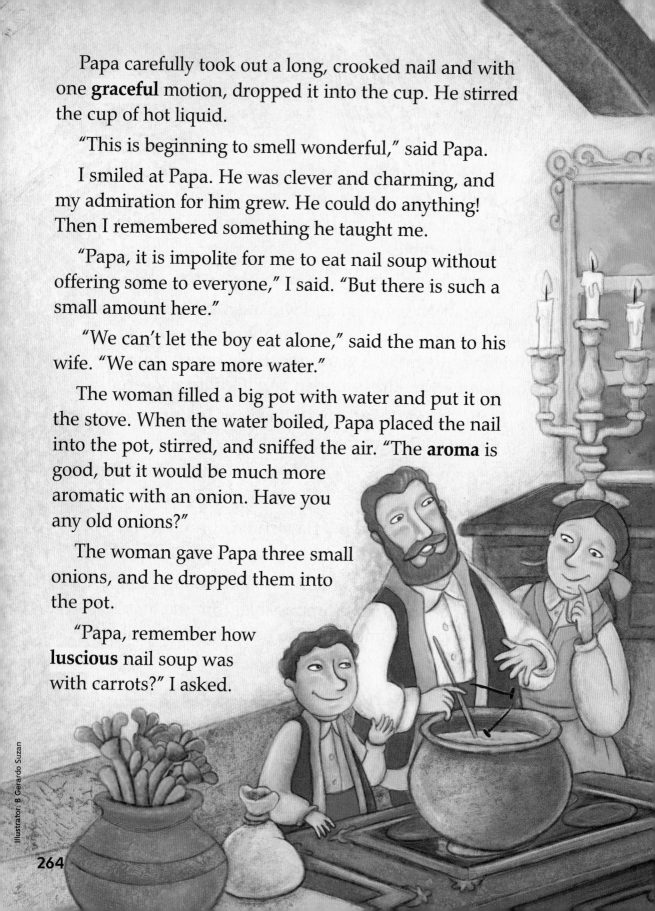

Papa carefully took out a long, crooked nail and with one **graceful** motion, dropped it into the cup. He stirred the cup of hot liquid.

"This is beginning to smell wonderful," said Papa.

I smiled at Papa. He was clever and charming, and my admiration for him grew. He could do anything! Then I remembered something he taught me.

"Papa, it is impolite for me to eat nail soup without offering some to everyone," I said. "But there is such a small amount here."

"We can't let the boy eat alone," said the man to his wife. "We can spare more water."

The woman filled a big pot with water and put it on the stove. When the water boiled, Papa placed the nail into the pot, stirred, and sniffed the air. "The **aroma** is good, but it would be much more aromatic with an onion. Have you any old onions?"

The woman gave Papa three small onions, and he dropped them into the pot.

"Papa, remember how **luscious** nail soup was with carrots?" I asked.

Illustrator: B Gerardo Suzan

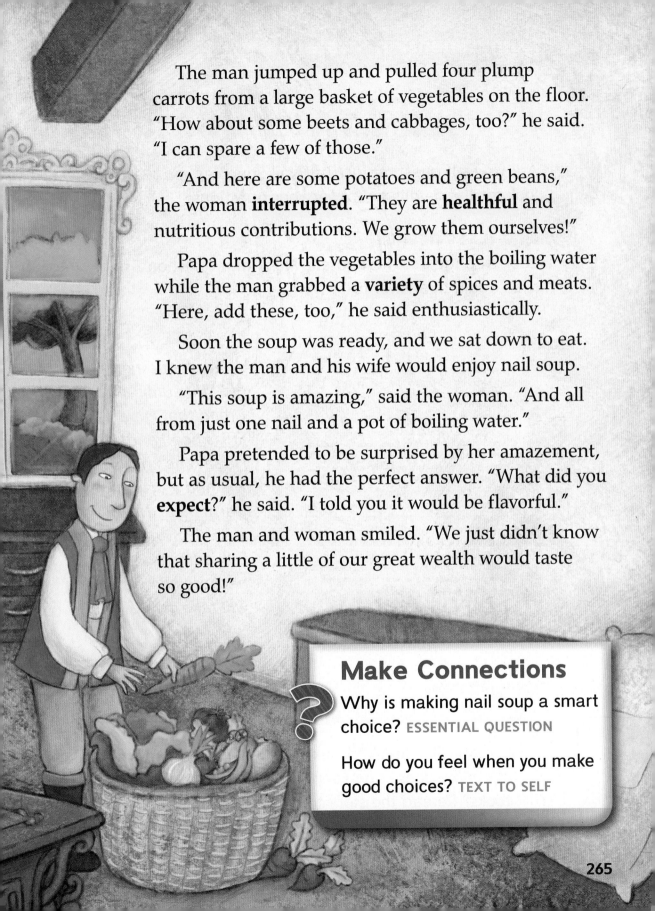

The man jumped up and pulled four plump carrots from a large basket of vegetables on the floor. "How about some beets and cabbages, too?" he said. "I can spare a few of those."

"And here are some potatoes and green beans," the woman **interrupted**. "They are **healthful** and nutritious contributions. We grow them ourselves!"

Papa dropped the vegetables into the boiling water while the man grabbed a **variety** of spices and meats. "Here, add these, too," he said enthusiastically.

Soon the soup was ready, and we sat down to eat. I knew the man and his wife would enjoy nail soup.

"This soup is amazing," said the woman. "And all from just one nail and a pot of boiling water."

Papa pretended to be surprised by her amazement, but as usual, he had the perfect answer. "What did you **expect**?" he said. "I told you it would be flavorful."

The man and woman smiled. "We just didn't know that sharing a little of our great wealth would taste so good!"

## Make Connections

Why is making nail soup a smart choice? ESSENTIAL QUESTION

How do you feel when you make good choices? TEXT TO SELF

# Ask and Answer Questions

Ask yourself questions about "Nail Soup" as you read. Then look for the details to answer your questions.

## Find Text Evidence

Look at page 263. Reread and think of a question. Then read again to answer it.

page 263

Once long ago, Papa and I were walking for miles on a long and winding country road. Finally we approached a large farmhouse surrounded by fields of healthy vegetables.

"Papa, I'm so hungry," I said.

Papa patted my head and winked. I smiled and nodded back. I admired my Papa. I knew he would find a way to get us a warm meal. We knocked on the door, and a well-dressed man and his wife answered.

"Hello," said Papa. "My son, Erik, is hungry. Could you please spare a morsel of food?"

The man shook his head. "We have lots of food, but we cannot afford to give any of it away," he said.

"Well, I could cook my **flavorful** nail soup if you would donate a small cup of hot water," said Papa.

The woman looked at her husband. "Soup from a nail?" she said. "That's impossible." But the man's curiosity overwhelmed him, so he brought a small cup of boiling water.

*I have a question. Why did Erik admire Papa?* <u>*I read that Papa patted Erik's head and winked. He says he knows Papa will find a way to get a warm meal.*</u> *Now I can answer my question. Erik admires Papa because he knows Papa will take care of him.*

## Your Turn

**COLLABORATE**

Reread "Nail Soup." Think of a question. You might ask: Why does Papa keep smelling the soup while it cooks? Reread the story to find the answer.

Illustrator: B Gerardo Suzan

# Point of View

Point of view is what a narrator thinks about events or other characters in a story. Look for details that show what the narrator thinks to figure out point of view.

## Find Text Evidence

*I read on page 263 that Erik, the story's narrator, nodded and smiled at Papa. Then he said he admired his Papa. This tells me he has a lot of respect and love for his father. He trusts he will take care of him.*

| Details |
|---|
| Erik smiles and nods. He knows Papa will get them a warm meal. |
| Papa knocks on a door and asks for food. Papa offers to do nail soup with these people |

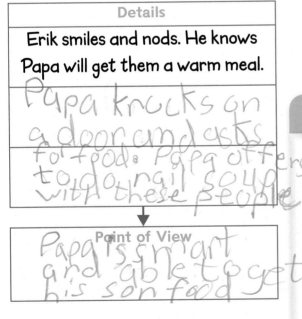

↓

| Point of View |
|---|
| Papa is smart and able to get his son food |

## Your Turn

Reread "Nail Soup." Look for more clues that show Erik's point of view about Papa. List them in the graphic organizer. Then tell Erik's opinion of his father. Do you agree with Erik's point of view about Papa?

*Go Digital!*
*Use the interactive graphic organizer*

# Folktale

"Nail Soup" is a folktale. A **folktale**:
- Is a short story passed from person to person
- Always has a problem the characters have to solve
- Usually has a message or lesson

 **Find Text Evidence**

*I can tell that "Nail Soup" is a folktale. There is a problem Erik and his Papa have to solve. The story also has a lesson. It teaches the man and his wife the importance of sharing.*

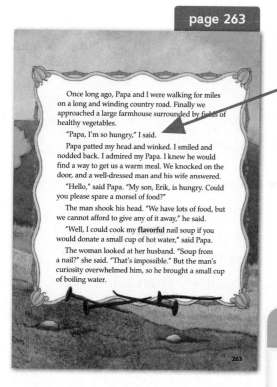

page 263

Once long ago, Papa and I were walking for miles on a long and winding country road. Finally we approached a large farmhouse surrounded by fields of healthy vegetables.

"Papa, I'm so hungry," I said.

Papa patted my head and winked. I smiled and nodded back. I admired my Papa. I knew he would find a way to get us a warm meal. We knocked on the door, and a well-dressed man and his wife answered.

"Hello," said Papa. "My son, Erik, is hungry. Could you please spare a morsel of food?"

The man shook his head. "We have lots of food, but we cannot afford to give any of it away," he said.

"Well, I could cook my **flavorful** nail soup if you would donate a small cup of hot water," said Papa.

The woman looked at her husband. "Soup from a nail?" she said. "That's impossible." But the man's curiosity overwhelmed him, so he brought a small cup of boiling water.

263

In this folktale, Erik has a problem. He is hungry. Papa finds a way to solve his problem.

A folktale often has a message that is stated at the end of the story.

 COLLABORATE

## Your Turn

Reread page 265. What lesson does the man and his wife learn? Tell a partner.

# Root Words

A root word is the simplest form of a word. When you read an unfamiliar word, look for a root word in it. Use the root word to figure out the unfamiliar word's meaning.

## Find Text Evidence

*On page 264 of "Nail Soup," I see the word* admiration. *I think the root word in* admiration *is* admire. *I know* admire *means "to respect or appreciate." Erik had a lot of* admiration *for his Papa. That means he "has respect" for him.*

He was clever and charming, and my admiration for him grew.

## Your Turn

Find the root word in each word. Use it to figure out the word's meaning.

**aromatic,** *page 264*

**amazement,** *page 265*

Illustrator: B Gerardo Suzan

Pages 262–265

# Write About the Text

Lizzie

I answered the question: *Do you think Erik was right to admire Papa? Use evidence to support your answer.*

**Student Model:** *Opinion*

**State an Opinion**
My opening sentence makes my opinion clear.

I think that Erik was right to admire Papa. Papa's plan to make nail soup was very clever. He found a way to get a meal for Erik and himself. This is one reason to admire Papa. Another reason is that he taught the couple an important lesson.

**Grammar**

The **linking verb** *was* connects the subject, *plan,* to the rest of the sentence.

*Grammar Handbook See page 481.*

altrendo images/Stockbyte/Getty Images

Papa tricked the couple into sharing their food. But they were happy and smiling at the end. Papa did more than feed himself and Erik. He also helped the couple learn to share. Erik was right to be proud of him.

**Show Feelings**
I included words to show how the characters feel.

**Supporting Details**
I supported my opinion with good reasons.

## Your Turn

In your opinion, did the man and his wife make good choices? Use text evidence to support your answer.

*Go Digital!*
*Write your response online.*
*Use your editing checklist.*

Illustrator: B Gerardo Suzan

**Essential Question**
How can you use what you know to help others?

*Go Digital!*

272

# USE YOUR SKILLS

We all have skills and talents. We might be artistic or smart. We might be good at sports or music.

▶ We can use our talents to help others.

▶ Our skills and talents also make us feel good about ourselves.

## Talk About It

Write words you have learned about using your talents. Talk with a partner about ways to helps others.

Talents

(inset)©Corbis

# Vocabulary

Use the picture and the sentence to talk with a partner about each word.

**achievement**

It is a big **achievement** to fly a kite on a very windy day.

What is your biggest achievement?

**apologized**

Kate **apologized** for breaking the dish.

When have you apologized for doing something?

**attention**

It is important to pay **attention** to directions.

What is something else you should pay attention to?

**audience**

The **audience** clapped and cheered at the end of the play.

When have you been part of an audience?

**confidence**

Jody read her report calmly and with **confidence**.

What does it mean to have confidence?

**embarrassed**

Tia was **embarrassed** when she forgot her lines in the play.

What was something that made you feel embarrassed?

**realized**

My soccer team celebrated when we **realized** we had won the game.

Describe a time when you realized something.

**talents**

One of Lila's **talents** is playing the violin.

What talents do you have?

COLLABORATE

## Your Turn

Pick three words. Write three questions for your partner to answer.

*Go Digital!* *Use the online visual glossary*

# The Impossible Pet Show

## Essential Question

**How can you use what you know to help others?**

Read how Daniel uses what he knows to save a pet show.

My best friend Carla Hernandez called me on Thursday afternoon. "Daniel, meet me in the park near the playground in five minutes. I have a great idea!" This worried me because Carla's great ideas almost always mean big trouble for me!

I dashed outside and jogged to the park. When I saw Carla, my heart sank because her gigantic dog Perro was with her. I liked everything about Carla *except* Perro. I've never had a pet, so I feel uncomfortable and nervous around animals. I'm **embarrassed** to say that I'm afraid of Carla's dog.

Carla smiled. "Isn't this the perfect location for a pet show?" she asked. "All the kids in the neighborhood can show off their pets' **talents** and demonstrate the things they do well. There are plenty of comfortable benches for our parents and friends to sit on. And since you don't have a pet to enter into the show, you will be the announcer."

"I'm sorry," I **apologized**, "but that's impossible! Crowds make me nervous and unsure. Besides, I don't like animals, remember?"

"That's nonsense," said Carla. "There's nothing to be concerned about because you'll be great!"

Just then, Perro leaped up, slobbered all over me, and almost knocked me down. "Yuck. Down, Perro! Stay!" I shouted. Perro sat as still as a statue. "Wow, you're good at that," said Carla. "Now let's get started because we have a lot to do."

By Saturday morning I had practiced announcing each pet's act a hundred times. My stomach was doing flip flops by the time the **audience** arrived. The size of the crowd made me feel even more anxious.

When the show began, I gulped and announced the first pet. It was a parakeet named Butter whose talent was walking back and forth on a wire. When Butter finished, everyone clapped and cheered. So far, everything was perfect, and I was beginning to feel calmer and more relaxed. I **realized** that being an announcer wasn't so bad after all.

Marcin Piwowarski

Then it was Carla and Perro's turn.

"Sit, Perro," she said, but Perro didn't sit.

Perro was not paying **attention** to Carla. He was too interested in watching Jack's bunnies jump in and out of their boxes. Suddenly, Perro leaped at the bunnies who hopped toward Mandy and knocked over her hamster's cage. Pudgy, the hamster, escaped and began running around in circles while Kyle's dog, Jake, howled. This was a disaster, and I had to do something.

"Sit!" I shouted at Perro. "Quiet!" I ordered Jake. "Stay!" I yelled. Everyone – kids and pets – stopped and stared at me. Even the audience froze.

"Daniel, that was incredible," said Carla. "You got the pets to settle down. That's quite an **achievement**."

Sadly, that was the end of our pet show. But now I have more **confidence** when I have to speak in front of people. And even though I am still nervous around animals, Perro and I have become great friends. And I've discovered my talent, too.

## Make Connections

How did Daniel use what he knows to help others?
**ESSENTIAL QUESTION**

Discuss whether you would like to take part in a pet show, and why. **TEXT TO SELF**

# Ask and Answer Questions

Stop and ask yourself questions about "The Impossible Pet Show" as you read. Then look for story details to answer your questions.

## Find Text Evidence

Reread page 277. Ask a question about what is happening. Then read again to find the answer.

page 277

I dashed outside and jogged to the park. When I saw Carla, my heart sank because her gigantic dog Perro was with her. I liked everything about Carla *except* Perro. I've never had a pet, so I feel uncomfortable and nervous around animals. I'm **embarrassed** to say that I'm afraid of Carla's dog.

Carla smiled. "Isn't this the perfect location for a pet show?" she asked. "All the kids in the neighborhood can show off their pets' **talents** and demonstrate the things they do well. There are plenty of comfortable benches for our parents and friends to sit on. And since you don't have a pet to enter into the show, you will be the announcer."

*I have a question. Why are Carla's ideas trouble for Daniel?* Daniel is uncomfortable around pets. Carla asks him to help at the pet show. *Carla's ideas are trouble because she is asking Daniel to do something he is not comfortable doing.*

COLLABORATE

## Your Turn

Reread "The Impossible Pet Show." Think of a question. You might ask: Why does Daniel think being an announcer isn't so bad? Reread page 278 to find the answer.

# Point of View

Point of view is what a narrator thinks about other characters or events in a story. Look for details that show what the narrator thinks. Use them to figure out the point of view.

 **Find Text Evidence**

*I read on page 277 that animals make Daniel nervous and uncomfortable. This will help me figure out what Daniel's point of view is about being an announcer for the pet show.*

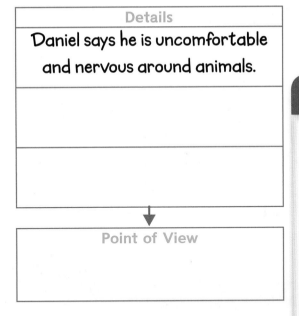

| Details |
|---|
| Daniel says he is uncomfortable and nervous around animals. |
| |
| |

Point of View

**Your Turn**

Reread "The Impossible Pet Show." Find more details that tell what Daniel thinks about being an announcer. List them in the graphic organizer. What is his point of view? Do you agree with Daniel's point of view about being an announcer at a pet show?

*Go Digital!*
*Use the interactive graphic organizer*

# Realistic Fiction

"The Impossible Pet Show" is realistic fiction.

**Realistic fiction:**

- Is a made-up story that could really happen
- Has dialogue and illustrations
- May be part of a longer book with chapters or part of a series about the same characters

 **Find Text Evidence**

*I can tell that "The Impossible Pet Show" is realistic fiction. The characters talk and act like real people. The events are made up, but they could really happen.*

**page 278**

"I'm sorry," I **apologized**, "but that's impossible! Crowds make me nervous and unsure. Besides, I don't like animals, remember?"

"That's nonsense," said Carla. "There's nothing to be concerned about because you'll be great!"

Just then, Perro leaped up, slobbered all over me, and almost knocked me down. "Yuck. Down, Perro! Stay!" I shouted. Perro sat as still as a statue. "Wow, you're good at that," said Carla. "Now let's get started because we have a lot to do."

By Saturday morning I had practiced announcing each pet's act a hundred times. My stomach was doing flip flops by the time the **audience** arrived. The size of the crowd made me feel even more anxious.

When the show began, I gulped and announced the first pet. It was a parakeet named Butter whose talent was walking back and forth on a wire. When Butter finished, everyone clapped and cheered. So far, everything was perfect, and I was beginning to feel calmer and more relaxed. I **realized** that being an announcer wasn't so bad after all.

**Dialogue** Dialogue is what the characters say to each other.

**Illustrations** Illustrations give more information or details about the characters and setting in the story.

**Your Turn**

Reread "The Impossible Pet Show." Find two events that help you figure out this is realistic fiction.

# Prefixes

A prefix is a word part added to the beginning of a word. A prefix changes the word's meaning. The prefixes *un-, non-,* and *im-* mean "not" or "opposite of." The prefix *pre-* means "before."

 **Find Text Evidence**

*On page 278, I see the word* unsure. *It has the root word* sure *and the prefix* un-. *I know that* sure *means "certain" and the prefix* un- *means "not." The word* unsure *must mean "not certain."*

Crowds make me nervous and unsure.

 **Your Turn**

Use the prefixes in each word to figure out its meaning.

    **uncomfortable,** *page 277*

    **impossible,** *page 278*

    **nonsense,** *page 278*

Marcin Piwowarski

# Write About the Text

Pages 276–279

Jamie

I answered the question: *In your opinion, should Carla have made Daniel the announcer in the Pet Show?*

## Student Model: *Opinion*

> I think Carla did the right
>
> thing when she made Daniel the
>
> announcer in the Pet Show. At
>
> first, I thought it was a bad idea
>
> because Daniel said he felt
>
> nervous. But I changed my opinion
>
> because Daniel calmed down
>
> when he presented the animals.

**Focus on a Topic**
My topic sentence states my opinion, so I can give my reasons in the rest of the paragraph.

**Linking Words**
I included linking words to connect my opinion and my reasons.

He could make the animals behave. Daniel found his talent when Carla made him the announcer. He wouldn't have discovered this talent if Carla had listened to him.

**Characters**
I used evidence from the story to show what David was like.

**Grammar**

This **contraction** is a short way of saying *would not*.

*Grammar Handbook*
*See page 485.*

**Your Turn**

In your opinion, would you be a good announcer in a pet show? Provide reasons why or why not.

*Go Digital!*
*Write your response online.*
*Use your editing checklist.*

Marcin Piwowarski

**Essential Question**
How do animals adapt to challenges in their habitat?

Go Digital!

286

# Adapt to Challenges

This ermine's fur is brown and white in the summer. It turns white in the winter and blends in with the snowy ground. This adaptation helps ermines escape its predators.

▶ Ermines are also fast runners and good climbers.

▶ They have an excellent sense of smell.

▶ Adaptations help ermines survive.

## Talk About It

Write words you have learned about adaptation. Talk with a partner about ways animals have adapted.

Adaptations

# Vocabulary

**Use the picture and the sentence to talk with a partner about each word.**

**alert**

Wolves howl to **alert** other wolves when danger is nearby.

How would you alert someone to talk quietly?

**competition**

Joe won the **competition** because he was the fastest runner.

What kind of competition have you participated in?

**environment**

The polar bear lives in a cold and snowy **environment**.

Describe a whale's environment.

**excellent**

Lily's **excellent** artwork won first place in the art show.

Tell about a time when something you did was excellent.

## prefer

Simon and his friends **prefer** walking to riding their bikes.

What kind of transportation do you prefer?

## protection

The skunk's scent provides **protection** from its enemies.

Tell what you use for protection on sunny days.

## related

Josh and Jen are **related** because they are both members of the same family.

Name two animals that are related.

## shelter

Our tent was a dry and safe **shelter** during the storm.

What is another kind of shelter people use?

COLLABORATE

# Your Turn

Pick three words. Write three questions for your partner to answer.

*Go Digital!*   *Use the online visual glossary*

# GRAY WOLF! RED FOX!

## Essential Question

How do animals adapt to challenges in their habitat?

Read how gray wolves and red foxes adapt to challenges.

290

©James Hager/Robert Harding World Imagery/Getty Images; (c)Photographs By Les Piccolo/Getty Images

Did you ever see a photograph of a gray wolf or a red fox? Don't they look a lot like dogs? Aren't they fantastic-looking animals? Well, dogs, foxes, and wolves are all **related**. They are all members of the same family. And while gray wolves and red foxes may look alike, they are different in many ways.

## LOOKS ARE EVERYTHING

The gray wolf is the largest member, or a part, of the wild dog family. An adult wolf is the size of a large dog. The red fox is smaller and weighs less. Both animals have **excellent** hearing. The red fox can even hear small animals digging holes underground.

And just take a look at those beautiful tails! The gray wolf and red fox both have long, bushy tails. The wolf's tail can be two feet long. The fox's tail is not as long but has a bright, white tip. In the winter, foxes use their thick, furry tails as **protection** from the cold.

The gray wolf and red fox are both mammals.

Foxes and wolves also have thick fur. Their coats can be white, brown, or black. However, red foxes most often have red fur, while a gray wolf's fur is usually more gray and brown.

United States of America

N
W E
S

**LEGEND**
- Red Fox only
- Gray Wolf only
- Both

## FINDING FOOD

Gray wolves and red foxes live in many different habitats. They live in forests, deserts, woodlands, and grasslands. But as more people build roads and shopping centers, both animals have lost their homes. The red fox has adapted well, or made changes, to fit into its **environment**. Now more foxes make their homes close to towns and parks. Wolves, however, stay far away from towns and people.

Foxes and wolves are not in **competition** for food. They have different diets. Red foxes **prefer** to hunt alone and eat small animals, birds, and fish. They also like to raid garbage cans and campsites for food. Wolves work together in packs, or groups, to hunt large animals, such as moose and deer.

**Gray wolves prefer to live and hunt in packs.**

292

## DAY-TO-DAY

Wolves live in packs of four to seven. They do almost everything together. They hunt, travel, and choose safe places to set up dens for **shelter**. Foxes, on the other hand, like to live alone. They usually sleep in the open or find an empty rabbit hole to call home.

The red fox hunts for food alone.

Both wolves and foxes communicate by barking and growling. The gray wolf also howls to **alert**, or warn, other wolves when there is danger nearby. The red fox signals in a different way. It waves its tail in the air to caution other foxes.

The gray wolf and red fox are members of the same family and have many things in common. But they really are two very different animals.

## Make Connections

How have the gray wolf and the red fox adapted to living in North America? **ESSENTIAL QUESTION**

Which animal would you like to learn more about? Why? **TEXT TO SELF**

# Reread

Stop and think about the text as you read. Are there new facts and ideas? Do they make sense? Reread to make sure you understand.

## Find Text Evidence

Do you understand how red foxes look different from gray wolves? Reread "Looks Are Everything" on page 291.

page 291

Did you ever see a photograph of a gray wolf or a red fox? Don't they look a lot like dogs? Aren't they fantastic-looking animals? Well, dogs, foxes, and wolves are all **related**. They are all members of the same family. And while gray wolves and red foxes may look alike, they are different in many ways.

**LOOKS ARE EVERYTHING**

The gray wolf is the largest member, or a part, of the wild dog family. An adult wolf is the size of a large dog. The red fox is smaller and weighs less. Both animals have **excellent** hearing. The red fox can even hear small animals digging holes underground.

And just take a look at those beautiful tails! The gray wolf and red fox both have long, bushy tails. The wolf's tail can be two feet long. The fox's tail is not as long but has a bright, white tip. In the winter, foxes use their thick, furry tails as **protection** from the cold.

*I read that <u>gray wolves are bigger than red foxes.</u> I also read that <u>the color of their fur and their tails look different.</u> Now I understand some of the ways the red fox and gray wolf look different.*

COLLABORATE

## Your Turn

Reread the section "Looks Are Everything." Look for details about how gray wolves and red foxes are alike.

# Compare and Contrast

When authors compare, they show how two things are alike. When they contrast, they tell how two things are different. Authors use signal words such as *both, alike, same,* or *different* to compare and contrast.

 **Find Text Evidence**

*How are red foxes and gray wolves alike and different? I will reread "Gray Wolf! Red Fox!" and look for signal words.*

| Wolves | Both | Foxes |
|---|---|---|
| The wolf's tail can be two feet long | Thick fur and long, bushy tails. | A fox's tail has a bright, white tip at the end. |

## Your Turn

Reread "Gray Wolf! Red Fox!" Find details that tell how red foxes and gray wolves are alike and different. Add these details to your graphic organizer. What signal words helped you?

*Go Digital!*
*Use the interactive graphic organizer*

# Expository Text

"Gray Wolf! Red Fox!" is an expository text.

**Expository text:**
- Gives facts and information to explain a topic
- May be about science topics
- Includes text features such as a map, photographs, and captions

## Find Text Evidence

*I can tell that "Gray Wolf! Red Fox!" is expository text. It explains how gray wolves and red foxes are alike and different. It includes a map, photographs, and captions.*

page 292

**WHERE DO THEY LIVE?**

Foxes and wolves also have thick fur. Their coats can be white, brown, or black. However, red foxes most often have red fur, while a gray wolf's fur is usually more gray and brown.

**FINDING FOOD**

Gray wolves and red foxes live in many different habitats. They live in forests, deserts, woodlands, and grasslands. But as more people build roads and shopping centers, both animals have lost their homes. The red fox has adapted well, or made changes, to fit into its **environment**. Now more foxes make their homes close to towns and parks. Wolves, however, stay far away from towns and people.

Foxes and wolves are not in **competition** for food. They have different diets. Red foxes **prefer** to hunt alone and eat small animals, birds, and fish. They also like to raid garbage cans and campsites for food. Wolves work together in packs, or groups, to hunt large animals, such as moose and deer.

United States of America

LEGEND
■ Red Fox only
▨ Gray Wolf only
■ Both

Gray wolves prefer to live and hunt in packs.

292

## Text Features

**Map** A map is a flat drawing of a place. It has a key that shows what colors and symbols mean.

**Caption** A caption explains a photograph or illustration.

COLLABORATE

## Your Turn

Look at the text features in "Gray Wolf! Red Fox!." Tell your partner about something you learned.

# Sentence Clues

Sentence clues are words or phrases in a sentence that help you figure out the meaning of an unfamiliar word. Sometimes clues define, or tell exactly, what a word means.

 **Find Text Evidence**

*I'm not sure what the word* member *means on page 291. I see the words "a part of" in the same sentence. This clue tells me that* member *means "a part of something."*

The gray wolf is the largest member, or a part, of the wild dog family.

 COLLABORATE

## Your Turn

Find context clues to figure out the meanings of these words.

**adapted,** *page 292*
**packs,** *page 292*

Talk about the sentence clues that helped you figure out the meanings.

Pages 290–293

# Write About the Text

Luke

I answered the question: *How have red foxes and gray wolves adapted to changes in their environment? Provide text evidence.*

## Student Model: *Informative Text*

**Strong Opening**
I wrote an interesting question to grab the reader's attention.

**Supporting Details**
I developed my topic with text evidence.

How could a small red fox beat a large gray wolf? The habitats of both animals changed when people built towns and roads. Guess which animal adapted better?

Wolves have moved away from towns and people. They live in wild areas where they can hunt deer.

But red foxes can live in more

places than gray wolves can.

They raid garbage cans and

campsites for food.

 Red foxes have adapted to

changes in their environment

better than gray wolves

have. That's how foxes

have beaten wolves!

(t)jimkruger/iStock/360/Getty Images; (twigs)McGraw-Hill Education

**Linking Words**
I used the word *but* to connect ideas.

**Grammar**

*Have* is a **helping verb** and *adapted* is the **main verb**.

*Grammar Handbook See page 484.*

**Your Turn**

How are red foxes and gray wolves the same and different in how they live? Provide text evidence.

*Go Digital!*
*Write your response online.*
*Use your editing checklist.*

W.3.2c, L.3.la See the California Standards section.

## Essential Question
How are people able to fly?

*Go Digital!*

Unimedia Images/Unimedia international/Newscom

300

# UP, UP, AND AWAY

People have wanted to fly for hundreds of years. Thanks to many inventors, there are lots of ways they can!

▶ People can cross the country in tiny planes, huge passenger jets, or colorful hot air balloons.

▶ Helicopters take small groups from here to there.

▶ And some adventurers fly solo high above the Earth.

## Talk About It

Write words about flight. Talk about how people have learned to fly.

Flight

# Vocabulary

**Use the picture and the sentence to talk with a partner about each word.**

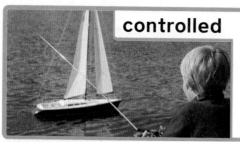

**controlled**

Tom **controlled** his toy boat's movements from the shore.

What is something you have controlled at home?

**direction**

The sign showed us which **direction** to go.

Point in the direction of the door.

**flight**

The first airplane **flight** took place many years ago.

Where would you like to go on an airplane flight?

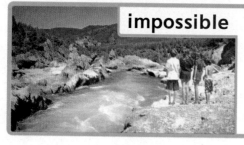

**impossible**

Crossing this river is **impossible**, so we will have to go a different way.

Name something that is impossible to do.

## launched

The space shuttle was **launched** and soared toward space.

What other things can be launched?

## motion

Julie enjoys the **motion** of the swing.

What kinds of motion do you like?

## passenger

Denise likes being a **passenger** in the car.

When was the last time you were a passenger?

## popular

Soccer is the most **popular** sport at our school.

Tell about a popular sport at your school.

### Your Turn    COLLABORATE

Pick three words. Write three questions for your partner to answer.

*Go Digital!*   *Use the online visual glossary*

(t) NASA-HQ-GRIN; (tc) mylife photos/Alamy; (bc) Randy Faris/Corbis; (b) MM Productions/Corbis

# Firsts in Flight

## Essential Question

**How are people able to fly?**

Read about how inventors learned how to fly.

Transtock/SuperStock

On December 17, 1903, the *Wright Flyer* flew for 12 seconds at Kitty Hawk.

**O**rville and Wilbur Wright stood on a cold, windy beach in Kitty Hawk, North Carolina. The brothers traveled a long way from their home in Dayton, Ohio to test their newest flying machine. Flying had been their dream since their father had given them a toy helicopter.

Orville and Wilbur Wright

The Wright brothers owned a bicycle shop in Dayton. In addition to selling, building, and repairing bicycles, they built flying machines. They flew the first one in 1899. However, the winds weren't strong enough to keep the machine in **motion**. So they looked for a place where the winds were stronger. As a result, they chose Kitty Hawk. It was not only windy there, but the sandy beaches made for soft landings.

Because their first **flight** was not successful, the Wright brothers learned a lot about flying. As a result, they built a better glider with bigger wings in 1900. This glider did not work very well either. The brothers did not give up. That's why they experimented with a new glider in 1902. Then in 1903, they built the *Wright Flyer*, their first airplane with an engine.

## Flying Firsts

By December 17, the brothers were ready to test the *Wright Flyer*. Orville started up the engines to power the plane. He **controlled** the plane, while Wilbur watched from the ground. The *Flyer* was **launched** into the sky. The plane moved in an upward **direction**, and the flight lasted twelve seconds. The Wright brothers had conquered gravity and unlocked the secrets of flying.

Alberto Santos-Dumont was the third man in the world to fly a plane with an engine.

Orville and Wilbur kept improving their planes, and their flights became longer. Soon, other people tried to fly airplanes.

## Will It Fly?

Do an experiment on flying using paper airplanes.

**Materials needed:**

• pencil  • paper  • ruler

**Directions:**

1. With a partner, fold two paper airplanes. Make the wing sizes different in each plane.

2. Gently throw one plane.

3. Measure and record how far the paper plane flew.

4. Take turns throwing the plane four more times. Each time, measure and record how far it flies.

5. Repeat the experiment with the other airplane.

6. Compare the plane's flights. Then discuss what you learned about flight.

Heritage Images/Corbis

Alberto Santos-Dumont was an inventor and pilot from Brazil. In 1906, he made the first official flight in front of an audience. The next year, the French pilot, Henri Farman, took along a **passenger** in his plane. They flew for one minute and fourteen seconds.

## Better Flying Machines

Because of these flights, airplane research became **popular** with inventors. Before long, better planes were traveling longer distances. In 1909, a French pilot flew an airplane across the English Channel. This plane was very different from the Wright brothers' plane. The new plane had only one long wing across its body. It looked a lot like today's airplanes.

This is what an airplane looked like in 1930.

Soon inventors began building airplanes that could carry more people. By 1920, several new companies offered passengers the chance to fly. Humans had done the **impossible**. They had figured out how to fly.

## Make Connections

How did the Wright brothers help people fly? ESSENTIAL QUESTION

Tell what you know about airplanes. Discuss other ways to fly. TEXT TO SELF

(b) Stockdisc/Getty Images (t) Everett Collection/SuperStock

# Reread

Stop and think as you read. Does the text make sense? Reread to make sure you understand.

 **Find Text Evidence**

Do you understand what the Wright brothers learned from their unsuccessful flights? Reread page 306.

> ### page 306
>
> Because their first **flight** was not successful, the Wright brothers learned a lot about flying. As a result, they built a better glider with bigger wings in 1900. This glider did not work very well either. The brothers did not give up. That's why they experimented with a new glider in 1902. Then in 1903, they built the *Wright Flyer*, their first airplane with an engine.
>
> **Flying Firsts**
>
> By December 17, the brothers were ready to test the *Wright Flyer*. Orville started up the engines to power the plane. He **controlled** the plane, while Wilbur watched from the ground. The *Flyer* was **launched** into the sky. The plane moved in an upward **direction**, and the flight lasted twelve

*I read that the Wright brothers' first flight was not successful. But they learned a lot about flying. Then they built a better glider with bigger wings. Now I understand why their unsuccessful flights were important.*

## Your Turn

COLLABORATE

How did other inventors use the Wright brothers' ideas? Reread pages 306 and 307.

# Cause and Effect

A cause is why something happens. An effect is what happens. They happen in time order. Signal words, such as *so, as a result, and because* help you find causes and effects.

 **Find Text Evidence**

*On page 305 I read that the Wrights had to find a windier place to fly. This is the effect. Now I can find the cause. The wind wasn't strong enough. The signal word* so *helped me find the cause and effect.*

| Cause | Effect |
|---|---|
| **First** The winds weren't strong enough. | So the brothers found a place where the winds were stronger. |
| **Next** | |
| **Then** | |
| **Finally** | |

COLLABORATE

## Your Turn

Reread "Firsts in Flight." Use signal words to help you find more causes and effects. Make sure they are in time order. Fill in the graphic organizer.

*Go Digital!*
*Use the interactive graphic organizer*

RI.3.3, RI.3.8 See the California Standards section.

# Expository Text

"Firsts in Flight" is an expository text. **Expository text:**
- May present causes and their effects in sequence
- May explain a science topic
- Includes text features such as headings, photographs, or sidebars

## Find Text Evidence

*I can tell that "Firsts in Flight" is an expository text. It gives facts and information about how people first started flying. It includes headings, photographs with captions, and a sidebar.*

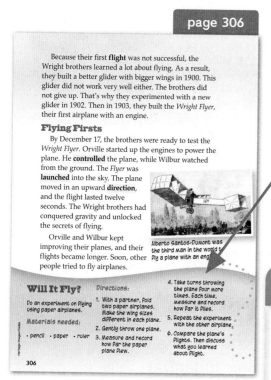

page 306

Because their first **flight** was not successful, the Wright brothers learned a lot about flying. As a result, they built a better glider with bigger wings in 1900. This glider did not work very well either. The brothers did not give up. That's why they experimented with a new glider in 1902. Then in 1903, they built the *Wright Flyer,* their first airplane with an engine.

### Flying Firsts

By December 17, the brothers were ready to test the *Wright Flyer.* Orville started up the engines to power the plane. He **controlled** the plane, while Wilbur watched from the ground. The *Flyer* was **launched** into the sky. The plane moved in an upward **direction,** and the flight lasted twelve seconds. The Wright brothers had conquered gravity and unlocked the secrets of flying.

Orville and Wilbur kept improving their planes, and their flights became longer. Soon, other people tried to fly airplanes.

Alberto Santos-Dumont was the third man in the world to fly a plane with an engine

### Will It Fly?

Do an experiment on flying using paper airplanes.

Materials needed:
• pencil • paper • ruler

Directions:
1. With a partner, fold two paper airplanes. Make the wing sizes different in each plane.
2. Gently throw one plane.
3. Measure and record how far the paper plane flew.
4. Take turns throwing the plane four more times. Each time, measure and record how far it flies.
5. Repeat the experiment with the other airplane.
6. Compare the plane's flights. Then discuss what you learned about flight.

306

## Text Features

**Sidebar** A sidebar gives more information about a topic. Sometimes a sidebar can be a science experiment or directions showing how to do something.

COLLABORATE

## Your Turn

Look at the text features in "Firsts in Flight." Tell your partner something you learned.

# Multiple-Meaning Words

Multiple-meaning words have more than one meaning. Find other words in the sentence to help you figure out the correct meaning of a multiple-meaning word.

## Find Text Evidence

*On page 306, I know* well *can mean "a deep hole with water in it" or "in a good way." The context clue* work *helps me figure out what* well *means in this sentence. I think* well *means "in a good way." The glider did not work in a good way.*

This glider did not work very well either.

## Your Turn

Find context clues. Use them to figure out the meaning of each word.
**seconds,** *page 306*
**fly,** *page 307*

Everett Collection/SuperStock

Pages 304–307

# Write About the Text

Mina

I answered the question: *How did the Wright brothers figure out how to fly? Support your answer with text evidence.*

**Student Model:** *Informative Text*

**Focus on a Topic**
My first sentence introduces the topic.

**Develop a Topic**
I included facts from the article to support my topic.

The Wright brothers figured out how to fly by experimenting. They started by building gliders. Although their first gliders did not work well, the two brothers kept trying. In 1903, they succeeded when their first airplane with an engine flew for twelve seconds.

**Grammar**

This **complex sentence** has an independent and a dependent clause.

*Grammar Handbook*
See page 477.

©Kris Timken/Blend Images LLC

**312**    W.3.2a, W.3.2b, L.3.1i See the California Standards section.

The Wright brothers had beaten gravity with this short flight. Then other people tried to fly airplanes, too. But it was the Wright brothers' hard work that first made flying possible!

**Strong Conclusions**
My last sentence sums up the paragraph by restating the main idea.

## Your Turn

Explain how inventions can help us even if they fail at first. Use text evidence to support your answer.

*Go Digital!*
*Write your response online.*
*Use your editing checklist.*

Transtock/SuperStock

**Essential Question**

How can others inspire us?

*Go Digital!*

Ira Block/National Geographic/Getty Images

314

# You Inspire Me

Danny talked to the firefighters in his neighborhood. He learned all about what they do. Danny thinks they are brave heroes. He wants to be a firefighter, too.

▶ People who are courageous and helpful inspire us.

▶ When we feel inspired, we want to help others, too.

## Talk About It

Talk with a partner about how we are inspired by others. Write words about inspiration.

Inspiration

# Vocabulary

**Use the picture and the sentence to talk with a partner about each word.**

### adventurous

Whitewater rafting is an **adventurous** and exciting activity.

What would you like to do that is adventurous?

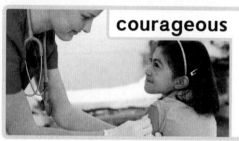

### courageous

Maya was **courageous** at the doctor's office.

Describe someone you know who is courageous.

### extremely

Some plants can grow in **extremely** dry places.

Tell about a time when you were extremely cold.

### weird

The Venus Flytrap is a **weird** and strange plant.

What is a synonym for weird?

# Poetry Words

**free verse**

Some of Emma's **free verse** poems rhyme, and some do not.

Explain why a limerick is not a free verse poem.

**narrative poem**

I wrote a **narrative poem** about the history of flight.

What kinds of stories make good narrative poems?

**repetition**

Using the same word several times in a poem is called **repetition**.

Why do poets use repetition?

**rhyme**

The words *night* and *right* **rhyme** because they end in the same sounds.

Why do poets use words that rhyme?

## Your Turn

COLLABORATE

Pick three words. Write three questions for your partner to answer.

*Go Digital!* **Use the online visual glossary**

# Ginger's Fingers

Diverse Images/Universal Images Group /Getty Images

Ginger's fingers are shooting stars,

They talk of adventurous trips to Mars.

Fingers talking without words,

Signing when sounds can't be heard.

Ginger's fingers are ocean waves,

They talk of fish and deep sea caves.

Fingers talking without words,

Signing when sounds can't be heard.

Ginger's fingers are butterflies,

They talk of a honey-gold sunrise.

Fingers talking without words,

Signing when sounds can't be heard.

## Essential Question

How can others inspire us?

Read about different ways
that people inspire others.

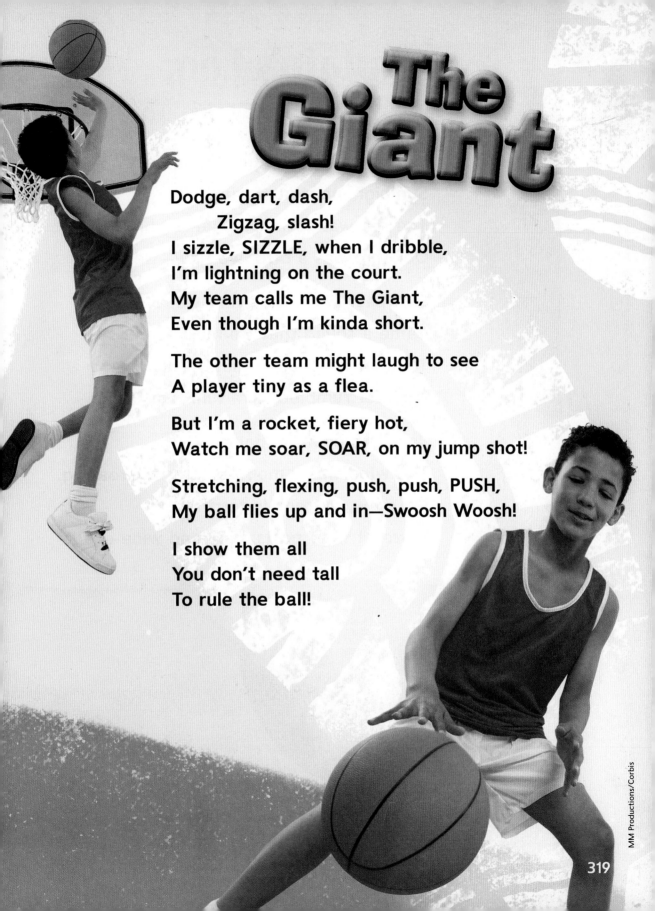

# The Giant

Dodge, dart, dash,
    Zigzag, slash!
I sizzle, SIZZLE, when I dribble,
I'm lightning on the court.
My team calls me The Giant,
Even though I'm kinda short.

The other team might laugh to see
A player tiny as a flea.

But I'm a rocket, fiery hot,
Watch me soar, SOAR, on my jump shot!

Stretching, flexing, push, push, PUSH,
My ball flies up and in—Swoosh Woosh!

I show them all
You don't need tall
To rule the ball!

# Captain's Log,
## May 12, 1868

We set sail from a port in Spain,

Sun high, no sign of rain.

The sea was satin, so blue—so blue.

Our ship was a bird, we flew—we flew.

Just past noon, how very weird,

Came a sound that we most feared.

Thunder rumbled, a giant drum.

Thunder rumbled, rum tum tum.

Rain was pouring, pouring.

The wind was a monster, roaring, roaring.

My crew, extremely terrified,

Froze at their posts, pale and wide-eyed.

A huge wave lifted up our ship,

My feet began to slip, slip, slip.

I knew that it was up to me,

To guide us through that stormy sea.

I grabbed a rope, reached for the mast,

And got back to the helm at last - at last

Shook off the rain, looked at my crew,

"Steady lads, I'll get us through."

The crew heard my call,

Each lad stood up tall.

All hands now on deck, we trimmed every sail.

Courageous, together, we rode out that gale.

## Make Connections

Talk about how the person in each poem is inspiring. **ESSENTIAL QUESTION**

In the poems, which person is most inspiring to you? Why? **TEXT TO SELF**

# Narrative and Free Verse

**Narrative** poetry: • Tells a story. • Often has stanzas, or groups of lines. • Often rhymes.

**Free verse** poetry: • Does not always rhyme. • Can have stanzas with different numbers of lines. • Can tell a story or express a poet's feelings.

 **Find Text Evidence**

*I can tell that "Captain's Log" is a narrative poem. It is a story of a ship's captain who inspires his crew during a bad storm.*

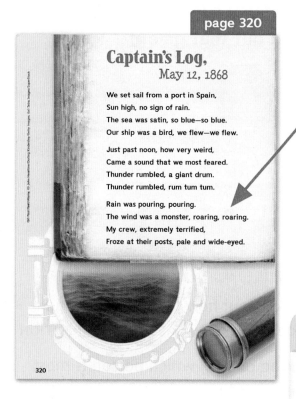

page 320

**Captain's Log,**
May 12, 1868

We set sail from a port in Spain,
Sun high, no sign of rain.
The sea was satin, so blue—so blue.
Our ship was a bird, we flew—we flew.

Just past noon, how very weird,
Came a sound that we most feared.
Thunder rumbled, a giant drum.
Thunder rumbled, rum tum tum.

Rain was pouring, pouring.
The wind was a monster, roaring, roaring.
My crew, extremely terrified,
Froze at their posts, pale and wide-eyed.

320

"Captain's Log" is a narrative poem that rhymes and has stanzas. It tells a story. This part describes the storm and how scared the crew on the ship was.

**Your Turn**

Reread "The Giant." Explain why it is a free verse poem.

# Theme

The theme is the main message or lesson in a poem. The details in a poem can help you figure out the theme.

 **Find Text Evidence**

*All the poems in this week are about inspirational people, but each poem has a different theme. I'll reread "The Giant" and look for details. I can use the details to figure out the theme.*

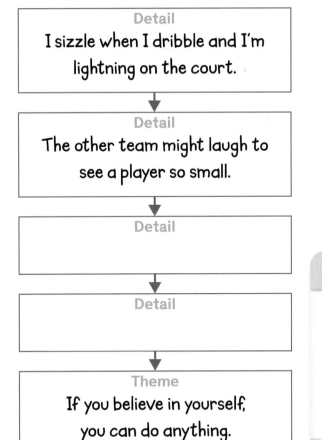

| Detail |
|---|
| I sizzle when I dribble and I'm lightning on the court. |

↓

| Detail |
|---|
| The other team might laugh to see a player so small. |

↓

| Detail |
|---|

↓

| Detail |
|---|

↓

| Theme |
|---|
| If you believe in yourself, you can do anything. |

**Your Turn**

Reread "The Giant." Find more details and list them in your graphic organizer. Make sure they support the theme.

*Go Digital!*
*Use the interactive graphic organizer*

# Repetition and Rhyme

**Repetition** means that words or phrases in a poem are repeated. A **rhyme** is two or more words that end with the same sounds, such as *pouring* and *roaring*.

## Find Text Evidence

Reread "Captain's Log" on pages 320–321. Listen for words or phrases that are repeated. Think about why the poet uses repetition.

page 320

## Captain's Log,
### May 12, 1868

We set sail from a port in Spain,
Sun high, no sign of rain.
The sea was satin, so blue—so blue.
Our ship was a bird, we flew—we flew.

*In the first stanza, the poet repeats the words* so blue *and* we flew. *These words also rhyme. This repetition gives the poem a musical quality. It helps me feel the waves and how the ship moves on the sea.*

### Your Turn
COLLABORATE

Reread "Captain's Log." Find examples of repetition and rhyme.

# Metaphor

A metaphor compares two things that are very different. It helps you picture, or visualize. "His teeth are white pearls" is a metaphor. It compares teeth to pearls. This metaphor helps me picture bright, white teeth.

## Find Text Evidence

*On page 318, I read that "Ginger's fingers are shooting stars." This is a metaphor. It compares the way Ginger's fingers move and sign to shooting stars. This metaphor helps me picture Ginger's fingers moving quickly and quietly.*

page 318

**Ginger's fingers are shooting stars,
They talk of adventurous trips to Mars.
Fingers talking without words,
Signing when sounds can't be heard.**

## Your Turn

COLLABORATE

Reread the poem "Ginger's Fingers." Find another metaphor. What two things are compared? Talk about how the metaphor helps you visualize.

# Write About the Text

Pages 318–321

Juan

I responded to the prompt: *Write a free verse poem about someone you think is inspiring. Use figurative language and repetition.*

**Student Model:** *Narrative Text*

## My Big Brother

My brother is a bear without the claws.

He's big and strong but never mean.

He likes to wrestle and shoot hoops.

**Figurative Language**
I began with a metaphor to introduce the subject of my poem.

**Strong Words**
I used precise words, such as *wrestle* and *shoot hoops,* to help readers visualize my brother.

He can pin opponents down, and

he can even slam dunk.

I've seen him be kind to small kids

and protect them from bullies.

He's the best brother, the best

brother you've ever seen.

**Repetition**
I ended my poem by repeating that my brother is the best to make sure the reader understands my message.

## Your Turn

Write a free verse poem about someone you believe is a good role model. Use figurative language and repetition.

*Go Digital!*
*Write your response online.*
*Use your editing checklist.*

©MM Productions/Corbis

# Take Action

## The Big Idea

### What are ways people can take action?

# Ben Franklin's STOVE

Back in 1742,
Snow fell fast and cold winds blew.

Ben Franklin's fireplace was bright,
Burning wood both day and night.

But Ben would rub his icy feet,
"Too much smoke, and where's the heat?

A fireplace does little good,
For it uses too much wood.

I'll build an iron stove instead,
It will burn less wood," Ben said.

Day after day, Ben's hammer rang
On that iron—CLINK, CLUNK, CLANG.

The stove Ben made helped hot air rise,
With no smoke to sting his eyes.

Now through the winter Ben could boast,
"My stove keeps me warm as toast!"

— By Charles Ashton

**Essential Question**

How do we get what we need?

Go Digital!

lemonade

# Give and Take

Everyone is thirsty. All the kids want a glass of Sue's lemonade. They wait in line for what they want and need. They will pay for it in different ways.

▶ Some will use money.

▶ Some will barter, or trade.

▶ Sue is getting what she needs, too. She is working to save money to buy a new bike.

## Talk About It

Write words you have learned about getting what you need. Talk with a partner about how to get what you need.

Get What You Need

# Vocabulary

**Use the picture and the sentence to talk with a partner about each word.**

**admit**

Josh had to **admit** to his mom that he got dirt on her clean sheets.

Tell about something you had to admit.

**barter**

Amy likes to **barter**, or trade, parts of her lunch with Kim.

What is another word for barter?

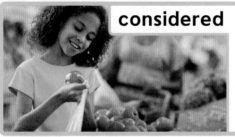

**considered**

Marta thought carefully as she **considered** which tomato to buy.

Name something you considered doing.

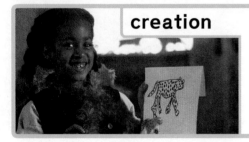

**creation**

Ella admired her **creation** in art class.

Tell about a creation you made.

## humble

My grandfather's house is **humble**, simple, and plain.

What is the opposite of *humble*?

## magnificent

Mr. Jacobs took a picture of the **magnificent** canyon.

What is a magnificent place you know?

## payment

Mom gave our neighbor **payment** for the vase.

What do people usually use for payment?

## reluctantly

The goats stepped **reluctantly** down the steep path.

Show how you would raise your hand reluctantly.

COLLABORATE

## Your Turn

Pick three words. Then write three questions for your partner to answer.

*Go Digital!* *Use the online visual glossary*

# Juanita and the Beanstalk

## ? Essential Question

**How do we get what we need?**

Read about what Juanita does to get what she needs.

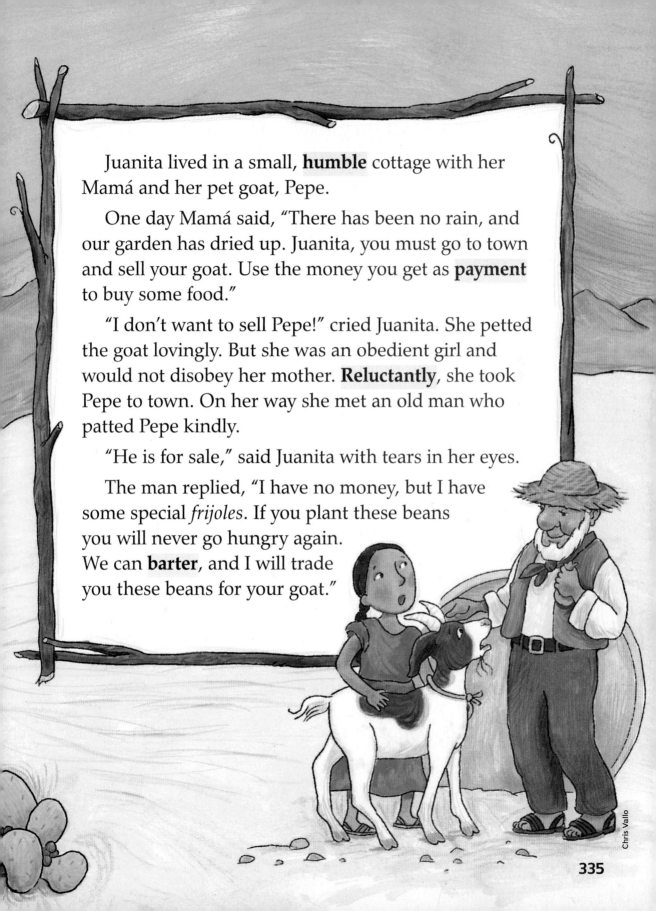

Juanita lived in a small, **humble** cottage with her Mamá and her pet goat, Pepe.

One day Mamá said, "There has been no rain, and our garden has dried up. Juanita, you must go to town and sell your goat. Use the money you get as **payment** to buy some food."

"I don't want to sell Pepe!" cried Juanita. She petted the goat lovingly. But she was an obedient girl and would not disobey her mother. **Reluctantly**, she took Pepe to town. On her way she met an old man who patted Pepe kindly.

"He is for sale," said Juanita with tears in her eyes.

The man replied, "I have no money, but I have some special *frijoles*. If you plant these beans you will never go hungry again. We can **barter**, and I will trade you these beans for your goat."

Chris Vallo

335

Juanita thought carefully as she **considered** the man's offer. He seemed caring and considerate. Certainly he would be kind to Pepe, so Juanita finally decided to sell Pepe. She accepted the beans.

When Juanita got home, Mamá was upset with her decision. "You have returned home with no food and no money!" she exclaimed.

Juanita had to **admit** that Mamá was right. All she had were three beans, and she still missed Pepe. Worst of all, Mamá was unhappy.

Juanita planted the beans in the backyard and went to bed. The next morning she woke up and went outside. A gigantic beanstalk as tall as the clouds stood where Juanita had planted the beans.

Juanita was curious. "I'm going to see what's up there," she said to herself, so Juanita climbed the beanstalk. At the top she saw a grand and **magnificent** palace in the middle of a field. She knocked on the door and a maid answered.

"Hide!" cried the maid. "The giant is coming now, and he doesn't like strangers." So Juanita quickly crawled under the table.

The giant stomped in carrying an unhappy hen in a cage. He said, "Lay, hen, lay!" Juanita's curiosity grew, and she peeked from under the table. Then she saw the hen's **creation**. Juanita gasped. It was a golden egg!

The poor hen reminded Juanita of Pepe. She wanted to give it a better home. She ran between the giant's legs and grabbed the cage. She raced to the beanstalk. The giant roared in anger and chased after her. Juanita was able to slide down the beanstalk, but the giant was too heavy. He caused the stalk to break and crash to the ground. The beanstalk was gone forever, and Juanita and the hen were safe.

The hen was happy to have a new home and laid many golden eggs. Mamá was happy to use the eggs to buy everything they needed. And Juanita was happy because she was able to trade a golden egg with the old man to get Pepe back!

## Make Connections

How does Juanita get what she needs? ESSENTIAL QUESTION

What are some ways you can get what you need? TEXT TO SELF

Chris Vallo

# Summarize

When you summarize, you retell the most important events in a story. Use details to help you summarize "Juanita and the Beanstalk".

### Find Text Evidence

Why does Juanita have to sell her pet goat? Identify important story events. Summarize them in your own words.

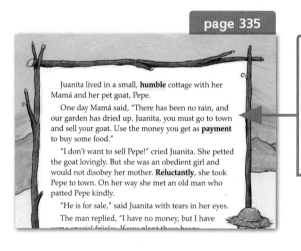

page 335

Juanita lived in a small, **humble** cottage with her Mamá and her pet goat, Pepe.

One day Mamá said, "There has been no rain, and our garden has dried up. Juanita, you must go to town and sell your goat. Use the money you get as **payment** to buy some food."

"I don't want to sell Pepe!" cried Juanita. She petted the goat lovingly. But she was an obedient girl and would not disobey her mother. **Reluctantly**, she took Pepe to town. On her way she met an old man who patted Pepe kindly.

"He is for sale," said Juanita with tears in her eyes.

The man replied, "I have no money, but I have

*I read that <u>it hadn't rained and Mamá's garden dried up. They needed money for food. Mamá told Juanita to sell Pepe, her pet goat.</u> These details help me summarize. Juanita had to sell her goat to get money for food.*

COLLABORATE

## Your Turn

Reread "Juanita and the Beanstalk." Summarize the most important events that tell how Juanita found the giant's palace.

Chris Vallo

# Point of View

A character often has thoughts about other characters or events in a story. This is the point of view. Look for details to figure out the character's point of view.

 **Find Text Evidence**

*What does Juanita think about Pepe? I can reread what she does and says. These details will help me figure out Juanita's point of view about the goat.*

| Details |
|---|
| Juanita tells Mamá that she does not want to sell Pepe. |
| She pets the goat lovingly. |
| |

↓

| Point of View |
|---|
| |

## Your Turn COLLABORATE

Reread "Juanita and the Beanstalk." Write details about Juanita's feelings for Pepe in the graphic organizer. Figure out her point of view. Do you agree with Juanita's point of view?

*Go Digital!*
*Use the interactive graphic organizer*

# Fairy Tale

"Juanita and the Beanstalk" is a fairy tale. A **fairy tale**:
- Is a made-up story with events that could not really happen
- Usually has magical characters or settings
- Almost always has a happy ending with a message

 **Find Text Evidence**

*I can tell that "Juanita and the Beanstalk" is a fairy tale. A huge beanstalk could not grow overnight in real life. There are also magical characters, such as a giant and a hen that lays golden eggs. The story has a happy ending, too.*

page 337

The giant stomped in carrying an unhappy hen in a cage. He said, "Lay, hen, lay!" Juanita's curiosity grew, and she peeked from under the table. Then she saw the hen's **creation**. Juanita gasped. It was a golden egg!

The poor hen reminded Juanita of Pepe. She wanted to give it a better home. She ran between the giant's legs and grabbed the cage. She raced to the beanstalk. The giant roared in anger and chased after her. Juanita was able to slide down the beanstalk, but the giant was too heavy. He caused the stalk to break and crash to the ground. The beanstalk was gone forever, and Juanita and the hen were safe.

The hen was happy to have a new home and laid many golden eggs. Mamá was happy to use the eggs to buy everything they needed. And Juanita was happy because she was able to trade a golden egg with the old man to get Pepe back!

**Make Connections**
How does Juanita get what she needs? ESSENTIAL QUESTION

What are some ways you can get what you need? TEXT TO SELF

337

Important **events** in a fairy tale could not really happen.

Fairy tales usually have a happy ending with a message.

COLLABORATE

## Your Turn

With a partner, find two details that show this is a fairy tale. How is it like other fairy tales you know?

# Root Words

A root word is the simplest form of a word. When you read an unfamiliar word, look for the root word. Then use the root word to figure out what the word means.

## Find Text Evidence

*On page 336 of "Juanita and the Beanstalk," I see the word* considerate. *I think the root word of* considerate *is* consider. *I know that to* consider *something means "to think about it." Being* considerate *means "thoughtful of others' feelings."*

Juanita thought carefully as she considered the man's offer. The man seemed caring and considerate.

COLLABORATE

## Your Turn

Find the root words. Use them to figure out the meanings of the following words.

**decision,** *page 336*
**curiosity,** *page 337*

Chris Vallo

Pages 334–337

# Write About the Text

Olivia

I responded to the prompt: *Add an event to the story. Write a dialogue between Juanita and Mamá at the end of the story.*

**Student Model:** *Narrative Text*

**Dialogue**
I made up a conversation to show what Mamá and Juanita are thinking and feeling.

**Vary Sentence Structures**
I used different kinds of sentences to make my story interesting to read.

"Mamá! Mamá! I'm back!" called Juanita.

"Where were you, Juanita? What happened?" Mamá cried.

Juanita said, "I planted the beans that I traded for Pepe. The beans grew into a huge beanstalk during the night. When I climbed the beanstalk, I saw a mean giant.

Maria Pavlova/E+/Getty Images

I rescued this hen from him. She lays golden eggs! They will help us get everything we need. But first of all I traded a golden egg to get Pepe back!"

"My smart girl! What a brave thing you did for us!" Mamá said proudly.

## Grammar

The **singular pronoun** *she* stands for *hen*. The **plural pronoun** *they* stands for *eggs*.

***Grammar Handbook*** See page 487.

**Strong Conclusion** My last paragraph shows that now Mamá is happy with Juanita.

## Your Turn

Add an event to the story. Write a dialogue between Juanita and the old man when she goes to get Pepe back.

*Go Digital!*
*Write your response online.*
*Use your editing checklist.*

**Essential Question**

How can we reuse what we already have?

Go Digital!

# Recycling

Old tires can be reused. They make great swings. They also can be used to build strong walls on land and to make reefs for animals under water.

▶ Almost everything we use can be recycled.

▶ Reusing things helps keep our Earth clean.

▶ We all should reuse and recycle what we can.

## Talk About It

Write words you have learned about recycling. Talk with a partner about ways you can reuse and recycle.

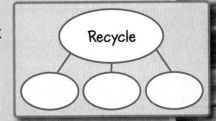

Recycle

# Vocabulary

**Use the picture and the sentence to talk with a partner about each word.**

**conservation**

Kara's light bulb saves energy and is a good example of **conservation**.

What is another example of conservation?

**discouraged**

Shawn felt **discouraged** when he and his mom couldn't find his lost football.

What would make you feel discouraged?

**frustration**

Diane gasped out of **frustration** when her computer screen went blank.

Tell about a time you showed frustration.

**gazed**

Tory **gazed** at the stars through her telescope.

When have you gazed at the stars?

**jubilant**

Ryan's team felt **jubilant** and delighted when they won the contest.

What word means almost the same as jubilant?

**recycling**

Sheila is **recycling** empty containers.

What are other things you could be recycling?

**remaining**

These seven puppies are **remaining** after we gave two away.

How many days of school are remaining this week?

BABY BULLDOGS

**tinkered**

Jon and his dad **tinkered** with the bike and got it working again.

Think of another word for tinkered.

## Your Turn

COLLABORATE

Pick three words. Write three questions for your partner to answer.

*Go Digital!* *Use the online visual glossary*

# The New HOOP

## ? Essential Question

**How can we reuse what we already have?**

Read to see how Kim and Marco reuse something to solve their problem.

Chris Vallo

348

Marco **gazed** at the basketball hoop and threw the ball up. It whizzed through the air. "Score!" he shouted as the ball fell through with a swish.

"You won this time, but I'll beat you next time, Marco!" said Kim as the two friends made their way home. "I wish we could play at home, too, instead of only at school. It's not fair." The basketball hoop in their neighborhood park had been ruined when a tree fell and crushed it.

"My dad says the Parks Department doesn't have enough money to buy a new hoop yet," grumbled Marco in **frustration**.

"I feel so **discouraged**," said Kim. "I guess there's nothing we can do."

Marco and Kim walked past the city's **recycling** center. They waved at the manager, Mr. Morse. His job was to separate the plastic, paper, and metal items people brought to him. He was transferring cardboard from an overflowing bin into large, empty containers.

Marco stared at all the old stuff. "That gives me an idea!" he said. "Mr. Morse, do you have anything we could reuse to make a basketball hoop?"

Mr. Morse picked up a plastic laundry basket. "We were going to recycle this basket, but I think it's reusable."

"It looks useless, old, and cracked," said Kim.

"No, it could be useful," said Marco. "We can cut off the bottom to make a fine hoop, and then an adult can help us attach it to a post."

Kim frowned. "I want a new basketball hoop," she said. "Not someone else's hand-me-down."

"Why?" wondered Marco. "Reusing things is a great way to practice **conservation**. It stops waste."

"I guess we can try," said Kim. "But I still don't believe it will be as good as a new one."

They took the basket to Marco's house. His older brother, Victor, got some leftover wood from an old building project. Together they **tinkered** with the materials and made a post and a backboard.

When Marco went to attach the basket to the backboard, he found his two cats napping in it. "I see someone has found a way to reuse the basket already!" he laughed. He let them sleep a few minutes longer.

When all the parts were ready, there was only one thing **remaining** to do. Marco, Kim, and Victor took everything to the park. Kim helped dig the hole for the post, but she was still unsure. Next, Marco helped Victor ease the backboard and basket carefully into the hole.

"It looks better than I thought it would!" said Kim.

"Here's the real test!" grinned Marco. He tossed her the basketball. Kim bounced the ball, aimed, and shot a perfect basket. She was **jubilant**.

"Wow, I was wrong," she said. "This recycled basketball hoop is really great. Now we can play whenever we want!"

"Yes, and I can beat you whenever I want," grinned Marco.

"Oh, no you can't!" laughed Kim. The two friends played basketball until dinner time.

## Make Connections

What problem do Kim and Marco have? How do they reuse something to solve it? ESSENTIAL QUESTION

Discuss how you reused something to solve a problem. How did it work? TEXT TO SELF

# Summarize

When you summarize, you retell the most important events in the story. Use events to help you summarize "The New Hoop."

 **Find Text Evidence**

You may not know why Kim and Marco feel frustrated and discouraged. Reread and identify important story events. Then summarize them in your own words.

> **page 349**
>
> Marco **gazed** at the basketball hoop and threw the ball up. It whizzed through the air. "Score!" he shouted as the ball fell through with a swish.
>
> "You won this time, but I'll beat you next time, Marco!" said Kim as the two friends made their way home. "I wish we could play at home, too, instead of only at school. It's not fair." The basketball hoop in their neighborhood park had been ruined when a tree fell and crushed it.
>
> "My dad says the Parks Department doesn't have enough money to buy a new hoop yet," grumbled Marco in **frustration**.
>
> "I feel so **discouraged**," said Kim. "I guess there's nothing we can do."

*I read that* _Kim said she wished she could play ball at home. The basketball hoop was broken, and there was no money to fix it. Marco grumbled. Kim said she felt discouraged._ *These details help me summarize. Kim and Marco are frustrated because they can't play basketball in their neighborhood.*

## Your Turn

COLLABORATE

Reread "The New Hoop." Summarize the most important events that tell how Kim and Marco solve their problem.

Chris Vallo

# Point of View

Point of view is what a character thinks about other characters or events in a story. Look at Marco's actions and words to figure out his point of view.

 **Find Text Evidence**

*What does Marco think about reusing recycled things? I can reread what he does and says. These details will help me figure out his point of view.*

| Details |
|---|
| Marco asks Mr. Morse if he has anything they could reuse to make a basketball hoop. |
| |
| |

↓

| Point of View |
|---|
| |

**Your Turn**

Reread "The New Hoop." Write about Marco's feelings about reusing things in your graphic organizer. Figure out his point of view. Do you agree with Marco's point of view about recycling? Why or why not?

*Go Digital!*
*Use the interactive graphic organizer*

# Realistic Fiction

"The New Hoop" is realistic fiction. **Realistic fiction**:
- Is a made-up story that could really happen
- Has illustrations that give information about the characters, setting, and events

### Find Text Evidence

*I can tell that "The New Hoop" is realistic fiction. Marco and Kim have a problem to solve. That could happen in real life. There are also illustrations that give details about the characters and setting.*

page 348

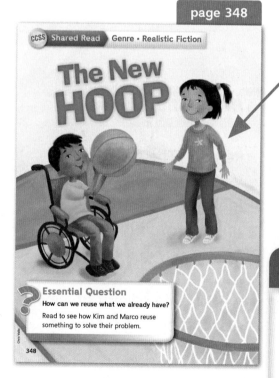

**CCSS** Shared Read > Genre · Realistic Fiction

## The New HOOP

**Essential Question**
How can we reuse what we already have?
Read to see how Kim and Marco reuse something to solve their problem.

348

**Illustrations** Illustrations give you more details about the characters, setting, or events in a story.

COLLABORATE
## Your Turn

Find two things in the story that could happen in real life. Talk about why "The New Hoop" is realistic fiction.

# Homographs

Homographs are words that are spelled the same but have different meanings. They are sometimes pronounced differently. Use nearby words as clues to help you figure out the meaning of a homograph.

 **Find Text Evidence**

*On page 349 in "The New Hoop" I see the word* can. *I know* can *means "to be able to" or "a metal container." I will reread sentences from the story to figure out which meaning fits. In this sentence,* can *means "to be able to."*

"I feel so discouraged," said Kim. " I guess there's nothing we can do."

## Your Turn

Use context clues to figure out the meaning for the following homographs.
   **fair,** *page 349*
   **fine,** *page 350*
   **post,** *page 350*

Chris Vallo

# Write About the Text

Pages 348–351

Jayla

I responded to the prompt: *Add an event to the story. Have Kim describe to her family how she and Marco solved their problem. Use sensory language.*

## Student Model: *Narrative Text*

**Set the Scene**
My first sentence tells where the conversation is taking place.

**Sensory Language**
I used vivid words to describe Kim's feelings about the hoop.

At the dinner table that night,

Kim's eyes were shiny with pride.

"There's a new basketball hoop at

the park, and we made it!" she said.

Her brother looked a little

doubtful. "How did you do that?"

he asked.

"We found an old, cracked

laundry basket," Kim explained.

**Develop Characters**
I used Kim's own words to show how her feelings changed about recycling old things.

"It was Marco's idea to use it. But I wasn't sure about how to recycle it. Victor helped us solve our problem. He used old wood to make the stand. After he attached the hoop, it worked just fine. I learned that recycling is a great idea!"

**Grammar**

The **object pronoun** *us* comes after the action verb *helped*. The **subject pronoun** *He* shows who *used*.

*Grammar Handbook*
*See page 488.*

**Your Turn**

Add an event to the end of the story. Have Marco explain to his class how he practiced conservation. Use sensory language.

*Go Digital!*
*Write your response online.*
*Use your editing checklist.*

©Peter Kneffel/dpa/Corbis

358

# TEAMWORK

Sasha is trained to rescue people. She and her team work together to search for and help people lost in the snow.

▶ There are many different kinds of teams.

▶ Team members must trust each other and communicate well.

▶ Teamwork gets the job done.

## Talk About It

Write words you have learned about teamwork. Talk with a partner about how teams work together.

Teamwork

# Vocabulary

Use the picture and the sentence to talk with a partner about each word.

### accidental

Jason felt bad about the **accidental** mess he made on the driveway.

What does the word accidental mean?

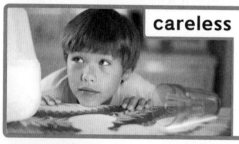

### careless

Harry was **careless** and not paying attention when he spilled his milk.

What is the opposite of careless?

### disasters

Tornadoes and other natural **disasters** often cause a lot of damage.

What are some other natural disasters you have heard about?

### equipment

Firefighters wear special **equipment** to fight fires.

What kind of equipment do firefighters need to do their jobs?

**harmful**

Poison ivy leaves may be **harmful** to your skin if you are allergic to them.

What other things might be harmful to you?

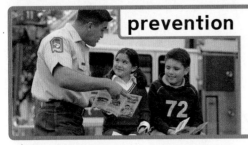

**prevention**

Dave is teaching Fran and Juan about fire **prevention**.

Why should you learn about fire prevention?

**purpose**

The **purpose** of Jay's helmet is to protect his head.

What purpose do gloves have?

**respond**

It is important for this ambulance to **respond** quickly to an emergency.

Why is it important to respond quickly to an emergency?

COLLABORATE

## Your Turn

Pick three words. Write three questions for your partner to answer.

*Go Digital!* *Use the online visual glossary*

# Rescue Dogs Save the Day

## Essential Question

**How do teams work together?**

Read how rescue dogs help in emergencies.

Rescue dogs are trained to go anywhere they are needed.

Rescue teams are there when we need them. They **respond** quickly to help people in trouble. They are brave heroes. But heroes aren't always people. Heroes can be dogs, too!

## Rescue Dogs Are Heroes

Rescue dogs are always ready to go to work. They team up with police, fire and other rescue workers. They are good at finding people who are lost. They rescue families after earthquakes and other **disasters**. They work in all types of weather. And the best news is that rescue dogs can do their jobs with no special **equipment**. All they need is their excellent hearing and a good nose!

Rescue dogs are smart and brave. They listen well to commands and do their jobs even when they are tired, thirsty, or hungry. They are friendly and get along well with their handlers, the people who work with them. They also must be obedient and do what they are told.

Certain breeds of dogs are easier to train to work in dangerous rescue situations than others. The Border Collie is one breed of dog used during disasters and emergencies. Border collies can work for a long time. They do not get tired easily, and that's important. But dogs need more than energy. They also need to follow commands, and that takes a lot of training.

# Getting Ready to Work

Rescue dogs begin their training as puppies. It can take up to two years to completely train a rescue dog. Then it is able to save people in **harmful** and dangerous situations.

The dogs learn to work outdoors in heat, cold, and bad weather. They run, jump, and climb for many hours every day. Rescue dogs also learn to ignore everything around them while they are working. This helps them to focus on the job and keeps them from making **careless** mistakes.

Rescue dogs must always be ready to dive in and help someone.

Everything a rescue dog learns to do has a **purpose**. Even friendship is not **accidental**. A dog and the people it works with must learn to communicate as a team. They trust each other. And when they have practiced and trained enough, they are ready to participate, or take part in, a real rescue mission.

## Best Rescue Dog Breeds

| These dogs make great rescue dogs. | | | | |
| --- | --- | --- | --- | --- |
| Dog Breed | **Labrador Retriever** | **German Shepherd** | **Bloodhound** | **Border Collie** |
| Rescue Trait | friendly | brave | great sense of smell | lots of energy and stamina |

# Good Dog!

When a hiker is lost, a rescue dog sniffs the air and the ground to find her. A dog's sense of smell is much stronger than a person's. Rescue dogs can even smell someone trapped under fifteen feet of snow. When a dog finds someone, it barks to alert its partner. The rescue worker trusts the dog, so the team works quickly to save a life. At the end of every rescue, the dog gets praise and treats for doing a great job.

Sometimes rescue teams go to schools to teach children about safety and disaster **prevention**. They show children how to stay safe and what to do during emergencies. This job is fun for rescue dogs. They get lots of attention for just doing what they do best – helping people. Rescue dogs really are heroes!

**This team works on snowy mountains.**

## Make Connections

How do rescue workers and dogs work together in an emergency? ESSENTIAL QUESTION

What do you think would be the best thing about working with a rescue dog? TEXT TO SELF

Tom Bear/Aurora/Getty Images

365

# Ask and Answer Questions

Stop and ask yourself questions as you read. Then reread to find details to support your answers.

## Find Text Evidence

Reread the section "Rescue Dogs Are Heroes" on page 363. Think of a question and then read to answer it.

> **page 363**
>
> Rescue teams are there when we need them. They **respond** quickly to help people in trouble. They are brave heroes. But heroes aren't always people. Heroes can be dogs, too!
>
> ### Rescue Dogs Are Heroes
>
> Rescue dogs are always ready to go to work. They team up with police, fire and other rescue workers. They are good at finding people who are lost. They rescue families after earthquakes and other **disasters**. They work in all types of weather. And the best news is that rescue dogs can do their jobs with no special **equipment**. All they need is their excellent hearing and a good nose!
>
> Rescue dogs are smart and brave. They listen well to commands and do their jobs even when

*I have a question. What do rescue dogs do?*

*I read that rescue dogs find people who are lost and rescue families after disasters. They work in all kinds of weather.* Now I can answer my question. Rescue dogs work hard to save lives.

## Your Turn

COLLABORATE

Reread "Getting Ready to Work." Think of a question. You might ask: How do dogs train to be rescue dogs? Reread the section to find the answer.

# Author's Point of View

A point of view is what an author thinks about a topic. Look for details that show what the author thinks. Decide if you agree with the author.

 **Find Text Evidence**

*What does the author think about rescue dogs? I can reread and look for details that tell me what the author thinks. This will help me figure out the author's point of view.*

| Details |
| --- |
| Rescue dogs are smart and brave. |
| They do not get tired easily, and that's important. |
|  |

↓

| Author's Point of View |
| --- |
|  |

**Your Turn**

Reread "Rescue Dogs Save the Day." Find details that tell what the author thinks about rescue dogs. What is the author's point of view? List details and point of view in your graphic organizer. Do you agree with the author's point of view? Why or why not?

*Go Digital!*
*Use the interactive graphic organizer*

# Expository Text

"Rescue Dogs Save the Day" is an expository text.

**Expository text:**

- May explain a science topic
- Includes text features such as headings, photographs, captions, and a chart

## 🔍 Find Text Evidence

*I can tell that "Rescue Dogs Save the Day" is an expository text. It gives facts and information about rescue dogs. It has photographs with captions. It also has headings and a chart.*

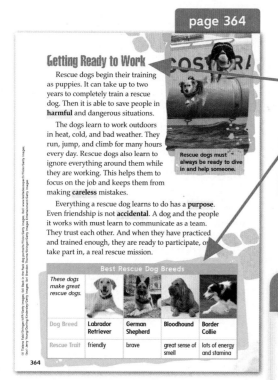

page 364

### Getting Ready to Work

Rescue dogs begin their training as puppies. It can take up to two years to completely train a rescue dog. Then it is able to save people in **harmful** and dangerous situations.

The dogs learn to work outdoors in heat, cold, and bad weather. They run, jump, and climb for many hours every day. Rescue dogs also learn to ignore everything around them while they are working. This helps them to focus on the job and keeps them from making **careless** mistakes.

Everything a rescue dog learns to do has a **purpose**. Even friendship is not **accidental**. A dog and the people it works with must learn to communicate as a team. They trust each other. And when they have practiced and trained enough, they are ready to participate, or take part in, a real rescue mission.

Rescue dogs must always be ready to dive in and help someone.

| Best Rescue Dog Breeds | | | |
|---|---|---|---|
| These dogs make great rescue dogs. | | | |
| Dog Breed | Labrador Retriever | German Shepherd | Bloodhound | Border Collie |
| Rescue Trait | friendly | brave | great sense of smell | lots of energy and stamina |

364

## Text Features

**Headings** A heading tells what a section of text is about.

**Chart** A chart presents information about the topic in a way that is easy to read.

COLLABORATE

## Your Turn

Look at the chart on page 364. Why do German Shepherds make good rescue dogs?

# Sentence Clues

As you read, you may come across a word you don't know. Look at other words in the same sentence. They can give you clues about the word's meaning.

 **Find Text Evidence**

*On page 363, I see the word* handlers. *I'm not sure what that word means. I see the words "people who work with them" in the same sentence. This helps me figure out that* handlers *are "the people who work with rescue dogs."*

They are friendly and get along well with their handlers, the people who work with them.

 **COLLABORATE**

## Your Turn

Find sentence clues. Use them to help you figure out the meanings of these words.

**obedient,** *page 363*
**participate,** *page 364*

Tom Bear/Aurora/Getty Images

# Write About the Text

Pages 362–365

Sebastián

I answered the question: *How do rescue workers and dogs work as a team to help people? Use text evidence to support your answer.*

**Introduce a Topic**
My first sentence states the main idea.

**Strong Paragraph**
The facts and details in my paragraph support my topic sentence.

**Student Model:** *Informative Text*

Rescue workers and dogs work together to save people in danger. Dogs help rescue workers, such as police and firefighters. The dogs help find people who are lost. These people might have been hurt in a natural disaster or an accident. Rescue dogs must train with their handlers for several years.

IPGGutenbergUKLtd/iStock/360/Getty Images

They learn to work as a team.
The two of them must learn to
communicate. Rescue dogs must
pay attention to the handlers'
commands and nothing else. With
good training, dogs help rescue
workers save many people.

Tiziana Fabi/Stringer/AFP/Getty Images

**Essential Question**

What do good citizens do?

*Go Digital!*

David L. Moore-HIO/Alamy

372

# CITIZENSHIP

Lou is helping his town get ready to honor its heroes. He is being a good citizen by participating in something that is important to his community.

▶ Being a good citizen means helping other people.

▶ It means following the rules and being respectful of others.

▶ Good citizenship helps make a community safe.

## Talk About It

Write words you have learned about citizenship. Talk about ways you can be a good citizen.

# Vocabulary

**Use the picture and the sentence to talk with a partner about each word.**

### citizenship

Planting a tree in your community is an example of good **citizenship**.

What is another example of good citizenship?

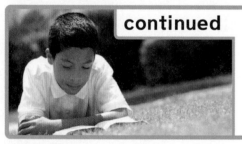

### continued

Justin **continued** to read his book all afternoon.

What is the opposite of *continued*?

### daring

One brave penguin made a **daring** dive into the cold sea.

Tell about something daring you have seen.

### horrified

Paul and his mother were **horrified** by the scary movie.

What does it mean to feel horrified?

**participate**

Barb and her friends like to **participate** in sack races at the picnic.

What are some games you like to participate in?

**proposed**

Mom **proposed** that they look online to find the answer to Tina's question.

Tell about something you proposed to your family.

**unfairness**

The baseball player discussed the **unfairness** of the referee's call.

What word means the opposite of unfairness?

**waver**

Ted's confidence started to **waver** when he forgot the answer.

Show how you would look if you start to waver.

## Your Turn

COLLABORATE

Pick three words. Write three questions for your partner to answer.

*Go Digital!*   *Use the online visual glossary*

# Dolores Huerta
## GROWING UP STRONG

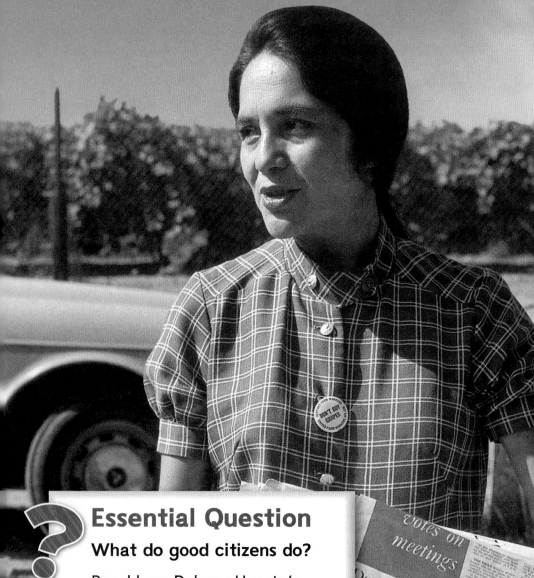

## Essential Question
**What do good citizens do?**

Read how Dolores Huerta's
actions helped many people.

**D**olores Huerta learned to help people by watching her mother. Good **citizenship** was important to her, and she taught Dolores that women can be strong leaders. When Dolores grew up, she had the same beliefs.

## Good Citizens

Dolores was born on April 10, 1930. She lived in a small town in New Mexico until she was three years old. Then she moved to California with her mother and two brothers. Dolores grew up watching her mother **participate** in community organizations. Her mother believed that all people deserved to be treated fairly.

When Dolores was a young girl, her mother owned a hotel and a restaurant. Many farm workers who lived in their town were poor and hungry. They were paid very little for their hard work. Dolores' mother let them stay at her hotel and eat at her restaurant for free. This taught Dolores and her brothers that good citizens get involved in the community by helping their neighbors.

Dolores Huerta helped farm workers who spent many hours working in fields.

## Dolores Goes to School

Dolores saw how hard life was for farm workers in California. She wanted everyone to be treated fairly. This attitude **continued** as she attended college and studied to become a teacher.

Many of the students that Dolores taught were the children of farm workers. These students were often tired and hungry. They came to school barefoot because they had no shoes. Dolores knew she needed to help them. As a result, she went to her school's principal and **proposed** some good ideas. She tried to get free lunches and milk for the children. She tried to get them new clothes and shoes.

Trying to help the children was a **daring** thing for Dolores to do. The other teachers did not agree with her ideas. Dolores risked a lot, but her beliefs did not **waver**. She decided to do something about the **unfairness** she saw. She wanted to find a better way to help farm workers and their families.

## Dolores: Strong and Fair

*This time line shows important dates in Dolores Huerta's life.*

1930     1940     1950     1960     1970     1980

**1933:** Moved to California

**1953–1955:** Worked as a teacher

**1955:** Met César Chávez

**1930:** Dolores is born

**1962:** Dolores and César started National Farm Worker's Association

**1975:** Helped pass laws to protect farm workers

## Dolores Stands Strong

Every day Dolores saw people working in unusually unsafe and disagreeable conditions. She was **horrified**. Many farm workers had little money to feed their families. Dolores decided to do something.

In 1955, Dolores met César Chávez. He wanted to make life better for farm workers, too. Dolores and César organized the

Dolores Huerta speaks out for farm workers at a rally in 1969.

workers into a group called the National Farm Workers Association. This group protected the rights of the farm workers. It helped make big farms treat them better. As a result, working conditions on the farms improved.

Growing up with a mother who cared about other people taught Dolores to be a good citizen. Her kind and brave acts helped farm workers and their families. Who is a good citizen? Dolores Huerta is!

1990    2000    2010

1998:
Earned Human Rights Award from President Clinton

## Make Connections

How did Dolores Huerta's actions make her a good citizen? **ESSENTIAL QUESTION**

What can you do to improve people's lives? **TEXT TO SELF**

# Ask and Answer Questions

Ask yourself questions as you read. Then read on or reread to find the answers.

## Find Text Evidence

Reread "Good Citizens" on page 377. Think of a question and then read to find the answer.

---

**page 377**

**D**olores Huerta learned to help people by watching her mother. Good **citizenship** was important to her, and she taught Dolores that women can be strong leaders. When Dolores grew up, she had the same beliefs.

**Good Citizens**

Dolores was born on April 10, 1930. She lived in a small town in New Mexico until she was three years old. Then she moved to California with her mother and two brothers. Dolores grew up watching her mother **participate** in community organizations. Her mother believed that all people deserved to be treated fairly.

When Dolores was a young girl, her mother owned

---

*I have a question. How did Dolores learn to be a good citizen? I read that <u>when Dolores was young, her mother let the farm workers eat and live for free at her hotel.</u> Now I can answer my question. Dolores learned to be a good citizen by watching her mother.*

## Your Turn

Reread "Dolores Goes to School." Think of a question. You might ask: How did Dolores try to help the children in her class? Reread the section to find the answer.

# Author's Point of View

Point of view is what an author thinks about a topic. Look for details that show what the author thinks. Decide if you agree with the author's point of view.

 **Find Text Evidence**

*What does the author think about Dolores Huerta? I can reread and look for details that tell me what the author thinks. This will help me figure out the author's point of view.*

| Details |
|---|
| Dolores' mother taught her to be a good citizen and a strong leader. |
| Helping her students was a daring thing for Dolores to do. |
| |

↓

| Author's Point of View |
|---|
| |

**Your Turn** COLLABORATE

Reread "Dolores Huerta, Growing Up Strong." Find more details that tell how the author feels about Dolores. What is the author's point of view? List them in your graphic organizer. Do you agree with the author's point of view about Dolores Huerta?

*Go Digital!*
*Use the interactive graphic organizer*

# Biography

"Dolores Huerta, Growing Up Strong" is a biography.
A **biography**:

- Tells the true story of a real person's life
- Is written by another person
- Includes text features such as timelines, photographs, and captions

## Find Text Evidence

*I can tell that "Dolores Huerta, Growing Up Strong" is a biography. The author gives facts and information about Dolores Huerta's life. There is also a timeline that shows important events in Dolores' life in time order.*

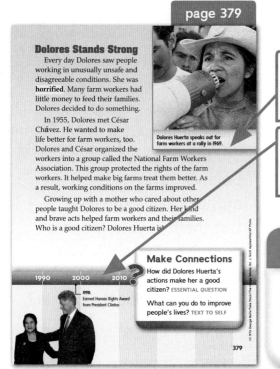

page 379

**Dolores Stands Strong**

Every day Dolores saw people working in unusually unsafe and disagreeable conditions. She was **horrified**. Many farm workers had little money to feed their families. Dolores decided to do something.

In 1955, Dolores met César Chávez. He wanted to make life better for farm workers, too. Dolores and César organized the workers into a group called the National Farm Workers Association. This group protected the rights of the farm workers. It helped make big farms treat them better. As a result, working conditions on the farms improved.

Growing up with a mother who cared about other people taught Dolores to be a good citizen. Her kind and brave acts helped farm workers and their families. Who is a good citizen? Dolores Huerta is!

Dolores Huerta speaks out for farm workers at a rally in 1969.

1990 2000 2010

1998: Earned Human Rights Award from President Clinton

**Make Connections**

How did Dolores Huerta's actions make her a good citizen? ESSENTIAL QUESTION

What can you do to improve people's lives? TEXT TO SELF

379

## Text Features

**Caption** A caption tells about a photograph. It gives information that is not included in the text.

**Timeline** A timeline shows the time order in which important dates and events happened.

COLLABORATE

## Your Turn

Look at the timeline on pages 378 and 379. In what year did Dolores Huerta meet César Chávez?

# Prefixes and Suffixes

A prefix is a word part added to the beginning of a word. A suffix is added at the end. To figure out the meaning of a word with a prefix and suffix, find the root word first.

## Find Text Evidence

*On page 379, I see the word* unusually. *I find the root word* usual *first. I know the prefix,* un- *means "not," and the suffix* -ly *means "in a way that." The word* unusually *must mean "not in a usual way."*

Everyday Dolores saw people working in unusually unsafe and disagreeable conditions.

## Your Turn

Find the root word. Then use the prefix and suffix to figure out the meanings of each word.

**unfairness,** *page 378*

**disagreeable,** *page 379*

Dr. Parvinder Sethi

# Write About the Text

Camilla

I answered the question: *How does the author explain what good citizenship means?*

---

**Student Model:** *Informative Text*

**Strong Opening**
My first sentence clearly states the topic.

**Supporting Details**
I used facts and details from the text to develop the topic.

    The author uses the life of Dolores Huerta to describe good citizenship. Dolores learned to be a good citizen by watching her mother. Her mom gave food and shelter to poor people. When Dolores grew up, she became a teacher. She helped her students by getting them shoes and food.

Mari/iStock/360/Getty Images

Later, Dolores helped farm workers get better working conditions and more pay for their work. Even though some people disagreed with her, Dolores did not stop. Dolores Huerta was a good citizen because she helped many people have better lives.

## Grammar

The word *their* is a **possessive pronoun** because it tells that the work was done by the farm workers.

***Grammar Handbook*** *See page 489.*

## Linking Words

I included words, such as *Even though,* to connect my ideas.

## Your Turn

How does the time line on pages 378–379 support the author's point of view about Dolores Huerta? Use text evidence to support your answer.

*Go Digital!*
*Write your response online.*
*Use your editing checklist.*

## Essential Question

**What are different kinds of energy?**

*Go Digital!*

©Simon Jarrett/Corbis

# We've Got the Power!

Carlos lives near a windmill farm. He loves to ride past on his bike and watch the turbines spin in the wind. Wind power makes electricity that heats his house and powers his lights.

► Energy comes from many different sources.

► Energy from the wind and the Sun are renewable. They can be used again and again.

## Talk About It

Write words you have learned about energy. Talk with a partner about the different kinds of energy.

# Vocabulary

Use the picture and the sentence to talk with a partner about each word.

**energy**

Good food gives Ron and his grandpa lots of **energy** to work together.

Where do cars get their energy?

**natural**

Cotton is a **natural** material used to make clothes.

Name a natural material that is used in buildings.

**pollution**

Water **pollution**, such as garbage and chemicals, can harm animals.

Name something that causes air pollution.

**produce**

The Sun can **produce** enough solar power to heat this family's home.

What word means the same as produce?

## renewable

Trees are a **renewable** resource because more will always grow.

What does the word renewable mean?

## replace

Soon Tina will **replace** her car with one that runs on electricity.

Name something that you can replace.

## sources

Wind and solar power are two energy **sources** we can use.

What are your energy sources?

## traditional

Cho and her mother like to eat **traditional** foods, such as rice and fish.

What is another word for traditional?

COLLABORATE

## Your Turn

Pick three words. Write three questions for your partner to answer.

*Go Digital!* **Use the online visual glossary**

## Essential Question

**What are different kinds of energy?**

Read why solar energy is a good source of power.

**This energetic snowboarder gets his power from the healthful foods he eats.**

390

# Here Comes Solar Power

What do you have in common with a car and a factory? You both need **energy** to run. Energy keeps things moving.

## Energy Today

You get your energy from eating healthful foods. Most factories, homes, and cars get their energy from fossil fuels. Coal, petroleum, and natural gas are fossil fuels. They have been the **traditional**, or usual, energy **sources** for more than a century. Today, most of the energy we use in the United States comes from burning fossil fuels.

But these fuels come from deep under the Earth's surface, and they are running out. They cannot be reused. Once a fossil fuel is gone, it's gone forever. So we need alternative energy sources to **replace** them. Scientists know that there is no other way to keep our country going and growing. So they are looking for new, alternative sources of energy that won't run out.

## Cheaper and Cleaner

Solar power is one source of **renewable** energy. And it is not expensive. As a result, many people are placing solar panels on the roofs of homes and large buildings. Solar panels look like giant mirrors, and they capture energy from the Sun.

On a bright day, the Sun's rays hit the solar panel and cause it to **produce** electricity. Then the electricity flows into the building. As a result, there is enough energy to raise the temperature inside homes, and turn on lights, stoves, and computers.

## The Future

More companies are turning to solar power to replace fossil fuels. It's **natural**. That means it isn't made, or changed, by people. Solar power is cheaper than fossil fuels, and it does not create **pollution**.

Today there are millions of people around the world using solar power to produce electricity for their homes and businesses. Someday solar power may completely replace fossil fuels.

**Solar panels are placed on the roofs of buildings.**

# GO SUNSHINE!

Renewable energy is where it's at. And solar power is at the top of our list. Here are the top reasons why solar energy is so hot!

- Solar power is cheaper than fossil fuels.

- It is renewable.

- It doesn't cause pollution and is good for our environment.

- Power from the Sun is always available.

- Solar power is natural.

Solar energy can do just about everything that fossil fuels do. Everyone should use solar power. It's good news for the planet!

Thanks to solar power, Paul can power up and listen to his MP3 player.

## Make Connections

Why is solar power a good source of energy? ESSENTIAL QUESTION

What are some ways you might use solar power? TEXT TO SELF

# Ask and Answer Questions

Ask yourself questions as you read "Here Comes Solar Power." Then look for details to support your answers.

 **Find Text Evidence**

Look at the section "Energy Today" on page 391. Think of a question. Then read to answer it.

page 391

## Energy Today

You get your energy from eating healthful foods. Most factories, homes, and cars get their energy from fossil fuels. Coal, petroleum, and natural gas are fossil fuels. They have been the **traditional**, or usual, energy **sources** for more than a century. Today, most of the energy we use in the United States comes from burning fossil fuels.

But these fuels come from deep under

*I have a question. What are fossil fuels? <u>I read that most factories, homes, and cars run on fossil fuels. They come from deep under the Earth's surface and are running out.</u> Now I can answer my question. Fossil fuels come from the Earth and will not always be there.*

## Your Turn

COLLABORATE

Think of one question about solar power. You might ask: How do solar panels work? Reread page 392 to answer it.

# Cause and Effect

A cause is why something happens. An effect is what happens. They happen in time order. Signal words, such as *so, as a result,* and *because* help you find causes and effects.

 **Find Text Evidence**

*On page 391 I read that scientists are looking for alternative sources of energy. This is the effect. Now I can find the cause. Fossil fuels are running out and we need new energy sources.*

| Cause ➡ | Effect |
|---|---|
| **First** <br> Fossil fuels are running out and we need new energy sources. ➡ | Scientists are looking for alternative sources of energy. |
| **Next** <br> Solar power is renewable and is not expensive. ➡ | |
| **Then** <br> The sun's rays hit the solar panel. ➡ | |

COLLABORATE

## Your Turn

Reread "Here Comes Solar Power." Use signal words to find more causes and effects. Write them in the graphic organizer.

*Go Digital!*
**Use the interactive graphic organizer**

# Expository Text

"Here Comes Solar Power" is an expository text.

**Expository text:**
- Often includes facts and information about a science topic.
- Includes text features such photographs, captions, headings, and a sidebar.

## Find Text Evidence

*I can tell that "Here Comes Solar Power" is an expository text. It has science facts and information. It has a sidebar that presents how the author feels about solar energy.*

page 393

TIME FOR KIDS

**GO SUNSHINE!**

Renewable energy is where it's at. And solar power is at the top of our list. Here are the top reasons why solar energy is so hot!

* Solar power is cheaper than fossil fuels.
* It is renewable.
* It doesn't cause pollution and is good for our environment.
* Power from the Sun is always available.
* Solar power is natural.

Solar energy can do just about everything that fossil fuels do. Everyone should use solar power. It's good news for the planet!

Thanks to solar power, Paul can power up and listen to his MP3 player.

**Make Connections**
Why is solar power a good source of energy? ESSENTIAL QUESTION

What are some ways you might use solar power? TEXT TO SELF

393

## Text Features

### Photographs and captions
Photographs and captions give extra information about a topic.

**Sidebar** A sidebar may present the author's opinion about a topic.

COLLABORATE

## Your Turn

Reread the sidebar on page 393. Tell a partner three reasons why people should use solar power.

# Homophones

Homophones are words that sound the same but have different meanings and different spellings. The words *sea* and *see* are homophones. Use context clues to figure out a homophone's meaning.

## Find Text Evidence

*I see the word* need *on page 391. Need and* knead *are homophones. Need means "to require something." Knead means "to mix with your hands." The words sound the same, but have different meanings and spellings. I can use context clues to figure out what* need *means. Here it means "to require."*

You both need energy to run.

COLLABORATE

## Your Turn

Use context clues to figure out what this word means. Then find its homophone.

**rays,** *page 392*

Corey Rich/Aurora Open/Corbis

# Write About the Text

Pages 390–393

William

I answered the question: *Do you think we should use solar energy instead of fossil fuels? Use text evidence to support your answer.*

**Opinions**
I clearly stated my opinion about solar power in my first sentence.

**Support Opinions**
I used text evidence to support my opinion.

> ## Student Model: *Opinion*
>
> I think the future of energy is
>
> in the Sun. The author explains
>
> that solar energy will not run out.
>
> Fossil fuels, such as coal or gas,
>
> cannot be replaced. Also, they
>
> must be changed before people
>
> can use them. Solar energy can
>
> be used without being changed.

Angela Lumsden/Moment/Getty Images

**398**    W.3.la, W.3.lb  See the California Standards section.

## Grammar

The **pronoun-verb contraction** *it's* is a short way of saying *it is.*

*Grammar Handbook*
*See page 490.*

Solar energy is natural. It doesn't pollute the air. As a result, it's better for the environment. I think that people should stop using fossil fuels because we can ← use solar energy for all the power we need.

## Connect Opinions and Reasons

I used the linking word *because* to help support my opinion in my last sentence.

## Your Turn

Does the author of "Here Comes Solar Power" do a good job of convincing readers to support solar power? Use reasons from the text to support your opinion.

*Go Digital!*
*Write your response online.*
*Use your editing checklist.*

# Diamond in the Rough

Dad called it a diamond in the rough,
A big, old field outside of town
Now just a dumping ground
A ton of trash
    A mile of mess
"No way!" my friends say.

But I just shake my head and smile.
I know.

I can clean it. Make it green.
Polish up that diamond in the rough.

## The Big Idea
How do we decide what's important?

I go each day,
Pick up trash,
Haul away sack after sack
    After sack.

My friends follow,
    Watching, watching,
Then roll up their sleeves.
They see it too—
    A diamond in the rough.


Together we yank up weeds,
    Rake things smooth,

Until finally, finally
    A baseball field.

Not the biggest
Not the best

But OURS
    A diamond in the rough.

        **— By Maureen Wong**

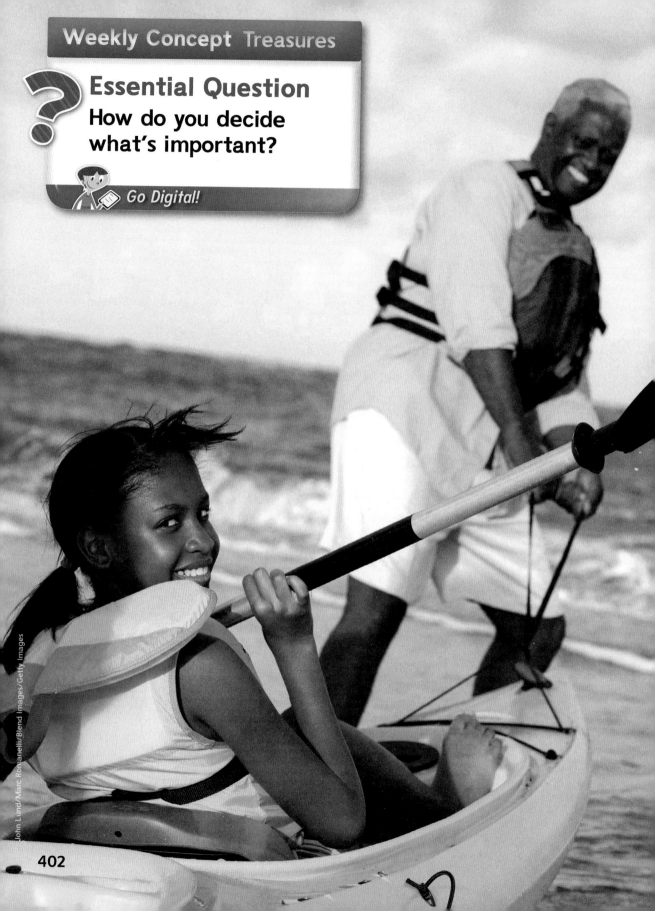

**Essential Question**
How do you decide
what's important?

*Go Digital!*

# WHAT WE VALUE

Spending time with my grandfather is important. He shares what he knows and helps me learn new things. He values spending time with me, too.

▶ Spending time with people and learning new things are valuable to me.

▶ Healthy habits and sharing are important, too.

## Talk About It

Write words you have learned about what's valuable. Talk with a partner about the things that you value.

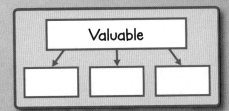

| Valuable | | |
|---|---|---|
|  |  |  |

# Vocabulary

Use the picture and the sentence to talk with a partner about each word.

**alarmed**

Jess was **alarmed** as he watched the barber cut his hair.

Show how you would look if you were alarmed by something.

**anguish**

Andy felt **anguish** when he realized his bike was missing.

What is another word that means the same as anguish?

**necessary**

Food is **necessary** for all living things.

What other things are necessary for living things?

**obsessed**

Paul is **obsessed** with space and wears his astronaut suit all the time.

Name something you are obsessed with.

**possess**

Dan and Meg **possess** a huge bunch of colorful balloons.

Tell about something you possess.

**reward**

Dad took us on vacation as a **reward** for getting good grades in school.

What reward would you like to get?

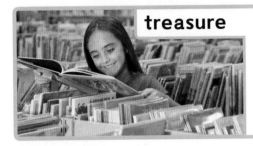

**treasure**

Lila found a real **treasure** at the book sale.

Tell about a treasure you have.

**wealth**

We are counting our money and will share our **wealth** by donating it.

What is another word for *wealth*?

COLLABORATE

## Your Turn

Pick three words. Write three questions for your partner to answer.

*Go Digital!* *Use the online visual glossary*

# ATHENA AND ARACHNE

? **Essential Question**

**How do you decide what's important?**

Read a myth that shows why valuing a talent can cause problems.

Jenny Reynish

## ⇢ SCENE ONE ⇠

*Athens, Greece, a long time ago, Arachne's home.*

**NARRATOR:** Long ago, Arachne and her friend Diana sat weaving.

**DIANA:** Oh, Arachne! That cloth is so beautiful.

*Arachne admires her cloth.*

**ARACHNE:** I know. Many people want to **possess** my cloth, but few can afford it. Only those with great **wealth** can buy it.

**DIANA:** Yes, it's true that people value your cloth. It is one of their most valued possessions. Your weavings are a real **treasure**. Some say that you learned your weaving skill, or talent, from the goddess Athena.

**ARACHNE:** It was not **necessary** for me to learn from a goddess. I was born with my talent. I am a much better weaver than Athena, and I'm sure I could beat her in a weaving competition!

*Diana is worried, stops weaving and looks at Arachne.*

**DIANA:** Ssshhh! I hope Athena isn't listening, or you're in big trouble!

**ARACHNE:** Nonsense! There's no reason to be **alarmed** or worried. Athena is much too busy to come down from Mount Olympus to compete with me.

## ⟶ SCENE TWO ⟵

*Mount Olympus, home of Athena. A messenger arrives.*

**MESSENGER:** Goddess Athena! I have news from Athens. The weaver Arachne says she can beat you in a weaving competition. She's **obsessed** with her skill and thinks she is the best weaver in Greece!

**ATHENA:** I'll show her who weaves the finest cloth! Her obsession with weaving must end. Please get me my cloak. *Messenger hands Athena her cloak.*

**ATHENA:** Arachne cannot talk about me that way! If she refuses to apologize, I will make her pay for her boastful words. Her **anguish** will be great!

## ⟶ SCENE THREE ⟵

*Arachne's home. There is a knock at the door.*

**ARACHNE:** Who's there?

**ATHENA:** Just an old woman with a question.

*Athena is hiding under her cloak. She enters the room.*

**ATHENA:** Is it true that you challenged the goddess Athena to a weaving competition?

**ARACHNE:** Yes, that's right. *Athena drops her cloak.*

**ATHENA:** Well, I am Athena, and I am here to compete with you!

**DIANA:** Arachne, please don't! It is unwise to compete with a goddess!

*Arachne and Athena sit down at the empty looms and begin to weave furiously.*

Jenny Reynish

**408**

**ARACHNE:** I am ready to win and get my **reward**!

**ATHENA:** There's no prize if you lose!

**NARRATOR:** Arachne and Athena both wove beautiful cloths. However, Arachne's cloth was filled with pictures of the gods being unkind.

**ATHENA:** Arachne, your weaving is beautiful, but I am insulted and upset by the pictures you chose to weave. You are boastful, and your cloth is mean and unkind. For that, I will punish you.

*Athena points dramatically at Arachne. Arachne falls behind her loom and crawls out as a spider.*

**ATHENA:** Arachne, you will spend the rest of your life weaving and living in your own web.

**NARRATOR:** Arachne was mean and boastful, so Athena turned her into a spider. That's why spiders are now called arachnids. Arachne learned that bragging and too much pride can lead to trouble.

⊰⇒ THE END ⇐⊱

## Make Connections

What does Arachne value? How does it cause her trouble? ESSENTIAL QUESTION

What do you value? Why do you value it? TEXT TO SELF

# Make Predictions

Use details in the story to predict what happens next. Was your prediction right? Read on to check it. Change your prediction if it is not right.

 **Find Text Evidence**

You may have made a prediction about Arachne at the beginning of "Athena and Arachne." What clues on page 407 helped you guess what might happen?

> **page 407**
>
> **DIANA:** Oh, Arachne! That cloth is so beautiful.
> *Arachne admires her cloth.*
> **ARACHNE:** I know. Many people want to **possess** my cloth, but few can afford it. Only those with great **wealth** can buy it.
> **DIANA:** Yes, it's true that people value your cloth. It is one of their most valued possessions. Your weavings are a real **treasure**. Some say that you learned your weaving skill, or talent, from the goddess Athena.
> **ARACHNE:** It was not **necessary** for me to learn from a goddess. I was born with my talent. I am a much better weaver than Athena, and I'm sure I could beat her in a weaving competition!

*I predicted that Arachne and Athena would compete. I read that Arachne says she is a better weaver than Athena and could beat her in a contest. I will read on to check my prediction.*

## Your Turn

What did you predict would happen when Athena went to see Arachne? Reread page 408 to check your prediction. Remember to make, confirm, and revise predictions as you read.

# Theme

The theme of a story is the author's message. Think about what the characters do and say. This will help you figure out the theme.

 **Find Text Evidence**

*In "Athena and Arachne," Arachne learns that bragging and too much pride can lead to trouble. This is the story's theme. I can reread to find details that help me figure out the theme.*

Detail

Arachne said that many people want to possess her cloth, but few can afford it. Only those with great wealth can buy it.

↓

Detail

↓

Detail

↓

Detail

↓

Theme

Bragging and too much pride can lead to trouble.

**Your Turn**

COLLABORATE

Read "Athena and Arachne." List important details about what Arachne says and does in your graphic organizer. Be sure the details tell about the theme.

*Go Digital!*
*Use the interactive graphic organizer*

# Myth/Drama

"Athena and Arachne" is a myth and a drama, or play. A **myth** tells how something came to be. A **drama**:

- Tells a story through dialogue and is performed
- Is separated into scenes and has stage directions

## Find Text Evidence

*I see that "Athena and Arachne" is a myth and a play. It is divided into three scenes. It uses dialogue and stage directions to tell how spiders came to weave webs.*

page 408

### → SCENE TWO ←

*Mount Olympus, home of Athena. A messenger arrives.*

**MESSENGER:** Goddess Athena! I have news from Athens. The weaver Arachne says she can beat you in a weaving competition. She's **obsessed** with her skill and thinks she is the best weaver in Greece!

**ATHENA:** I'll show her who weaves the finest cloth! Her obsession with weaving must end. Please get me my cloak. *Messenger hands Athena her cloak.*

**ATHENA:** Arachne cannot talk about me that way! If she refuses to apologize, I will make her pay for her boastful words. Her **anguish** will be great!

### → SCENE THREE ←

*Arachne's home. There is a knock at the door.*

**ARACHNE:** Who's there?

**ATHENA:** Just an old woman with a question.

*Athena is hiding under her cloak. She enters the room.*

**ATHENA:** Is it true that you challenged the goddess Athena to a weaving competition?

**ARACHNE:** Yes, that's right. *Athena drops her cloak.*

**ATHENA:** Well, I am Athena, and I am here to compete with you!

**Scene** A scene is a part of a play. Scenes tell the story in time order.

**Stage Directions** Stage directions tell what the characters do and how they move.

**Dialogue** Dialogue is the words the characters speak.

COLLABORATE

## Your Turn

Find more examples of scenes, dialogue, and stage directions in "Athena and Arachne." Tell your partner how they help tell the story.

Jenny Reynish

# Root Words

A root word is the simplest form of a word. It helps you figure out the meaning of a related word.

## Find Text Evidence

*In "Athena and Arachne," I see the word* competition. *I think the root word of* competition *is* compete. *I know* compete *means "to be in a contest." I think a* competition *is "a contest where people try to win."*

I am a much better weaver than Athena, and I'm sure I could beat her in a weaving competition!

## Your Turn

Find the root word. Then use it to figure out the meaning of each word.

**possessions,** *page 407*

**obsession,** *page 408*

Jenny Reynish

# Write About the Text

Holly

I answered the question: *Do you think it was fair of Athena to turn Arachne into a spider? Give reasons from the text to support your claim.*

**Student Model:** *Opinion*

**State an Opinion**

My first sentence explains my opinion about the topic.

> Athena was right about
>
> Arachne, but I do not think it was
>
> fair to turn her into a spider for
>
> the rest of her life. Arachne was
>
> a boastful and unkind person. But
>
> Athena's response was too strong.
>
> Why didn't she change Arachne
>
> for one day to teach her a lesson?

**Grammar**

The word *a* is an **article,** and the words *boastful* and *unkind* are **adjectives.**

*Grammar Handbook See page 491.*

sarahwolfephotography/Moment Open/Getty Images

**414** W.3.1a, L.3.1a See the California Standards section.

Maybe Arachne wouldn't have changed, but Athena should have given her a chance at least. ← **Sentence Length** I combined sentences to make my writing more interesting.

Instead, Athena turned her into a ← **Supporting Details** I gave reasons to support my opinion.

spider forever. Athena was just as mean as Arachne.

## Your Turn

Who is a better friend, Diana or Arachne? Use reasons from the text to support your claim.

*Go Digital!*
*Write your response online.*
*Use your editing checklist.*

Jenny Reynish

**Essential Question**
How can weather affect us?

*Go Digital!*

Ryan McVay/Lifesize/Getty Images

416

# WEATHER AFFECTS US

How's the weather? Turn on the weather report or look outdoors to find out. Is it sunny? Is it raining? It's important to know what the weather is. What's today's forecast? Warm and rainy with a side of fun.

▶ Weather is what is happening outdoors right now.

▶ It affects how we dress and what we do.

▶ Sometimes severe weather affects the way we live.

## Talk About It

Write words you have learned about weather. Talk with a partner about how weather affects you.

Weather

# Vocabulary

**Use the picture and the sentence to talk with a partner about each word.**

**argue**

James and his grandfather sometimes discuss movies and **argue** about them.

What are some words that mean the opposite of argue?

**astonished**

Tammy and Kim were **astonished** and amazed at the big bug they found.

What is another word for *astonished*?

**complained**

Ben **complained** about his dinner because he didn't like peas.

Tell about a time when you complained about something.

**conditions**

Mark's umbrella was ruined by the windy **conditions**.

What are the weather conditions today?

## forbidding

This sign is **forbidding** us to swim in the pond.

Think of some words that mean the same as *forbidding*.

## forecast

The weatherman says that the **forecast** today is sunny and warm.

Why do you look at a weather forecast?

## relief

It was a **relief** that Mom found my dog, and he was okay.

Tell about a time when you felt relief.

## stranded

Patricia was **stranded** at home during the rainstorm.

Why might you be stranded in bad weather?

## Your Turn

COLLABORATE

Pick three words. Write three questions for your partner to answer.

*Go Digital!* *Use the online visual glossary*

# The Big Blizzard

?

## Essential Question

How can weather affect us?

Read how a blizzard affects the Hernandez family in New York City.

420

Rosa and Eddie Hernandez huddled close to the radio and listened carefully to the scratchy voice of the news announcer.

"The blizzard of 1947 is the biggest snowstorm in New York City history! Tremendous amounts of snow and terrible weather **conditions** caused the city's subway system to shut down yesterday from Wall Street to Spanish Harlem. Parents are even **forbidding** their children to go outside because it is so dangerous. The weather **forecast** for today predicts that the snow will stop. In the meantime, Mayor O'Dwyer's message to all New Yorkers is this: Help each other in the face of this disaster."

"Oh, mamá!" whispered Rosa. "Will papá ever get home from work?"

Mamá gave Rosa a big hug. "He must be stuck at work and unable to get home," she said. "He is **stranded**, but don't worry. The snow is slowing down now, and I'm sure he will make it home soon."

Mamá went into the kitchen to make lunch. She came out carrying her coat and scarf.

"We are out of milk and bread, so I need to try to get to Maria's Market," said mamá.

Rosa and Eddie jumped up and begged to go with her. Mamá had kept them inside for two days because it was snowing too hard to go out.

"No," said mamá. "It's too cold."

Stacey Schuett

Rosa and Eddie knew they shouldn't **argue** with mamá, but they were tired of being indoors.

"Oh please, take us outside! We can all go to the store together!" said Eddie.

"Okay," said mamá with a sigh. "But we have to stick together and stay close to each other."

Mamá helped Rosa and Eddie bundle up in their uncomfortable, but warm, wool clothes. When they got outside, they were **astonished** and amazed to find a wall of snow several feet high! Luckily, their neighbor Mr. Colón arrived with two metal shovels.

"Who wants to help dig out?" he asked.

Mamá, Rosa, and Eddie took turns shoveling snow. It was hard work, but no one fussed or **complained**. When they were done, they looked across the street. Maria's Market was still snowed in. Mrs. Sanchez, the owner, was trying to clear the snow with a small broom.

"Mr. Colón, may we borrow your shovels, *por favor*?" asked Rosa. "I think we need to give Mrs. Sanchez a hand."

Shoveling the walk in front of the store was easy. It was a piece of cake for Rosa and Eddie. They laughed and threw snowballs, too. Mrs. Sanchez was grateful for their help. "*Gracias,*" she said, and gave mamá milk and bread from her store as thanks.

As Rosa and Eddie crossed the snowy street with mamá to go home, they heard a deep, familiar voice.

"Is that my Rosa and Eddie?"

"Papá!" they shouted and ran over to him. Rosa told him breathlessly about how they helped Mr. Colón and Mrs. Sanchez.

"It is such a **relief** and a comfort to finally be home," said papá. "I am so proud of you for helping our neighbors."

## Make Connections

How does the weather affect the Hernandez family? ESSENTIAL QUESTION

Tell about a time when you or your family helped out in bad weather. TEXT TO SELF

Stacey Schuett

# Make Predictions

Use details in the story to tell, or predict, what happens next. Was your prediction right? Read on to check it. Change it if it is not right.

 **Find Text Evidence**

You may have made a prediction about *papá* as you read "The Big Blizzard." What details on page 421 helped you tell what might happen?

---

**page 421**

Street to Spanish Harlem. Parents are even **forbidding** their children to go outside because it is so dangerous. The weather **forecast** for today predicts that the snow will stop. In the meantime, Mayor O'Dwyer's message to all New Yorkers is this: Help each other in the face of this disaster."

"Oh, mamá!" whispered Rosa. "Will papá ever get home from work?"

Mamá gave Rosa a big hug. "He must be stuck at work and unable to get home," she said. "He is **stranded**, but don't worry. The snow is slowing down now, and I'm sure he will make it home soon."

Mamá went into the kitchen to make lunch. She came out carrying her coat and scarf.

"We are out of milk and bread, so I need to try to get

---

*I predicted that papá would come home soon. I read that <u>the radio announcer said the snow would stop. Mamá told Rosa that she was sure he would make it home soon.</u> I will read on to check my prediction.*

---

## Your Turn

What did you predict would happen when Mr. Colón arrived with two metal shovels? Read page 422. Was your prediction correct? Did it need to be revised?

# Theme

The theme of a story is the author's message. Think about what the characters do and say. This will help you figure out the theme.

 **Find Text Evidence**

*In "The Big Blizzard," Mayor O'Dwyer tells New Yorkers to help one another. I think this is an important detail about the theme. I will read to find more details about the characters' actions. Then I can figure out the story's theme.*

> Detail
>
> Mayor O'Dwyer's message to all New Yorkers is, "Help one another in the face of this disaster."

↓

> Detail
>
> The Hernandez family helps Mr. Colón shovel snow.

↓

> Detail

↓

> Detail

↓

> Theme

 COLLABORATE

## Your Turn

Reread "The Big Blizzard." Find more important details and write them in your graphic organizer. Then use the details to figure out the theme.

*Go Digital!*
*Use the interactive graphic organizer*

# Historical Fiction

"The Big Blizzard" is historical fiction. **Historical fiction**:
- Is a made-up story that takes place in the past
- Has illustrations that show the setting and how people lived, and often helps create a mood

## Find Text Evidence

*I can tell that "The Big Blizzard" is historical fiction. The characters and events are made up. The story is based on real events that happened in 1947 in New York City.*

page 422

Rosa and Eddie knew they shouldn't **argue** with mamá, but they were tired of being indoors.

"Oh please, take us outside! We can all go to the store together!" said Eddie.

"Okay," said mamá with a sigh. "But we have to stick together and stay close to each other."

Mamá helped Rosa and Eddie bundle up in their uncomfortable, but warm, wool clothes. When they got outside, they were **astonished** and amazed to find a wall of snow several feet high! Luckily, their neighbor Mr. Colón arrived with two metal shovels.

"Who wants to help dig out?" he asked.

Mamá, Rosa, and Eddie took turns shoveling snow. It was hard work, but no one fussed or **complained**. When they were done, they looked across the street. Maria's Market was still snowed in. Mrs. Sanchez, the owner, was trying to clear the snow with a small broom.

"Mr. Colón, may we borrow your shovels, *por favor*?" asked Rosa. "I think we need to give Mrs. Sanchez a hand."

422

The story and characters are made up, but the events could happen in real life. Events in historical fiction happened a long time ago.

Illustrations show details of the setting and how people lived.

## Your Turn

COLLABORATE

Find two details about the past in the story and in the illustrations. Talk about why "The Big Blizzard" is historical fiction.

# Idioms

An idiom is a group of words that mean something different from the meaning of each word in it. The phrase *under the weather* is an idiom. It doesn't mean someone is outside in bad weather. It means that someone feels sick.

 **Find Text Evidence**

*On page 422, the phrase* stick together *is an idiom. I can use clues in the story to help me figure out that it means "to stay close together in a group."*

Oh please, take us outside! We can all go to the store together!" said Eddie.

"Okay," said mamá." But we have to <u>stick together</u> and stay close to each other."

## Your Turn COLLABORATE

Talk about these idioms from "The Big Blizzard."
**bundle up,** *page 422*
**give Mrs. Sanchez a hand,** *page 422*
**a piece of cake,** *page 423*

Stacey Schuett

Pages 420–423

# Write About the Text

Harrison

I responded to the prompt: *Write a letter from Rosa to a relative telling how she felt during the blizzard. Use details from the text.*

**Student Model:** *Narrative Text*

**Strong Opening**
I began with an exclamation to grab the reader's attention.

**Linking Words**
I used the word *but* to connect and compare ideas.

Dear Grandma,

   Last week was scary and so exciting! We had to stay inside for two whole days because of the blizzard. At first, Eddie and I were happy to miss school, but then we felt cooped up inside. We could see piles of snow from the window, and we wanted to play in it. At last, mamá let us go outside.

McGraw-Hill Education

**Supporting Details**
I included details and descriptions from the text.

Before we could play, we had to shovel a path through the snow so mamá could get to the market. Then Eddie and I had a lot of fun throwing snowballs! It was the happiest snow day that I have ever had.

Love,

Rosa

**Grammar**

This is an **adjective that compares** more than two things.

*Grammar Handbook
See page 492.*

## Your Turn

Write a letter from mamá to a friend. Tell what she, Rosa, and Eddie did when they went out into the blizzard. Use details from the text.

*Go Digital!
Write your response online.
Use your editing checklist.*

Stacey Schuett

## Essential Question
### Why are goals important?

Go Digital!

**SUCCESS!**

Kayla had a goal. She wanted to win her race in the Special Olympics. Her goal was important to her, so she worked hard. Kayla is so proud of herself today.

▶ Goals are important.

▶ They help us focus and learn new things.

▶ Achieving our goals makes us feel good about ourselves.

## Talk About It

Write words you have learned about goals. Talk with a partner about why goals are important.

Goals

# Vocabulary

**Use the picture and the sentence to talk with a partner about each word.**

**communicated**

Mora and her friends **communicated** by writing emails to each other.

What are some ways you have communicated with friends?

**essential**

A toothbrush is an **essential** tool for cleaning teeth.

What is an *essential* tool for planting seeds?

**goal**

Nick reached his **goal** and learned to swim.

Tell about a goal that you have.

**motivated**

Jerry was **motivated** to learn to play his guitar, so he practiced every day.

What have you been motivated to learn to do?

## professional

Ted works as a **professional** police officer.

Where would a professional musician work?

## research

Melanie's mom is a scientist, and she uses a microscope to do **research**.

What animal would you like to research?

## serious

Winnie pays attention because she is **serious** about getting good grades.

What is another word for *serious*?

## specialist

Dr. Morrison is a **specialist** in sports medicine.

What does it take to be a specialist?

COLLABORATE

## Your Turn

Pick three words. Write three questions for your partner to answer.

*Go Digital!*   *Use the online visual glossary*

# ROCKETING INTO SPACE

## Essential Question

**Why are goals important?**

Read how one man used his education and experience to reach his goals.

When James A. Lovell, Jr. was a boy, he loved to build rockets and launch them into the sky. But his dreams went a lot farther than his rockets. Like many boys who grew up in the 1930s, Lovell dreamed of being a pilot. And as he watched his rockets soar, he knew someday he would, too.

# HIGH FLYING DREAMS

Lovell was born in Cleveland, Ohio, in 1928. He worked hard in school and planned to go to a special college to study **astronomy** and rockets. Unfortunately, he didn't have enough money to attend. Lovell had to figure out another way to reach his **goal**.

Lovell was **motivated** to find a way to fly rockets. So, he went to college near his home for two years and then signed up for flight training at the United States Naval Academy. After four years at the academy, Lovell joined the United States Navy and became a **professional** naval test pilot. His job was to fly planes before anyone else was allowed to fly them.

James A. Lovell, Jr. became an astronaut in 1962. He flew four space missions.

NASA

435

## PILOT TO ASTRONAUT

As a pilot, Lovell spent more than half of his flying time in jets. He taught other pilots how to fly. He also worked as a **specialist** in air flight safety. Soon, the National Aeronautics and Space Administration, or NASA, put out a call for astronauts. Lovell applied for the job because he had all the **essential** skills needed to fly into space. As a result, NASA chose him. By 1962, James Lovell was an astronaut! He had finally reached his goal.

## BIG CHALLENGES

Lovell flew on three space missions, and then, in April 1970 he became commander of the Apollo 13 mission. This was a big responsibility and a great honor. This was also one of the biggest **challenges** of Lovell's life.

Apollo 13 was supposed to land on the Moon. Two days after leaving Earth, however, the spacecraft had a **serious** problem. One of its oxygen tanks exploded. The crew did not have enough power or air to breathe. They could not make it to the Moon.

Lovell **communicated** with the experts at NASA. No one knew what to do at first. Then the team on the ground did some **research** and came up with a solution. The astronauts followed the team's directions and built an invention using plastic bags, cardboard, and tape. It worked! It cleaned the air in the spacecraft. But the next problem was even bigger. How were the astronauts going to get back to Earth?

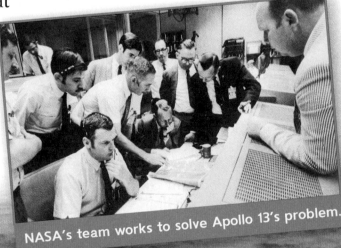

NASA's team works to solve Apollo 13's problem.

## A JOB WELL DONE

The NASA team decided the astronauts would use the **lunar,** or moon, module as a lifeboat. James and the other two astronauts climbed into the smaller spacecraft and shut the hatch tight. They moved away from the main spaceship. With little power, water, food, or heat, the astronauts listened carefully to the team at NASA.

The trip back to Earth was dangerous and scary. For almost four days, the astronauts traveled in a cramped capsule. They were cold, thirsty, and hungry. Then, with millions of people watching on television, the module fell to Earth.

The Apollo 13 crew splashed down safely on April 17, 1970.

Years later, James Lovell said that Apollo 13 taught him how important it was for people to work together. His favorite memory was when the capsule splashed down in the Pacific Ocean and the diver knocked on the window to let them know they were safe.

## A DREAM COME TRUE

DID YOU EVER DREAM OF GOING INTO SPACE? CHECK OUT SPACE CAMP!

Space camps have been around for more than 30 years. They make science, math, and technology exciting so kids will want to learn more. And like the NASA training programs, these camps teach the importance of teamwork and leadership.

## Make Connections

How did James A. Lovell's goals as a child help him as an adult? ESSENTIAL QUESTION

Tell about one of your goals and how you might achieve it. TEXT TO SELF

# Reread

Stop and think about the text as you read. Are there new facts and ideas? Do they make sense? Reread to make sure you understand.

 **Find Text Evidence**

Do you understand what James A. Lovell, Jr. did to become a pilot? Reread "High Flying Dreams" on page 435.

page 435

in 1928. He worked hard in school and planned to go to a special college to study **astronomy** and rockets. Unfortunately, he didn't have enough money to attend. Lovell had to figure out another way to reach his **goal**.

Lovell was **motivated** to find a way to fly rockets. So, he went to college near his home for two years and then signed up for flight training at the United States Naval Academy. After four years at the academy, Lovell joined the United States Navy and became a **professional** naval test pilot. His job was to fly planes before

*I read that James Lovell <u>went to college and then to the United States Naval Academy. He signed up for flight training and became a professional naval test pilot</u>. James Lovell became a pilot by going to school. He never gave up.*

## Your Turn

COLLABORATE

How did James Lovell help get his Apollo 13 space ship back home? Reread pages 436 and 437.

NASA

# Problem and Solution

Some informational texts describe a problem, tell the steps taken to solve the problem, and give the solution. Signal words, such as *problem, solution, solve,* and *as a result,* show there is a problem and the steps to a solution.

 **Find Text Evidence**

*James Lovell wanted to fly rockets but didn't have enough money to go to a special college. That was his problem. What steps did he take to solve his problem? What was the solution?*

Problem
James wanted to fly rockets, but he didn't have enough money to go to a special college.

↓

James went to college near his home.

↓

He became a test pilot.

↓

He joined NASA and became an astronaut.

↓

Solution
As an astronaut, James Lovell was able to fly in rocket ships.

**Your Turn**

Reread "Big Challenges." What was James Lovell's problem on Apollo 13? Find the steps he took to solve it and write them in your graphic organizer. Then write the solution.

*Go Digital!*
*Use the interactive graphic organizer*

# Biography

"Rocketing Into Space" is a biography. A **biography**:
- Tells the true story of a real person's life
- Is written by another person
- Includes text features such as keywords, photographs and captions

 **Find Text Evidence**

*I can tell that "Rocketing Into Space" is a biography. It is the true story of James Lovell's life. It has photographs with captions and key words that are important to the biography.*

**page 436**

### PILOT TO ASTRONAUT

As a pilot, Lovell spent more than half of his flying time in jets. He taught other pilots how to fly. He also worked as a **specialist** in air flight safety. Soon, the National Aeronautics and Space Administration, or NASA, put out a call for astronauts. Lovell applied for the job because he had all the **essential** skills needed to fly into space. As a result, NASA chose him. By 1962, James Lovell was an astronaut! He had finally reached his goal.

### BIG CHALLENGES

Lovell flew on three space missions, and then, in April 1970 he became commander of the Apollo 13 mission. This was a big responsibility and a great honor. This was also one of the biggest **challenges** of Lovell's life.

Apollo 13 was supposed to land on the Moon. Two days after leaving Earth, however, the spacecraft had a **serious** problem. One of its oxygen tanks exploded. The crew did not have enough power or air to breathe. They could not make it to the Moon.

Lovell **communicated** with the experts at NASA. No one knew what to do at first. Then the team on the ground did some **research** and came up with a solution. The astronauts followed the team's directions and built an invention using plastic bags, cardboard, and tape. It worked! It cleaned the air in the spacecraft. But the next problem was even bigger. How were the astronauts going to get back to Earth?

NASA's team works to solve Apollo 13's problem.

436

## Text Features

**Keywords** Keywords are important words. They are in dark type.

**Photographs** Photographs and their captions show more about the events in the person's life.

COLLABORATE

## Your Turn

Find another keyword. Why is this an important word in James Lovell's biography?

# Greek and Latin Roots

Many words have word parts, such as Greek or Latin roots, in them. The Greek root *astro* means "star," and *naut* means "ship." The Latin root *luna* means "moon."

 **Find Text Evidence**

*On page 435, I see the word* astronomy. *I remember that* astro *comes from a Greek root that means "star." I think* astronomy *must have something to do with the stars. It may mean "the study of the stars."*

He worked hard in school and planned to go to a special college to study astronomy and rockets.

## Your Turn

Use the Greek or Latin roots to figure out the meaning of each word.

astronauts, *page 436*
lunar, *page 437*

NASA

# Write About the Text

Pages 434–437

Yusuf

I answered the question: *What does the author want readers to understand from this biography? Use text evidence to support your answer.*

## Student Model: *Informative Text*

**Focus on a Topic**
I introduced the topic in my first sentence.

   The author wants to show readers that James Lovell became a success through hard work. As a boy, his dream was to be a pilot. Lovell studied hard. He wanted to go to a special college to study rockets, but he couldn't afford it. Instead, Lovell went to another college for two years.

**Ideas in Order**
I used sequence to order the events.

MHImages/iStock/360/Getty Images

Then he joined the United States Navy and became a test pilot. By 1962, Lovell had successfully reached his goal. He was an astronaut! The author describes how James Lovell continued to work hard as an astronaut.

**Grammar**

The **adverb** *successfully* tells how James Lovell reached his goal.

*Grammar Handbook* See page 493.

**Strong Conclusion**
My concluding statement restates the main idea of the paragraph.

## Your Turn

How did Lovell handle the problems he had during his life? Use text evidence to support your answer.

*Go Digital!*
*Write your response online.*
*Use your editing checklist.*

NASA

### Essential Question

How can learning about animals help you respect them?

Go Digital!

Peter Dazeley/Photographer's Choice/Getty Images

# Respecting Animals

My name is Max and I'm a Great Horned Owl. My job here at the wildlife preserve is to help kids like Nora learn all about owls. All animals deserve respect.

▶ Learning about animals helps you respect them.

▶ The more you know about animals, the more you can do to help them.

## Talk About It

Write words you have learned about respecting animals. Talk with a partner about ways you can help protect animals.

(r)Taylor S. Kennedy/National Geographic RF/Getty Images

# Vocabulary

Use the picture and the sentence to talk with a partner about each word.

**endangered**

The giant panda is an **endangered** animal and needs to be protected.

Name another endangered animal.

**fascinating**

Maya thought the butterflies on her shirt were **fascinating** and interesting.

Tell about something you find fascinating.

**illegal**

The sign says it is **illegal** to swim here because the beach is closed.

What word means the opposite of illegal?

**inhabit**

Many animals, including moose, **inhabit** forests.

What animals inhabit the ocean?

**requirement**

Food is an important **requirement** for all living things.

Name another requirement for living things.

**respected**

The players **respected** their football coach because he was smart and fair.

Who is respected in your school?

**unaware**

The Karr family is **unaware** that there is a giraffe watching them.

What word means the opposite of unaware?

**wildlife**

Zebras are one kind of **wildlife** that live in Africa.

What kind of wildlife lives near your home?

## Your Turn

COLLABORATE

Pick three words. Write three questions for your partner to answer.

*Go Digital!* *Use the online visual glossary*

# Butterflies
## Big and Small

## ? Essential Question

**How can learning about animals help you respect them?**

Read how respecting butterflies can help them survive.

Monarch butterflies like to land in the same trees when they migrate.

There are more than 725 species, or kinds, of butterflies fluttering around the United States and Canada. These **fascinating** creatures taste leaves with their feet and only see the colors red, yellow, and green. The Monarch butterfly and the Western Pygmy Blue butterfly share these same traits, but they are also different in many ways.

## Size and Color

The Western Pygmy Blue butterfly is the smallest butterfly in the world. It is just about a half-inch across from wing tip to wing tip. That's smaller than a dime!

Monarch butterflies are much bigger. They measure about four inches across.

Size is not the only way Monarchs are different from Pygmy Blues. Monarch butterflies are a bright orange color with black markings. That makes them easy to see. Pygmy Blue butterflies are mostly brown and blue, and they blend in with their surroundings. Many people walk right by Pygmy Blues, **unaware** that they are even there.

This diagram shows the parts of a butterfly.

### Western Pygmy Blue Butterfly

wing

antennae

head

thorax

leg

abdomen

# Moving Around

Almost all butterflies migrate, or move to different areas. The Monarch's journey is the longest migration of any butterfly in the world. It spends summers in the northern United States and Canada. Then it migrates south to Mexico in early fall. Many Monarchs travel more than 3,000 miles.

Western Pygmy Blue butterflies **inhabit** southwestern deserts and marshes from California to Texas. They migrate short distances north to Oregon, and also to Arkansas, and Nebraska.

Both Monarchs and Blue Pygmies migrate when the weather gets chilly. Butterflies are cold-blooded insects. They are hot when the weather is hot and cold when the weather is cold. As a result, both butterflies migrate to stay warm. They also journey north or south to find food.

# Finding Food

The Western Pygmy Blue drinks the nectar of many kinds of flowers. It finds the sweet, thick liquid easily, so its population has steadily grown. However, Monarch butterflies are not so lucky.

This Western Pygmy Blue butterfly stops to eat.

**Butterfly Migration**

CANADA
Great Lakes

UNITED STATES

Pacific Ocean

MEXICO

N
W — E
S

**Map Key**
← Monarch butterfly migration route
← Western Pygmy Blue butterfly migration route

Just like the Pygmy Blue, Monarch butterflies sip nectar from flowers. But the Monarch butterfly has one main food **requirement** — the milkweed. Monarch butterflies must find this plant along their migration route. But what happens if there are no milkweed leaves?

When people build houses and roads, there are fewer places for Monarchs to find milkweed. If the Monarch cannot find food, its population will decrease. The Western Pygmy Blue and Monarch butterflies are not **endangered**, or at risk for becoming extinct now, but biologists are worried. Many other butterflies are endangered because people destroy their habitats.

# Help Butterflies

Like all **wildlife**, Monarch and Pygmy Blue butterflies should be **respected**. People need to preserve butterfly habitats. To help, they can work to change laws, plant milkweed, and make it **illegal** to destroy animal habitats.

Learning about butterflies and what they need to survive is important. That way there will be plenty of Western Pygmy Blue and Monarch butterflies for future generations to enjoy.

Monarch butterflies feed on milkweed.

## Make Connections

How can people learn to respect butterflies? **ESSENTIAL QUESTION**

Talk about some butterflies you've seen. How are they alike and different? **TEXT TO SELF**

# Reread

Stop and think about the text as you read. Are there new facts and ideas? Do they make sense? Reread to make sure you understand.

 **Find Text Evidence**

Do you understand some ways the Monarch butterfly is different from the Western Pygmy Blue butterfly? Reread "Size and Color" on page 449.

page 449

There are more than 725 species, or kinds, of butterflies fluttering around the United States and Canada. These **fascinating** creatures taste leaves with their feet and only see the colors red, yellow, and green. The Monarch butterfly and the Western Pygmy Blue butterfly share these same traits, but they are also different in many ways.

**Size and Color**

The Western Pygmy Blue butterfly is the smallest butterfly in the world. It is just about a half-inch across from wing tip to wing tip. That's smaller than a dime!

Monarch butterflies are much bigger. They measure about four inches across.

Size is not the only way Monarchs are different from Pygmy Blues. Monarch butterflies are a bright orange color with black markings. That makes them easy to see. Pygmy Blue butterflies are mostly brown and blue, and they blend in with their surroundings. Many people walk right by Pygmy Blues, **unaware** that they are even there.

*I read that <u>the Western Pygmy Blue butterfly is smaller than a dime and is mostly brown and blue in color. The Monarch butterfly is about four inches wide and is orange and black.</u> Now I understand some of the ways these two butterflies are different.*

COLLABORATE

## Your Turn

How are Monarch butterflies and Western Pygmy Blue butterflies alike? Reread "Moving Around" on page 450 to find out.

# Compare and Contrast

When authors compare, they show how two things are alike. When authors contrast, they tell how the things are different. Authors use signal words, such as *both, alike, same,* or *different,* to compare and contrast.

## Find Text Evidence

*How are the Monarch butterfly and Western Pygmy Blue butterfly alike and different? I will reread "Butterflies Big and Small" and look for signal words.*

Monarch Butterflies — Colorful and big

Both — Taste leaves with their feet

Western Pygmy Blue Butterflies — Blend in with their surroundings, very small

COLLABORATE

## Your Turn

Reread "Butterflies Big and Small." Find details that tell how Monarch butterflies and Western Pygmy Blue butterflies are alike and different. Write them in the graphic organizer. What signal words helped you?

*Go Digital!*
*Use the interactive graphic organizer*

# Expository Text

"Butterflies Big and Small" is an expository text.
**Expository text**:

- May give information about a science topic
- Has headings that tell what a section is about
- Includes text features such as diagrams and maps

## Find Text Evidence

*I can tell that "Butterflies Big and Small" is expository text. It give facts about Monarch and Western Pygmy Blue butterflies. This science article also has headings, a diagram, and a map.*

page 449

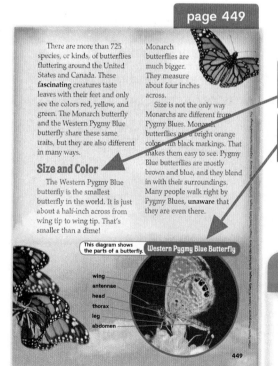

There are more than 725 species, or kinds, of butterflies fluttering around the United States and Canada. These **fascinating** creatures taste leaves with their feet and only see the colors red, yellow, and green. The Monarch butterfly and the Western Pygmy Blue butterfly share these same traits, but they are also different in many ways.

### Size and Color

The Western Pygmy Blue butterfly is the smallest butterfly in the world. It is just about a half-inch across from wing tip to wing tip. That's smaller than a dime!

Monarch butterflies are much bigger. They measure about four inches across.

Size is not the only way Monarchs are different from Pygmy Blues. Monarch butterflies are a bright orange color with black markings. That makes them easy to see. Pygmy Blue butterflies are mostly brown and blue, and they blend in with their surroundings. Many people walk right by Pygmy Blues, **unaware** that they are even there.

This diagram shows the parts of a butterfly.    Western Pygmy Blue Butterfly

wing
antennae
head
thorax
leg
abdomen

449

## Text Features

**Headings**  Headings tell what a section of text is mostly about.

**Diagram**  A diagram is a simple picture with labels.

COLLABORATE

## Your Turn

Look at the text features in "Butterflies Big and Small." Tell your partner about something you learned.

# Context Clues

Context clues are words or phrases that help you figure out the meaning of an unfamiliar word. In many science texts, context clues appear in the same paragraph as an unfamiliar word.

 **Find Text Evidence**

*On page 450, I'm not sure what the word* migrate *means. I will look for clues in the paragraph. I read that butterflies "move to different areas" and "travel more than 3,000 miles." I also see the word "journey." I think* migrate *means to move or travel to different places.*

Almost all butterflies migrate, or move to different areas. The Monarch's journey is the longest migration of any butterfly in the world. It spends summers in the northern United States and Canada. Then it migrates south to Mexico in early fall. Many Monarchs travel more than 3,000 miles.

## Your Turn

COLLABORATE

Find context clues. Use them to figure out the meanings of the following words.

**cold-blooded,** *page 450*
**nectar,** *page 451*

Don Farrall/Photographer's Choice RF/Getty Images

# Write About the Text

Pages 448–451

Collin

I responded to the prompt: *Describe butterfly migration. Use evidence from the text.*

**Student Model:** *Informative Text*

**Main Idea**
My topic sentence explains why it is important for butterflies to migrate.

> Most butterflies migrate to stay warm. That is because they are cold-blooded. The Monarch butterfly flies longer than any other butterfly when it migrates. Monarchs live in the northern United States and Canada in summer. When it gets chilly in the fall, they fly all the way to Mexico.

**Grammar**

This is an example of an **adverb that compares.**

*Grammar Handbook* See page 494.

Western Pygmy Blue butterflies do not fly as far. They migrate from the southwestern United States to Oregon, Arkansas, and Nebraska. These routes may seem very long, but butterflies must travel that far in order to survive.

**Supporting Details**
I developed the topic with evidence from the text.

**Strong Conclusion**
My final sentence sums up why it is important for butterflies to migrate.

## Your Turn

How did text features, such as the map on page 450, help you understand the article?

*Go Digital!*
*Write your response online.*
*Use your editing checklist.*

## Essential Question
## What makes you laugh?

*Go Digital!*

Bob Elsdale/Photonica/Getty Images

# LET'S LAUGH

Lots of things make you laugh - jokes, funny stories, silly pictures. Just look at these pink pigs. Aren't they funny?

▶ Having a good sense of humor is important.

▶ Laughing makes you feel good.

▶ Laughing helps you share feelings with friends.

## Talk About It

Talk with a partner about what you think is humorous. Write words about things that make you laugh.

Humorous

# Vocabulary

Use the picture and the sentence to talk with a partner about each word.

**entertainment**

Grandpa and Devon think playing chess is great **entertainment**.

What do you like to do for entertainment?

**humorous**

Evan couldn't stop laughing at Nick's **humorous** story.

Tell a humorous story to a partner.

**ridiculous**

Jess wore a **ridiculous** clown nose and made his friends giggle.

What is another word for *ridiculous*?

**slithered**

The long, thin snake **slithered** across the floor.

Move your hands to show what slithered looks like.

# Poetry Words

## narrative poem

My favorite **narrative poem** tells about Paul Revere's ride.

What story would you tell in a narrative poem?

## rhyme

The words *moon* and *spoon* **rhyme** because they end in the same sound.

Name another word that rhymes with *moon* and *spoon*.

## rhythm

Ben's poem has a **rhythm** that sounds like a drumbeat.

Why might a poet include rhythm in a poem?

## stanza

Each **stanza** in Maggie's poem has five lines.

Write a poem with two stanzas.

COLLABORATE

## Your Turn

Pick three words. Then write three questions for your partner to answer.

*Go Digital!* **Use the online visual glossary**

# The Camping Trip

We roughed it at Old Piney Park,
With tents and hot dogs after dark.

I'd barely yawned and gone to sleep,
When I felt something creep, creep, creep.

A slimy something crawled on me,
Across my toe, up to my knee.

## ? Essential Question

**What makes you laugh?**

Read two poems about funny situations.

Daryll Collins

462

Ridiculous! Hard to believe,
That creature slithered up my sleeve.

It was not humorous or fun.
I hollered "Rattlesnake! Let's run!"

We all jumped up and stomped around,
Our tent collapsed flat on the ground.

Ten flashlights clicked on to reveal,
That creepy crawly by my heel.

I blushed bright red, "Oops, I was wrong."
Snake?
No, a lizard—one-inch long.

— Constance Andrea Keremes

463

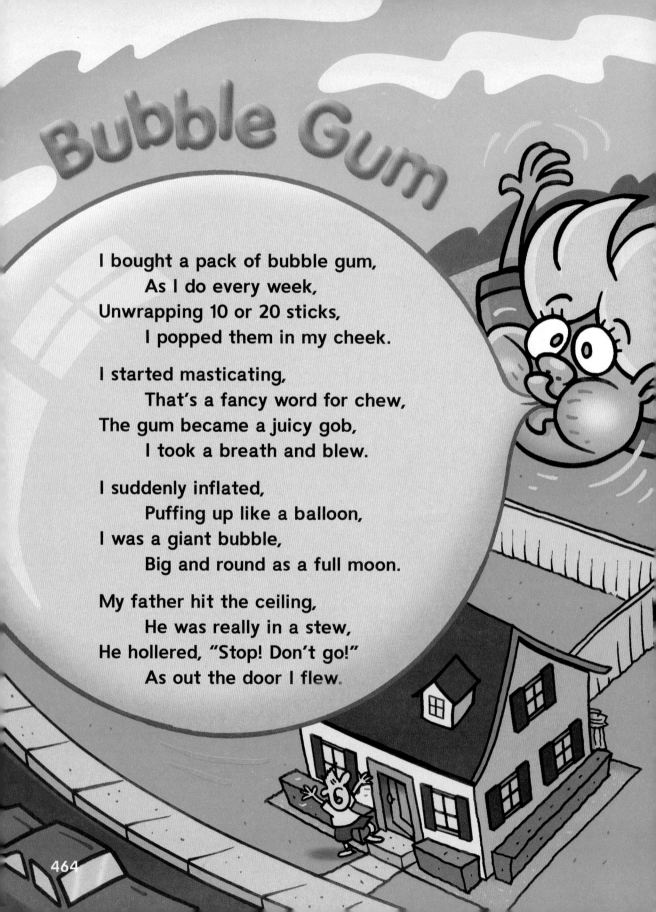

# Bubble Gum

I bought a pack of bubble gum,
    As I do every week,
Unwrapping 10 or 20 sticks,
    I popped them in my cheek.

I started masticating,
    That's a fancy word for chew,
The gum became a juicy gob,
    I took a breath and blew.

I suddenly inflated,
    Puffing up like a balloon,
I was a giant bubble,
    Big and round as a full moon.

My father hit the ceiling,
    He was really in a stew,
He hollered, "Stop! Don't go!"
    As out the door I flew.

The neighbors' eyes were popping.
    They dropped everything to see.
I was the entertainment of the day.
    Forget about TV.

If you like bubble gum, beware—
    Chew just one stick a day,
Or you'll become a bubble, too
    And float up   Up   AWAY!

I saw my friends below me,
    And let loose a mighty roar.
WHOOSH!
All my air blew out,
    And I was just a kid once more.

— Diana Kent

## Make Connections

Which poem made you laugh? Talk about what funny thing happens in each of the poems. ESSENTIAL QUESTION

Which poem has the funniest events or characters? TEXT TO SELF

# Narrative Poem

**Narrative** poetry: • Tells a story. • Can have any number of lines and stanzas.

A **stanza**: • Is a group of lines that form part of a poem.
• Often has rhyme and rhythm.

## Find Text Evidence

*I can tell that "Bubble Gum" is a narrative poem. It tells a story. It also has stanzas. Each stanza has four lines. The second and fourth lines rhyme.*

page 464

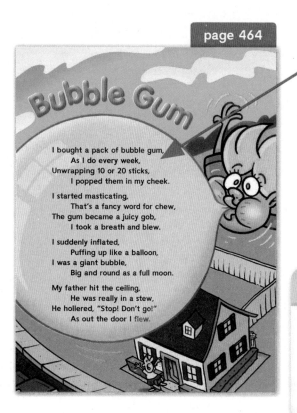

Bubble Gum

I bought a pack of bubble gum,
    As I do every week,
Unwrapping 10 or 20 sticks,
    I popped them in my cheek.

I started masticating,
    That's a fancy word for chew,
The gum became a juicy gob,
    I took a breath and blew.

I suddenly inflated,
    Puffing up like a balloon,
I was a giant bubble,
    Big and round as a full moon.

My father hit the ceiling,
    He was really in a stew,
He hollered, "Stop! Don't go!"
    As out the door I flew.

*This is a stanza. It is a group of lines. There are four stanzas on this page.*

COLLABORATE

## Your Turn

Reread the poem "The Camping Trip." Explain why it is a narrative poem. Tell how many stanzas are in it.

# Point of View

Point of view in a poem is what the narrator thinks about an event, a thing, or a person. Look for details that show the narrator's point of view.

 **Find Text Evidence**

*In "The Camping Trip" I read that the narrator feels something creeping on him. He calls it slimy. He says it slithered. The details tell me he is either afraid of or dislikes small, creepy crawly things. This is the narrator's point of view.*

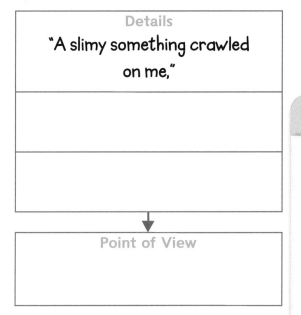

Details

"A slimy something crawled on me,"

↓

Point of View

COLLABORATE

**Your Turn**

Reread "The Camping Trip." Find more details about how the narrator feels about the creepy creature. Write them in the graphic organizer. Then write the narrator's point of view. Do you agree with the narrator's point of view? Why or why not?

*Go Digital!*
*Use the interactive graphic organizer*

# Rhythm and Rhyme

Poets use rhythm and rhyme make a poem interesting to listen to and fun to read.

 **Find Text Evidence**

Reread the poem "Bubble Gum" on pages 464–465 aloud. Listen for words that rhyme. Clap your hands as you read the poem to follow the poem's rhythm.

page 464

I bought a pack of bubble gum,
    As I do every week,
Unwrapping 10 or 20 sticks,
    I popped them in my cheek.

I started masticating,
    That's a fancy word for chew,

*In the second and fourth lines of the poem, the words* week *and* cheek *rhyme. I clapped my hands to find the rhythm. I like the way the poem has a pattern of sounds that repeat themselves.*

COLLABORATE

## Your Turn

Find more examples of rhythm and rhyme in "The Camping Trip" on pages 462–463.

Daryll Collins

# Idioms

An idiom is a group of words that means something different from the usual meaning of each word in it. The phrase *lend a hand* is an idiom. It doesn't mean "to give someone your hand." It means "to help someone do something."

**Find Text Evidence**

*On page 462 in "The Camping Trip," the phrase* roughed it *is an idiom. I can use clues in the poem to help me figure out that it means "to live without the usual comforts of home."*

page 462

We *roughed it* at Old Piney Park,
With tents and hot dogs after dark.

**Your Turn**

COLLABORATE

Talk about these idioms from "Bubble Gum."
**hit the ceiling,** *page 464*
**eyes were popping,** *page 465*

Daryll Collins

# Write About the Text

Pages 462–465

Jen

I responded to the prompt: *Write a narrative poem about something that is funny. Include rhyme or rhythm.*

**Rhyme**
I used rhymes, such as *play* and *clay,* to make the poem fun to read.

**Grammar**

This **preposition** tells where Mom was taking the dirty clothes.

*Grammar Handbook See page 495.*

---

**Student Model:** *Narrative Text*

### A Trick on Mom

One Saturday morning my cousin

came over to play.

As my mom cleaned the house and

swished the broom,

We built a fort with boxes.

We   made animals out of clay.

Then we saw Mom taking dirty

clothes to the laundry room.

"Quick! Let's hide behind the door!"

Tara said.

When Mom came in, we popped

out and screeched, "Boo!"

Mom gasped and dropped the

clothes. She yelled, "Whoops!"

We all laughed, but then

Mom gave us all the

folding to do!

## Dialogue and Description
I used dialogue and described events to tell the story.

## Precise Words
I used strong verbs to help readers visualize the action.

## Your Turn

Write your own narrative poem about something funny. Include rhyme or rhythm.

*Go Digital!*
*Write your response online.*
*Use your editing checklist.*

# Contents

# Sentences

## Sentences and Fragments

A **complete sentence** is a group of words that tells a complete thought. A **sentence fragment** is a group of words that does not tell a complete thought.

*The rocket. (does not tell a complete thought)*
*The rocket soars into the clouds. (tells a complete thought)*

**Your Turn** Write each group of words. Tell whether it is "complete" or "fragment." Write it.

1. My little brother.
2. My father takes a picture.
3. The engines roar.

## Types of Sentences

When you write or talk, you use different kinds of sentences.

| | |
|---|---|
| A **statement** tells something. It ends with a period. | *My father likes to cook.* |
| A **question** asks something. It ends with a question mark. | *What are we having for lunch?* |
| A **command** tells you to do something and ends in a period. | *Help me set the table.* |
| An **exclamation** shows strong feeling. It ends with an exclamation mark. | *This will be the best meal ever!* |

**Your Turn** Write each sentence. Tell what type it is.

1. Can my friend join us for dinner?
2. Pasta is his favorite meal.
3. I can't believe how hungry we are!
4. Call us when it's ready.

## Subjects in Sentences

Every sentence has two parts. The **complete subject** in a sentence tells what or whom the sentence is about. The complete subject of a sentence can be more than one word.

*Rain* pours down from the sky.
*All of my friends* run for cover.

**Your Turn** Write each sentence. Draw a line under the complete subject of each sentence.

1. Lightning flashes.
2. Thunder rumbles in the distance.
3. A gust of wind shakes the tree.
4. Sheets of rain strike the window.
5. Do storms like these happen often?

## Predicates in Sentences

Every sentence has a subject and a **predicate**. The **complete predicate** tells what the subject does or is. The complete predicate can be one or more words.

The dog **howled**.
The girl **will feed him dinner**.

**Your Turn** Write each sentence. Draw a line under the complete predicate of each sentence.

1. The cat sneezes.
2. The bird flaps its wings.
3. The thirsty dog pushes his bowl.
4. My friends and I laugh.
5. Did the dog smile?

# Sentences

## Simple Sentences

A simple sentence expresses only one idea. It contains only one subject and one predicate.

*The young man wants to fly airplanes.*

**Your Turn** Write each sentence. Circle the subject and underline the predicate.

1. He reads about airplanes.
2. His friend was a pilot.
3. The man enrolls in a training program.
4. All of his classmates share his interest.
5. It will be quite an adventure!

## Compound Sentences

A **compound sentence** expresses two or more complete thoughts, which are **combined** using a comma and a **coordinating conjunction**. A coordinating conjunction is a small word that links two things, such as *and, but,* or *or.*

*I walk to school. You ride the bus. (two simple sentences)*
*I walk to school, **but** you ride the bus. (one compound sentence)*

**Your Turn** Write each pair of simple sentences as a compound sentence.

1. Sam runs down the hall. The dog chases him.
2. Tara goes outside. It starts to rain.
3. Tara gets a ride. Sam decides to walk in the rain.
4. The school bell rings. The students go inside.
5. The rain turns to snow. Students are sent home early.

## Complex Sentences

A **complex sentence** has an independent clause and one or more dependent clauses. An **independent clause** contains a subject and predicate and tells a complete thought.

A **dependent clause** contains a subject and predicate, and begins with a **subordinating conjunction**, such as *after, although, before, because, if, since, until, when, where, while.* Place a **comma** after the dependent clause when it is at the start of a sentence. *When we got there, the game began.*

**Your Turn** Write each sentence. Circle the independent clause. Underline the dependent clause.

1. People stopped to talk when they saw us there.
2. Because we sold so many, we raised a lot of money.

## Run-On Sentences

A **run-on sentence** contains two or more independent clauses without the proper conjunctions or punctuation.

*I cooked dinner my family liked it they asked for seconds.*
You can correct run-on sentences using these strategies.

| | |
|---|---|
| Break the independent clauses into separate sentences. | *I cooked dinner. My family liked it. They asked for seconds.* |
| Create a compound subject or compound predicate. | *I cooked dinner. My family liked it and asked for seconds.* |
| Create a compound sentence using coordinating conjunctions. | *I cooked dinner, and my family liked it. They asked for seconds.* |
| Create a complex sentence using subordinating conjunctions. | *I cooked dinner. Since my family liked it, they asked for seconds.* |

**Your Turn** Correct each run-on sentence.

1. This was my first time cooking my mother helped.
2. Did you make the dessert I didn't have time.
3. I cooked the meal I didn't have to do the dishes.

# Nouns

## Common and Proper Nouns

A **noun** names a person, place, thing, or idea. A **common noun** names any person, place, or thing. A **proper noun** names a particular person, place, or thing, and begins with a capital letter.

> The **student** studied the **atlas**. (common)
> **Tom** located **Mount Rushmore**. (proper)

**Your Turn** Write each sentence. Underline each common noun. Circle each proper noun.

1. The book had many maps.
2. Can Joanne find our state?
3. Which country in Africa did your parents visit?
4. The library has a huge globe.

## Concrete and Abstract Nouns

A **concrete noun** names a person, place, or thing that can be seen or touched. An **abstract noun** names a quality, concept, or idea that cannot be seen or touched. Many abstract nouns have no plural form.

> **Barbara** set the **book** on the **desk**. (concrete)
> **Reading** gives me great **joy**. (abstract)

**Your Turn** Write each sentence. Underline each concrete noun. Circle each abstract noun.

1. My cousin is afraid of the dark.
2. The dog slept under his bed.
3. His father read for an hour.
4. Silence filled the house.

## Singular and Plural Nouns

A **singular noun** names one person, place, thing, or idea. A **plural noun** names more than one. Add -s to form the plural of most nouns. Add -es to form the plural of nouns ending in s, x, ch, or sh. If a noun ends in a consonant + y, change y to i and add -es. If a noun ends in a vowel + y, add -s. If a noun ends in -f, you sometimes change f to v and add -es.

girl girls      store stores      bench benches
city cities      key keys      leaf leaves

**Your Turn** Write each sentence. Underline each singular noun. Circle each plural noun.

1. My mother bought two jackets.
2. Look at those hats near the door.
3. The boys found bats and balls.

## Special Plurals and Collective Nouns

Some nouns change their spelling to name more than one. Others don't change at all.

man men      woman women      child children
tooth teeth      mouse mice      foot feet
fish fish      sheep sheep      goose geese
moose moose      deer deer

A **collective noun** names a group that acts together as one thing. It can be singular or plural.
*Our **band** will play after the three other **bands**.*

**Your Turn** Write each sentence. Use the correct form of the noun in ( ).

1. As a joke, we played "Three Blind (Mouse)" first.
2. All the (man) and (woman) laughed.
3. (Child) danced in front of the stage.

# Nouns

## Singular and Plural Possessive Nouns

A **possessive noun** is a noun that shows who or what owns or has something. Add an **apostrophe (')** + *s* to a singular noun to make it possessive.

> My **dentist's** office is in my **uncle's** town.

Add an **apostrophe** to the end of most plural nouns to make them possessive. Add an **apostrophe** + *s* to form the plural of possessive nouns that don't end in *-s*.

> The **children's** mother visited three **teachers'** rooms.

**Your Turn** Write each sentence. Change the word in ( ) into a possessive noun.

1. I like listening to my (parents) stories.
2. They talk about my (family) adventures.
3. They told me about my (aunt) wedding.
4. My mother sat at the (children) table.

## Combining Sentences: Nouns

Two sentences can be combined by joining two nouns in the subject or predicate with the conjunction *and*.

> Kendra went to her room. Scott went to his room. Kendra **and** Scott went to their rooms.

**Your Turn** Combine the nouns in the sentence pairs to form one sentence.

1. Dad went to the city. Mom went to the city.
2. Dad visited a museum. Dad visited a gallery.
3. They saw a movie. They saw a jazz concert.
4. Did Mom enjoy it? Did Dad enjoy it?

# Verbs

## Action Verbs

An **action verb** is a word that shows action. Some action verbs tell about actions that are hard to see.

*The boy **dreamed** that he **scored** the winning goal.*

**Your Turn** Write each sentence. Underline each action verb.

1. He practices hard every day.
2. The team runs across the field.
3. The coach carries a bag of soccer balls.
4. He drops one and kicks it hard.
5. Look at how quickly the team chases it!

## Linking Verbs

A **linking verb** does not express action. A linking verb connects a subject to another part of the sentence. The most common present-tense linking verbs are *am, are,* and *is.* The most common past-tense linking verbs are *was* and *were.*

*Roberto **is** a writer. His last two books **were** wonderful.*

**Your Turn** Write each sentence and underline each linking verb.

1. Carla is a fast reader.
2. Her book shelves are full.
3. Both of her parents are teachers.
4. They were happy to loan us books.
5. Carla learned to read when she was four years old.

481

# Verbs

## Present-Tense Verbs

**Present-tense verbs** tell what is happening now. When the subject is not *I* or *you,* add *-s* to tell what one person or thing is doing. Add *-es* to verbs that end in *sh, ch, s, z,* or *x.* Change *y* to *i* and add *-es* to verbs that end with a consonant and *y.*

> Jen **looks** up and **watches** the birds. She **studies** them.

**Your Turn** Write each sentence in the present tense. Use the correct form of the verb in ( ).

1. My older sister (know) how to repair things.
2. She (fix) clocks and watches.
3. My sister (try) to figure out what's wrong.
4. She (make) a list and (cross) out each item.

## Past-Tense Verbs

**Past-tense verbs** tell about an action that has already happened. Add *-ed* to most verbs to form the past tense.

> The farmer **planted** the seeds last week.

If the verb ends in a consonant plus *y,* change the *y* to *i* before adding *-ed.* If the verb ends with a vowel and a consonant, double the final consonant before adding *-ed.* If the verb ends with a consonant and *e,* drop the *e* before adding *-ed.*

> She **raised** her cup and **sipped** from the cup she **carried.**

**Your Turn** Write each sentence in the past tense. Use the correct form of the verb in ( ).

1. We (hurry) to finish our work.
2. She (want) to be done before dark.
3. The farmer (tug) at the weeds.
4. She and I (care) for the plants every day.

## Future-Tense Verbs

A **future-tense verb** tells about action that is going to happen. Use the verb *will* to write about the future.

*My family **will visit** the park this weekend.*

**Your Turn** Write each sentence in the future tense. Use the correct form of the verb in ( ).

1. Next summer I (take) my first train ride.
2. My family (cross) the country by car.
3. We (stay) with my grandparents.
4. My sister and I (learn) how to sail.
5. It (be) the best summer vacation ever!

## Subject-Verb Agreement

A **present-tense verb** must agree with its subject. Do not add *-s* or *-es* to a present-tense verb when the subject is plural or *I* or *you*.

*My **sister sends** me a message, and **I answer** right away.*

**Your Turn** Write each sentence in the present tense. Use the correct form of each verb in ( ).

1. She (write) e-mails quickly.
2. My brother (spend) all day on the phone.
3. My mother (wish) he would clean his room.
4. "I'll do it later," he (say).
5. My sister (advise) him to do it now.

# Verbs

## Verbs *Be, Do,* and *Have*

The verbs *be, do,* and *have* have special forms.

| Subject | Present Tense | Past Tense |
|---|---|---|
| I | am, do, have | was, did, had |
| You | are, do, have | were, did, had |
| Singular subjects | is, does, has | was, did, had |
| We | are, do, have | were, did, had |
| Plural subjects | are, do, have | were, did, had |

> I **am** happy with my phone, but his phone **has** a problem.
> **Were** the pages you **had** clear, or **did** you need new ones?

**Your Turn** Write each sentence. Use the correct form of the verb in ( ).

1. You (be) beginning to feel sleepy now.
2. I (be) standing beside you.
3. Your brother (have) an alarm clock once.
4. Where (do) he keep it now?

## Main and Helping Verbs

Sometimes a verb can be more than one word. The **main verb** tells what the subject is or does. The **helping verb** helps the main verb show an action. *Have* and *be* can be used as helping verbs.

> Beth **is writing** a letter. She **had sent** one already.

**Your Turn** Write each sentence. Circle the helping verb. Underline the main verb.

1. We are going on a field trip.
2. The class will visit a television studio.
3. My cousin has worked there for years.

## Contractions with *Not*

A **contraction** combines a verb with the word *not*. An **apostrophe (')** takes the place of the missing letters. Some contractions have irregular spellings, such as *won't* (will not) and *can't* (cannot).

> Carol **isn't** feeling well. She **hasn't** eaten all day.

**Your Turn** **Write each sentence. Combine the two words in ( ) to form a contraction.**

1. She (did not) bring a lunch today.
2. I (do not) understand why.
3. This (is not) the first time.
4. She (does not) know if she should buy lunch.
5. (Will not) someone share a sandwich with her?

## Combining Sentences: Verbs

When two sentences have the same subject, you can combine the predicates. Use the conjunction **and** to join the predicates.

> *Joe runs to the door. Joe opens it.*
> *Joe runs to the door and opens it.*

**Your Turn** **Combine the predicates in the sentence pairs to form one sentence.**

1. The boy stumbled. The boy fell.
2. The teacher raced over. The teacher helped him up.
3. He brushed off his clothes. He laughed.
4. The boy went to the bench. He sat down.
5. We went over. We made sure he was fine.

# Verbs

## Irregular Verbs

An **irregular verb** has a special spelling to show the past tense. Some verbs have a special spelling when used with the helping verb *have*.

| Present | Past | Past with the verb *have* |
|---|---|---|
| am/are/is (be) | was/were | been |
| begin | began | begun |
| bring | brought | brought |
| come | came | come |
| do/does (do) | did | done |
| eat | ate | eaten |
| give | gave | given |
| go | went | gone |
| grow | grew | grown |
| hide | hid | hidden |
| run | ran | run |
| say | said | said |
| see | saw | seen |
| sing | sang | sung |
| sit | sat | sat |
| tell | told | told |

**Your Turn** Write each sentence. Use the correct form of the verb in ( ).

1. Last night, our show (begin) late.
2. The audience (sit) patiently in their seats.
3. My parents had (come) to see the show.
4. I (tell) them to sit near the front.
5. They have (see) me in many plays before.

# Pronouns

## Pronouns

**Pronouns** take the place of nouns. A **personal pronoun** refers to specific people or things. An **indefinite pronoun** does not refer to specific people or things.

Personal pronouns: *I, you, he, she, it, we, they, me, her, him, us, them*

Common indefinite pronouns: *anyone, anything, everyone, no one, nothing, somebody, something*

> *We promised to tell no one. I won't say anything about it.*

**Your Turn** **Write each sentence. Circle the personal pronouns. Underline the indefinite pronouns.**

1. We talked to the police officer.
2. Something didn't seem right to us.
3. She gave me a phone number to call.
4. I could talk to anyone at the station.
5. "They want to help everyone," she told us.

## Singular and Plural Pronouns

**Singular pronouns** include *I, you, he, she, it, me, her,* and *him.* Indefinite pronouns are usually treated as singular.

**Plural pronouns** include *we, you, they, us,* and *them.*

> *He gives **them** money. **They** give **him** change. **Everybody** is happy.*

**Your Turn** **Write each sentence. Circle the singular pronouns. Underline the plural pronouns.**

1. We wanted to give my mother a gift.
2. I found it on sale at the mall.
3. I bought two because they were on sale.
4. We hope that she likes them.

# Pronouns

## Subject Pronouns

A **subject pronoun** tells who or what did an action in a sentence. *I, you, he, she, it, we,* and *they* are subject pronouns.
**She** *calls us into the dining room.* **We** *are ready to eat.*

**Your Turn** Write each sentence. Change the words in ( ) into subject pronouns.

1. (My grandmother) cooks our dinner.
2. (My brother and sister) sit at the table.
3. Can (my brother) have a glass of juice?
4. (My sister and I) have a surprise dessert for our parents.
5. No one enjoys food as much as (my father) does!

## Object Pronouns

An **object pronoun** comes after an action verb or prepositions such as *for, at, of, on, with, about,* and *to.* The pronouns *me, you, him, her, it, us,* and *them* are object pronouns.

*The clerk gave* **us** *two tickets. My parents put* **them** *in a safe place.*

**Your Turn** Write each sentence. Change the words in ( ) into object pronouns.

1. My parents called (my sister and me) downstairs.
2. We gave (my parents) our attention.
3. They looked at (my sister).
4. "Tell (the two children) about our vacation," Mom said.
5. "Let's start (our vacation) today!" Dad exclaimed.

# Pronoun-Verb Agreement

A present-tense action verb must **agree** with its subject pronoun. Add *-s* to most action verbs in the present tense when you use the pronouns *he, she,* and *it*. Do not add *-s* to an action verb in the present tense when you use the pronouns *I, we, you,* and *they*.

> **He understands** what **they say**.

**Your Turn** Write each sentence. Use the correct present-tense forms of the verbs in ( ).

1. She (create) a secret code.
2. We (help) write a message.
3. It (give) directions to a special place.
4. Did you (try) to figure it out?
5. They (succeed) and (find) the hidden treasure.

# Possessive Pronouns

A **possessive pronoun** takes the place of a possessive noun. It shows who or what owns something. *My, your, her, his, its, our,* and *their* are possessive pronouns that are used before other nouns. *Mine, yours, his, hers, its, ours,* and *theirs* are possessive pronouns that can stand alone.

> *Jim used **his** camera on **our** trip. **Mine** was in **my** room.*

**Your Turn** Write each sentence. Change the words in ( ) into possessive pronouns.

1. I borrowed (my sister's) camera.
2. She showed me how to use (the camera's) buttons.
3. I saw three hawks and took (the hawks') picture.
4. Mine came out better than (your pictures).
5. Shall we show (your and my) pictures to Mom?

# Pronouns

## Pronoun-Verb Contractions

A **contraction** is a shortened form of two words that are combined. An **apostrophe** (') replaces missing letters.

*It's hard work, but **you'll** be proud when **we're** done.*

**Your Turn** Write each sentence. Form contractions.

1. (I will) be working at the animal shelter today.
2. (They are) having a dog wash.

## Reflexive Pronouns

A **reflexive pronoun** shows that a subject does something for or to itself. The ending *-self* is used for singular pronouns. The ending *-selves* is used for plural pronouns.

*Mom made **herself** a snack. We got **ourselves** one, too.*

**Your Turn** Write each sentence. Replace the words in ( ).

1. My father teaches (my father) sign language.
2. We like to give (to us) new challenges.
3. I found (for me) a tutor.

## Pronoun-Antecedent Agreement

The **antecedent** is the noun or nouns to which a pronoun refers. A pronoun must agree with the number and gender of its antecedent.

***My sister** thinks **she** is late. **My brothers** think **they** are late.*

**Your Turn** Write each sentence. Choose the correct pronoun. Then underline the antecedent.

1. My father says that (he, she) will go jogging.
2. My friend and I decide that (he, we) will join him.

# Adjectives

## Adjectives

An **adjective** is a word that describes a noun. Some adjectives tell **what kind** or **how many**. *Few, many,* and *several* are special adjectives that tell how many.

> ***Several*** *students with* ***blue*** *banners ran onto the* ***crowded*** *field.*

**Your Turn** Write each sentence. Circle each adjective and underline the noun being described.

1. It was an exciting game.
2. The band played a happy song.
3. We gave the team a huge cheer.
4. Three players lifted up the coach.
5. Did you see who scored the final goal?

## Articles

The words *the, a,* and *an* are special adjectives called **articles**. Use *a* before singular nouns that begin with a consonant. Use *an* before singular words that begin with a vowel. Use *the* before singular and plural nouns.

> ***An*** *otter left* ***a*** *trail along* ***the*** *river.*

**Your Turn** Write each sentence. Circle each article.

1. We followed the animal's tracks.
2. Dad was sure it was a deer.
3. We looked through an opening in the bushes.
4. A baby moose stood in the meadow.
5. I took a picture of it for the school paper.

# Adjectives

## This, That, These, and Those

*This, that, these,* and *those* are special adjectives that tell **how many** and **how close**. *This* and *that* refer to singular nouns. *These* and *those* refer to plural nouns.

*I drew **this** sketch here and **those** sketches over there.*

**Your Turn** Write each sentence. Choose the correct adjective in ( ) to complete the sentence.

1. My mother likes (this, these) painting.
2. My father prefers (that, those) posters.
3. (This, These) rooms need more art.

## Adjectives That Compare

Add *-er* to an adjective to compare two nouns. Add *-est* to compare more than two nouns. When the adjective ends in a consonant and *y*, change the *y* to *i* before adding *-er* or *-est*. When the adjective ends in *e*, drop the *e* before adding *-er* or *-est*. For adjectives that have a single vowel before a final consonant, double the final consonant before adding *-er* or *-est*. For long adjectives, use **more** in front of the adjective instead of adding *-er*. Use **most** in front of the adjective instead of adding *-est*.

*I chose the **smallest** and **scariest** book on the list.*
*My sister picked a **more difficult** book than mine.*

**Your Turn** Write each sentence. Use the correct form of the adjective in ( ).

1. I wrote a (short) book report than my sister's.
2. I asked the (smart) student in our class for help.
3. He had chosen the (easy) book of all.
4. This book is (interesting) than the first one.

# Adverbs

## Adverbs

An **adverb** is a word that tells more about a verb. Adverbs tell *how, when,* or *where* an action takes place.

> She **often** reads **quietly** in class.

**Your Turn** Write each sentence. Circle each adverb. Then underline the verb it tells about.

1. The boat moved slowly across the sea.
2. Sea gulls flew nearby.
3. A whale suddenly swam to the surface.
4. We ran fast to take a picture.
5. Soon it disappeared underwater.

## Adverbs That Tell *How*

Some adverbs tell *how* an action takes place. Adverbs that tell *how* often end with *-ly*.

> The telephone rang **loudly**.

**Your Turn** Write each sentence. Circle each adverb. Then underline the verb it tells about.

1. I quickly answered the phone.
2. A man talked rapidly to me.
3. I tried hard to understand.
4. I calmly asked him to repeat himself.
5. I wrote the information carefully.

# Adverbs

## Adverbs That Tell *When* or *Where*

Some adverbs tell **when** or **where** an action takes place.
*Later, we went **outside** for a walk.*

**Your Turn** Write each sentence. Circle each adverb. Then underline the verb it tells about.

1. I soon heard a sound.
2. Then I looked up.
3. A plane appeared overhead.
4. Next I saw parachutes open.
5. Sky divers eventually landed nearby.

## Adverbs That Compare

For most adverbs, use **more** in front of the adverb to compare two actions. Use **most** in front of the adverb to compare more than two actions. For shorter adverbs, add **-er** to the adverb to compare two actions. Add **-est** to compare more than two actions. When the adverb ends in a consonant and *y*, change the y to *i* before adding -er or -est.
*I ran **faster** than my friend, but he swam **more gracefully**.*

**Your Turn** Write each sentence. Use the correct form of the adverb in ( ).

1. I practiced (hard) than my brother did.
2. My father may arrive (soon) than my mother.
3. My mother drives (carefully) than he does.
4. I speak (quietly) in the car than I do on the field.
5. Dad listens (closely) of all the parents I know.

# Prepositions

## Prepositions

A **preposition** comes before a noun or a pronoun. A preposition shows how the noun or pronoun is linked to another word in the sentence. Some common prepositions are *in, into, at, of, from, on, with, to,* and *by.*

The girl *in* the raincoat ran *to* the house.

**Your Turn** Write each sentence. Circle each preposition.

1. Clouds appeared in the sky.
2. Rain fell on the town.
3. We were at the cinema.
4. We called our parents from the lobby.
5. They would meet us by the front door.

## Prepositional Phrases

A **prepositional phrase** is a group of words that begins with a preposition and ends with a noun or pronoun. The noun or pronoun is the **object** of the preposition. A prepositional phrase can be used as an adjective or an adverb.

The man *at the beach* (adjective) swam *in the water* (adverb).

**Your Turn** Write each sentence. Underline each prepositional phrase. Then circle the object of the preposition.

1. Fish jumped into the air.
2. Children played with their friends.
3. A girl in sandals gathered shells.
4. A lifeguard watched us from his chair.
5. You found a starfish and showed it to me.

# Mechanics: Abbreviations

## Titles

An **abbreviation** is the shortened form of a word. It usually begins with a capital letter and ends with a period. You can abbreviate the titles before a name.

*Mr.* Scott Fletcher     *Ms.* Bethany Collins
*Mrs.* Miko Anaki     *Dr.* Steinberg

**Your Turn** Write each name using the correct abbreviation and capitalization.

1. mrs Patricia Barry
2. Mister Ed West
3. Doctor Paula hanson
4. ms susie blair

## Days of the Week

You can abbreviate the days of the week.

*Sun.*    *Mon.*    *Tues.*    *Wed.*    *Thurs.*    *Fri.*    *Sat.*

## Months of the Year

You can abbreviate the months of the year. Do not abbreviate the months May, June, or July.

*Jan.*   *Feb.*   *Mar.*   *Apr.*   *Aug.*   *Sept.*   *Oct.*   *Nov.*   *Dec.*

**Your Turn** Write each sentence with the correct abbreviation.

1. Our first game was on September 19.
2. We go on Monday and Tuesday this week.
3. Can you be here on January 22?
4. I can't make a Wednesday meeting.
5. We will finish on Thursday, March 15.

# States

When you write an address, you may use United States Postal Service abbreviations for the names of states. The abbreviations are two capital letters with no period at the end. Do not use a comma between the city and the state when using these abbreviations.

| | | | | | |
|---|---|---|---|---|---|
| Alabama | AL | Kentucky | KY | Ohio | OH |
| Alaska | AK | Louisiana | LA | Oklahoma | OK |
| Arizona | AZ | Maine | ME | Oregon | OR |
| Arkansas | AR | Maryland | MD | Pennsylvania | PA |
| California | CA | Massachusetts | MA | Rhode Island | RI |
| Colorado | CO | Michigan | MI | South Carolina | SC |
| Connecticut | CT | Minnesota | MN | South Dakota | SD |
| Delaware | DE | Mississippi | MS | Tennessee | TN |
| District of Columbia | DC | Missouri | MO | Texas | TX |
| | | Montana | MT | Utah | UT |
| Florida | FL | Nebraska | NE | Vermont | VT |
| Georgia | GA | Nevada | NV | Virginia | VA |
| Hawaii | HI | New Hampshire | NH | Washington | WA |
| Idaho | ID | New Jersey | NJ | West Virginia | WV |
| Illinois | IL | New Mexico | NM | Wisconsin | WI |
| Indiana | IN | New York | NY | Wyoming | WY |
| Iowa | IA | North Carolina | NC | | |
| Kansas | KS | North Dakota | ND | | |

**Your Turn** Write the U.S. Postal Service Abbreviation for each of the following.

1. Sacramento, California
2. Ft. Worth, Texas
3. Sarasota, Florida
4. Springfield, New Jersey
5. Portland, Maine

# Mechanics: Capitalization

## First Word in a Sentence

Capitalize the first word in a sentence. Capitalize the first word of a direct quotation, or the exact words a person says.

*Maura said, "This is my new backpack."*

**Your Turn** **Write each sentence. Use capital letters.**

1. the dog chewed through her old backpack.
2. she said, "he didn't mean to do it."
3. "was he hungry?" I asked.
4. This one is nice, But the old one was better.

## Letters

Capitalize all of the major words in a letter's greeting. Capitalize only the first word in the closing of a letter.

*Dear Sir or Madam:      Sincerely yours,*

## Proper Nouns: Names and Titles of People

Capitalize names and initials that stand for names. Capitalize titles or abbreviations of titles when they come before the names of people. Capitalize the pronoun *I*.

*Mr. Renaldo and I paid Dr. E. M. Carlson a visit.*

**Your Turn** **Write each part of the letter with the correct capitalization.**

1. dear mrs. price,
2. t. j. and i are doing a survey.
3. Have you read gov. grant's new book?
4. very truly yours,

# Proper Nouns: Names of Places

Capitalize the names of cities, states, countries, and continents. Do not capitalize articles or prepositions that are part of the names.

*We flew from the **United States of America** to **Africa**.*

Capitalize the names of geographical features.

***Lake Superior** is north of the other **Great Lakes**.*

Capitalize the names of streets and highways. Capitalize the names of buildings and bridges.

***Golden Gate Bridge***     ***Empire State Building***

Capitalize the names of stars and planets.

*I asked, "How far from **Earth** is the star **Sirius**?"*

**Your Turn** **Rewrite each sentence. Use capital letters where needed.**

1. Our teacher used to live in colorado.
2. Lucy once visited the grand canyon.
3. A telescope can help you see rigel, a bright star.
4. The observatory is near la plata river.
5. The night sky in north america is different from australia.

# Mechanics: Capitalization

## Other Proper Nouns

Capitalize the names of schools, clubs, teams, businesses, and products.

>  I joined the **Health Club** at **Parker Elementary**.

Capitalize the days of the week, months of the year, and holidays. Do not capitalize the names of the seasons.

>  **Labor Day** is the first **Monday** in **September**.

Capitalize abbreviations when they refer to people or places.

>  **Ms. Webb** studied the **Mt. St.** Helens eruption.

Capitalize the first, the last, and all important words in the title of a book, poem, article, song, short story, film, video, television program, and newspaper.

>  She wrote an article called "**A Year** in the **Danger Zone**."

**Your Turn** **Rewrite each sentence. Use capital letters where needed.**

1. We saw the film "volcano!" on monday.
2. The young geologists club hosted.
3. After the movie, mr. Isham gave a talk.
4. He will come back after memorial day.
5. Can we go to elmwood middle school to hear him?

# Mechanics: Punctuation

## End Marks for Sentences

A **period (.)** ends a statement or a command.

A **question mark (?)** ends a question.

An **exclamation mark (!)** ends an exclamation.

*Why is that light flashing? I'm scared! It was a false alarm.*

**Your Turn** Write each sentence. Use the correct end punctuation.

1. We heard the siren outside
2. It was incredibly loud
3. Who called the fire department
4. Do they know it's a false alarm
5. Go ask the teacher for advice

## Periods for Abbreviations

Use a period at the end of an abbreviation. Use a period after initials.

*We will visit **Dr. E. X.** Young on **Oct.** 21.*

**Your Turn** Write each sentence. Insert periods where needed.

1. Ms Mehta teaches us how to cook.
2. We'll return on Apr 13 for our next class.
3. Prof Ruiz is also in our class.
4. We meet both Mon and Tues next week.
5. My brother A J will drive to Pine St to get us.

# Mechanics: Punctuation

## Colons

Use a **colon** after the greeting of a business letter.
  *Dear Senator:*

Use a **colon** to separate the hour and minute when you write the time of day.
  *Thank you for speaking with me at 10:30 today.*

**Your Turn** **Write each sentence. Insert colons.**

1. Dear Judge Michaels
2. I'm sorry I missed our 930 interview.
3. The 830 bus was late this morning.

## Commas in Letters

Use a **comma (,)** between the name of a city and the complete name of a state. Do not use a comma before the postal service abbreviation for a state.
  *Plymouth, Massachusetts      Tucson AZ*

Use a **comma** between the day and the year in a date.
  *March 6, 2005      Tuesday, June 12, 2010*

Use a **comma** after the greeting and closing in a friendly letter.
  *Dear Uncle Walter,      Sincerely yours,*

**Your Turn** **Write each sentence. Add commas where needed.**

1. Dear Aunt Jobeth
2. Have you ever been to Miami Florida?
3. We moved there on July 15 2011.
4. We had been living in Fort Worth Texas.

## Commas in Sentences

Use a **comma** before *and, but,* or *or* in a compound sentence. Use a comma after a dependent clause at the start of a sentence.

> *When the bell rang, the students looked up, and the teacher spoke.*

Use **commas** to separate three or more items in a series.

> *We put away the toys, games, and craft materials.*

Use a **comma** after the words *yes* or *no* when they begin a sentence. Use a comma after the name of a person being spoken to.

> *Yes, my desk is clean.*       *Adam, is your desk clean?*

**Your Turn** Write each sentence. Add commas.

1. I used yellow red and blue for my poster.
2. Jen started a new one and I finished it.
3. No it wasn't as good as the first one.
4. Is there enough or should I make more?
5. Leroy I think we have more than enough!

## Apostrophes

Use an **apostrophe (')** with a noun to show possession. Use an apostrophe in a **contraction** to show where a letter or letters are missing.

> *Our uncle's horses aren't where they should be.*

**Your Turn** Write each sentence. Add apostrophes.

1. I got the keys to my mothers car.
2. We cant see them from the road.
3. "Whats causing that dust cloud?" I asked.
4. "Thats probably them," my mother said.
5. We could see all the horses tracks in the dirt.

# Mechanics: Punctuation

## Commas and Quotation Marks

Use **quotation marks** at the beginning and at the end of the exact words a person says. Use **commas** to set off a direct quotation.

*"I like it," she said, "but it's too expensive."*

**Your Turn** Write each sentence. Add commas and quotation marks where necessary.

1. I asked Aren't they on sale?
2. She replied I wish they were.
3. Let's try another store I said.
4. What about that one? she asked.
5. The price here she said is better!

## Italics or Underlining

Use italics or underlining for the title of a book, movie, play, magazine, or newspaper.

*I read <u>The Big Book of Adventures</u> at the library.*

**Your Turn** Write each sentence. Underline the titles.

1. I was looking for The Little Book of Secrets.
2. I read a review of it in the Chicago Tribune.
3. Does the movie Tiny Truths still mention the book?
4. My aunt saw Big Lies, Little Lies on stage in New York.
5. I'm writing a book called The Whole Story.

# California Common Core State Standards

At the bottom of some pages in this book, you will see letters and numbers. What do these numbers and letters mean? In **RL.3.1**, **RL** stands for **R**eading Standards for **L**iterature. The number **3** stands for Grade 3. The number **1** is the standard number.

| Subject Area | Grade Level | Standard Number |
|:---:|:---:|:---:|
| RL | 3 | 1 |

This California standard means that you can ask and answer questions to show that you understand the stories you are reading.

1. Ask and answer questions to demonstrate understanding of a text, referring explicitly to the text as the basis for the answers.

The standard also means that you will learn to find the answers to specific questions right there in the stories you read.

The Grade 3 California Standards for Reading and Language Arts have six subject areas.

RL  =  Reading Standards for Literature

RI  =  Reading Standards for information Text

RF  =  Reading Standards for Foundational Skills

W  =  Writing Standards

SL  =  Speaking and Listening Standards

L  =  Language Standards

Your standards in all of these subject areas follow. **Take a look!**

# English Language Arts & Literacy in History/Social Studies, Science, and Technical Subjects

## Grade 3

| Reading Standards for Literature | |
|---|---|
| **Key Ideas and Details** | |
| RL.3.1 | Ask and answer questions to demonstrate understanding of a text, referring explicitly to the text as the basis for the answers. |
| RL.3.2 | Recount stories, including fables, folktales, and myths from diverse cultures; determine the central message, lesson, or moral and explain how it is conveyed through key details in the text. |
| RL.3.3 | Describe characters in a story (e.g., their traits, motivations, or feelings) and explain how their actions contribute to the sequence of events. |
| **Craft and Structure** | |
| RL.3.4 | Determine the meaning of words and phrases as they are used in a text, distinguishing literal from nonliteral language. (See grade 3 Language standards 4–6 for additional expectations.) |
| RL.3.5 | Refer to parts of stories, dramas, and poems when writing or speaking about a text, using terms such as chapter, scene, and stanza; describe how each successive part builds on earlier sections. |
| RL.3.6 | Distinguish their own point of view from that of the narrator or those of the characters. |
| **Integration of Knowledge and Ideas** | |
| RL.3.7 | Explain how specific aspects of a text's illustrations contribute to what is conveyed by the words in a story (e.g., create mood, emphasize aspects of a character or setting). |
| RL.3.8 | (Not applicable to literature) |
| RL.3.9 | Compare and contrast the themes, settings, and plots of stories written by the same author about the same or similar characters (e.g., in books from a series). |
| **Range of Reading and Level of Text Complexity** | |
| RL.3.10 | By the end of the year, read and comprehend literature, including stories, dramas, and poetry, at the high end of the grades 2–3 text complexity band independently and proficiently. |

## Standards for Informational Text

### Key Ideas and Details

**RI.3.1**    Ask and answer questions to demonstrate understanding of a text, referring explicitly to the text as the basis for the answers.

**RI.3.2**    Determine the main idea of a text; recount the key details and explain how they support the main idea.

**RI.3.3**    Describe the relationship between a series of historical events, scientific ideas or concepts, or steps in technical procedures in a text, using language that pertains to time, sequence, and cause/effect.

### Craft and Structure

**RI.3.4**    Determine the meaning of general academic and domain-specific words and phrases in a text relevant to a *grade 3 topic or subject area.* (See grade 3 Language standards 4–6 for additional expectations.)

**RI.3.5**    Use text features and search tools (e.g., key words, sidebars, hyperlinks) to locate information relevant to a given topic efficiently.

**RI.3.6**    Distinguish their own point of view from that of the author of a text.

### Integration of Knowledge and Ideas

**RI.3.7**    Use information gained from illustrations (e.g., maps, photographs) and the words in a text to demonstrate understanding of the text (e.g., where, when, why, and how key events occur).

**RI.3.8**    Describe the logical connection between particular sentences and paragraphs in a text (e.g., comparison, cause/effect, first/second/third in a sequence).

**RI.3.9**    Compare and contrast the most important points and key details presented in two texts on the same topic.

### Range of Reading and Level of Text Complexity

**RI.3.10**    By the end of the year, read and comprehend informational texts, including history/social studies, science, and technical texts, at the high end of the grades 2–3 text complexity band independently and proficiently.

# Grade 3

## Reading Standards for Foundational Skills

### Phonics and Word Recognition

| RF.3.3 | Know and apply grade-level phonics and word analysis skills in decoding words both in isolation and in text. |
|---|---|
| RF.3.3a | Identify and know the meaning of the most common prefixes and derivational suffixes. |
| RF.3.3b | Decode words with common Latin suffixes. |
| RF.3.3c | Decode multisyllable words. |
| RF.3.3d | Read grade-appropriate irregularly spelled words. |

### Fluency

| RF.3.4 | Read with sufficient accuracy and fluency to support comprehension. |
|---|---|
| RF.3.4a | Read on-level text with purpose and understanding. |
| RF.3.4b | Read on-level prose and poetry orally with accuracy, appropriate rate, and expression on successive readings. |
| RF.3.4c | Use context to confirm or self-correct word recognition and understanding, rereading as necessary. |

## Writing Standards

### Text Types and Purposes

| W.3.1 | Write opinion pieces on topics or texts, supporting a point of view with reasons. |
|---|---|
| W.3.1a | Introduce the topic or text they are writing about, state an opinion, and create an organizational structure that lists reasons. |
| W.3.1b | Provide reasons that support the opinion. |
| W.3.1c | Use linking words and phrases (e.g., *because, therefore, since, for example*) to connect opinion and reasons. |
| W.3.1d | Provide a concluding statement or section. |
| W.3.2 | Write informative/explanatory texts to examine a topic and convey ideas and information clearly. |
| W.3.2a | Introduce a topic and group related information together; include illustrations when useful to aiding comprehension. |
| W.3.2b | Develop the topic with facts, definitions, and details. |

| W.3.2c | Use linking words and phrases (e.g., *also, another, and, more, but*) to connect ideas within categories of information. |
|---|---|
| W.3.2d | Provide a concluding statement or section. |
| W.3.3 | Write narratives to develop real or imagined experiences or events using effective technique, descriptive details, and clear event sequences. |
| W.3.3a | Establish a situation and introduce a narrator and/or characters; organize an event sequence that unfolds naturally. |
| W.3.3b | Use dialogue and descriptions of actions, thoughts, and feelings to develop experiences and events or show the response of characters to situations. |
| W.3.3c | Use temporal words and phrases to signal event order. |
| W.3.3d | Provide a sense of closure. |

### Production and Distribution of Writing

| W.3.4 | With guidance and support from adults, produce writing in which the development and organization are appropriate to task and purpose. (Grade-specific expectations for writing types are defined in standards 1–3 above.) |
|---|---|
| W.3.5 | With guidance and support from peers and adults, develop and strengthen writing as needed by planning, revising, and editing. (Editing for conventions should demonstrate command of Language standards 1–3 up to and including grade 3.) |
| W.3.6 | With guidance and support from adults, use technology to produce and publish writing (using keyboarding skills) as well as to interact and collaborate with others. |

### Research to Build and Present Knowledge

| W.3.7 | Conduct short research projects that build knowledge about a topic. |
|---|---|
| W.3.8 | Recall information from experiences or gather information from print and digital sources; take brief notes on sources and sort evidence into provided categories. |
| W.3.9 | (Begins in grade 4) |

### Range of Writing

| W.3.10 | Write routinely over extended time frames (time for research, reflection, and revision) and shorter time frames (a single sitting or a day or two) for a range of discipline-specific tasks, purposes, and audiences. |
|---|---|

# Grade 3

## Speaking and Listening Standards

### Comprehension and Collaboration

| | |
|---|---|
| SL.3.1 | Engage effectively in a range of collaborative discussions (one-on-one, in groups, and teacher-led) with diverse partners *on grade 3 topics and texts,* building on others' ideas and expressing their own clearly. |
| SL.3.1a | Come to discussions prepared, having read or studied required material; explicitly draw on that preparation and other information known about the topic to explore ideas under discussion. |
| SL.3.1b | Follow agreed-upon rules for discussions (e.g., gaining the floor in respectful ways, listening to others with care, speaking one at a time about the topics and texts under discussion). |
| SL.3.1c | Ask questions to check understanding of information presented, stay on topic, and link their comments to the remarks of others. |
| SL.3.1d | Explain their own ideas and understanding in light of the discussion. |
| SL.3.2 | Determine the main ideas and supporting details of a text read aloud or information presented in diverse media and formats, including visually, quantitatively, and orally. |
| SL.3.3 | Ask and answer questions about information from a speaker, offering appropriate elaboration and detail. |

### Presentation of Knowledge and Ideas

| | |
|---|---|
| SL.3.4 | Report on a topic or text, tell a story, or recount an experience with appropriate facts and relevant, descriptive details, speaking clearly at an understandable pace. |
| SL.3.4a | Plan and deliver an informative/explanatory presentation on a topic that: organizes ideas around major points of information, follows a logical sequence, includes supporting details, uses clear and specific vocabulary, and provides a strong conclusion. |
| SL.3.5 | Create engaging audio recordings of stories or poems that demonstrate fluid reading at an understandable pace; add visual displays when appropriate to emphasize or enhance certain facts or details. |
| SL.3.6 | Speak in complete sentences when appropriate to task and situation in order to provide requested detail or clarification. (See grade 3 Language standards 1 and 3 for specific expectations.) |

## Language Standards

### Conventions of Standard English

| | |
|---|---|
| L.3.1 | Demonstrate command of the conventions of standard English grammar and usage when writing or speaking. |
| L.3.1a | Explain the function of nouns, pronouns, verbs, adjectives, and adverbs in general and their functions in particular sentences. |
| L.3.1b | Form and use regular and irregular plural nouns. |
| L.3.1c | Use abstract nouns (e.g., *childhood*). |
| L.3.1d | Form and use regular and irregular verbs. |
| L.3.1e | Form and use the simple (e.g., *I walked; I walk; I will walk*) verb tenses. |
| L.3.1f | Ensure subject-verb and pronoun-antecedent agreement. |
| L.3.1g | Form and use comparative and superlative adjectives and adverbs, and choose between them depending on what is to be modified. |
| L.3.1h | Use coordinating and subordinating conjunctions. |
| L.3.1i | Produce simple, compound, and complex sentences. |
| L.3.1j | Write legibly in cursive or joined italics, allowing margins and correct spacing between letters in a word and words in a sentence. |
| L.3.1k | Use reciprocal pronouns correctly. |
| L.3.2 | Demonstrate command of the conventions of standard English capitalization, punctuation, and spelling when writing. |
| L.3.2a | Capitalize appropriate words in titles. |
| L.3.2b | Use commas in addresses. |
| L.3.2c | Use commas and quotation marks in dialogue. |
| L.3.2d | Form and use possessives. |
| L.3.2e | Use conventional spelling for high-frequency and other studied words and for adding suffixes to base words (e.g., *sitting, smiled, cries, happiness*). |
| L.3.2f | Use spelling patterns and generalizations (e.g., word families, position-based spellings, syllable patterns, ending rules, meaningful word parts) in writing words. |
| L.3.2g | Consult reference materials, including beginning dictionaries, as needed to check and correct spellings. |

# Grade 3 · Language Standards (continued)

## Knowledge of Language

| | |
|---|---|
| L.3.3 | Use knowledge of language and its conventions when writing, speaking, reading, or listening. |
| L.3.3a | Choose words and phrases for effect. |
| L.3.3b | Recognize and observe differences between the conventions of spoken and written standard English. |

## Vocabulary Acquisition and Use

| | |
|---|---|
| L.3.4 | Determine or clarify the meaning of unknown and multiple-meaning word and phrases based on *grade 3 reading and content,* choosing flexibly from a range of strategies. |
| L.3.4a | Use sentence-level context as a clue to the meaning of a word or phrase. |
| L.3.4b | Determine the meaning of the new word formed when a known affix is added to a known word (e.g., *agreeable/disagreeable, comfortable/uncomfortable, care/ careless, heat/preheat*). |
| L.3.4c | Use a known root word as a clue to the meaning of an unknown word with the same root (e.g., *company, companion*). |
| L.3.4d | Use glossaries or beginning dictionaries, both print and digital, to determine or clarify the precise meaning of key words and phrases in all content areas. |
| L.3.5 | Demonstrate understanding of word relationships and nuances in word meanings. |
| L.3.5a | Distinguish the literal and non-literal meanings of words and phrases in context (e.g., *take steps*). |
| L.3.5b | Identify real-life connections between words and their use (e.g., *describe people who are friendly or helpful*). |
| L.3.5c | Distinguish shades of meaning among related words that describe states of mind or degrees of certainty (e.g., *knew, believed, suspected, heard, wondered*). |
| L.3.6 | Acquire and use accurately grade-appropriate conversational, general academic, and domain-specific words and phrases, including those that signal spatial and temporal relationships (e.g., *After dinner that night we went looking for them*). |